# PRAISE FOR
## *THE KNOWLEDGE MANAGER'S HANDBOOK*

'I've been working in KM for 20 years and I still picked up some new ideas in this book that will make my work easier. This is a book knowledge managers will find themselves returning to again and again.'

**Nancy Dixon, Common Knowledge Associates**

'A brilliant book with practical and grounded approaches, believable case studies and fabulous tips that made me want to revisit my entire KM programme!'

**Murni Shariff, Senior Manager, Knowledge Management and Institutional Capability, PETRONAS Malaysia**

'A long-awaited knowledge manager's handbook based on a simple, comprehensive and pragmatic roadmap on how to successfully implement KM in an organization. The tips and real case studies provided throughout the book nicely illustrate the concepts presented. A must-have in your KM book collection!'

**Professor Vincent Ribière, Managing Director and Co-founder, Institute for Knowledge and Innovation Southeast Asia (IKI-SEA)**

'If you are new to KM, this will be the book to help you get started quickly and surely. If you are already an experienced knowledge manager, you'll be surprised how this book can help you check your blind spots and show you how to move forward.'

**Mavis Lee, Head of Knowledge Management, Singapore Army, Training and Doctrine Command**

'This is the most comprehensive book I have ever read on the implementation of KM. Whether you are just starting out or a seasoned professional, it is all here. Absolutely a first-rate reference.'

**Robert H Buckman, retired Chairman and CEO, Bulab Holdings, Inc**

'Exploiting knowledge management for business gain or competitive advantage is a broad, multifaceted affair that brings with it many questions; this book not only identifies them, but gives sensible answers to them too.'

**Colin Cadas, Associate Fellow KM, Rolls-Royce plc**

'For knowledge practitioners, no other KM book comes close. Milton and Lambe cover a comprehensive set of topics and challenges spanning the conception of KM to post-implementation, as well as treatments on change management and sustainability, two of the hardest problems in any KM journey. Valuable in-depth case studies further enhance the value of this practitioner's bible.'

**Eric Tsui, Professor and Associate Director, KM and Innovation Research Centre, The Hong Kong Polytechnic University**

We dedicate this book to the knowledge managers around the world from whom we have learned so much, to our colleagues with whom we have learned, and to our families, for their patience and understanding in supporting the often challenging life of a professional knowledge manager.

We also thank Linda Davies, Jessica Magnusson, Dan Ranta, Doreen Tan and Tan Xinde, whose real-life KM stories are included as Chapters 27 through 31. Your willingness to share the lessons from your journeys is a beacon to knowledge managers everywhere.

# The Knowledge Manager's Handbook

A step-by-step guide to embedding effective knowledge management in your organization

Nick Milton and
Patrick Lambe

KoganPage

LONDON  PHILADELPHIA  NEW DELHI

First published in Great Britain and the United States in 2016 by Kogan Page Limited

| | | |
|---|---|---|
| 2nd Floor, 45 Gee Street | 1518 Walnut Street, Suite 900 | 4737/23 Ansari Road |
| London | Philadelphia PA 19102 | Daryaganj |
| EC1V 3RS | USA | New Delhi 110002 |
| United Kingdom | | India |

© Nick Milton and Patrick Lambe, 2016

The right of Nick Milton and Patrick Lambe to be identified as the authors of this work has been asserted by them in accordance with the Copyright, Designs and Patents Act 1988.

ISBN      978 0 7494 7553 6
E-ISBN   978 0 7494 7554 3

**British Library Cataloguing-in-Publication Data**

A CIP record for this book is available from the British Library.

**Library of Congress Cataloging-in-Publication Data**

Names: Milton, N. J. (Nick J.), author. | Lambe, Patrick, 1960 author.
Title: The knowledge manager's handbook : a step-by-step guide to embedding
   effective knowledge management in your organization / Nick Milton and
   Patrick Lambe.
Description: London : Philadelphia : Kogan Page, 2016.
Identifiers: LCCN 2015048235 (print) | LCCN 2016006038 (ebook) | ISBN
   9780749475536 (paperback) | ISBN 9780749475543 (ebook)
Subjects: LCSH: Knowledge management. | BISAC: BUSINESS & ECONOMICS /
   Information Management. | BUSINESS & ECONOMICS / Knowledge Capital. |
   BUSINESS & ECONOMICS / Management.
Classification: LCC HD30.2 .M5465 2016 (print) | LCC HD30.2 (ebook) | DDC
   658.4/038–dc23
LC record available at http://lccn.loc.gov/2015048235

Typeset by Graphicraft Limited, Hong Kong
Print production managed by Jellyfish
Printed and bound by CPI Group (UK) Ltd, Croydon CR0 4YY

# CONTENTS

# ABOUT THE AUTHORS

## Dr Nick Milton

Dr Nick Milton is director and co-founder of Knoco Ltd (**www.knoco.com**), and has worked in the knowledge management field since 1992.

Working with Knoco Ltd, Nick has helped develop and deliver KM strategies, implementation plans and services in a wide range of different organizations around the globe. He has a particular interest in Lessons Learned programmes, managing major lessons capture programmes in fields such as mergers and acquisitions and high-technology engineering, and also specializes in the development of KM Frameworks. Prior to founding Knoco, Nick spent two years at the centre of the team that made BP the leading KM company in the world at the time, acting as the team Knowledge Manager, developing and implementing BP's knowledge of KM development and implementation, and coordinating the BP KM Community of Practice. Prior to this he acted as Knowledge Manager for BP Norway for five years.

Nick is the author of *The Lessons Learned Handbook* and *Knowledge Management for Teams and Projects*, co-author of *Knowledge Management for Sales and Marketing*, *Performance through Learning: Knowledge management in practice* and *Designing a Successful KM Strategy: A guide for the knowledge management professional*. He is a member of the ISO working group looking to develop a KM standard. Nick blogs most days at **www.nickmilton.com** and can be found on Twitter at @nickknoco.

## Patrick Lambe

Patrick Lambe is founding partner of Straits Knowledge, a knowledge management consulting and research company headquartered in Singapore (**www.straitsknowledge.com**). He has been working in knowledge management since 1998.

With Straits Knowledge, Patrick has conducted knowledge audits and supported clients in developing and implementing knowledge management strategies across Asia and the Middle East. He has a particular specialization in knowledge organization and taxonomy development, with clients in the United States, Europe, the Middle East and Asia. Before working in KM, Patrick's background was in library science and learning and development. Patrick is two-term former president of the Information and Knowledge Management Society, and founding President of the International Society for Knowledge Development Singapore Chapter. He is a Visiting Professor in KM at Bangkok University, an Adjunct Professor in KM at the Hong Kong Polytechnic University, and a member of the Editorial Advisory Board of the top-ranked *Journal of Knowledge Management*.

Patrick is the author of *Organising Knowledge: Taxonomies, knowledge and organisational effectiveness* and *The Blind Tour Guide: Surviving and prospering in the new economy*, and co-author of *KM Approaches, Methods and Tools: A guidebook* and *Knowledge Management Competencies: A framework for knowledge managers*. He is a member of the AIIM Knowledge Management Standards Committee seeking to develop an organizational standard for knowledge management. Patrick blogs at **www.greenchameleon.com** and can be found on Twitter at @plambesg.

# FOREWORD

Although humans of a speculative nature have been thinking about knowledge since there has been written language (and most likely before that), it is only recently that anybody has tried to think about how to 'manage' knowledge in an effective manner within organizations and governments.

The reasons for this are varied, and it would be presumptuous of me to try and list them here. Suffice to say there wasn't much need or incentive to do so until it was acknowledged and widely understood that knowledge has serious economic potential – maybe even more than the traditional sources of wealth: land, labour and capital.

The confluence of several economic forces spurring on this revelation led such thinkers as Peter Drucker, Ikujiro Nonaka and others to begin writing in the late 1980s on knowledge, knowledge work and, most importantly, how one could realistically manage knowledge with the existing tools and models.

This led to pioneer organizations across many industries to attempt to do just this – somehow to figure out what knowledge they had, or had potential to acquire, and try to manage it effectively, efficiently and with measures to judge how well they were doing.

Many of these early attempts failed; mainly because there was no agreement even within organizations as to what knowledge actually was, and how it might be different from data, information, judgment, etc. To this problem was added a powerful techno-utopian fantasy (especially in the Anglophone countries) that an organization's knowledge could somehow be digitized and easily made accessible to whomever needed it.

However, the subject has survived all this – and much more – because of the very apparent need for any organization to actually know what it knows, use what it knows, and to know new things. Anyone with even a modicum of sense cannot fail to think this is worth doing in the 21st century.

And here are two very experienced knowledge practitioners and thinkers to help all of us get through the difficulties of bringing forth a desperately needed new practice – still not taught much in business schools or recognized by economists – with clarity, insight, many good examples and good writing. Hooray for them!!!

*Laurence Prusak*

# Introduction

> There is nothing more difficult to take in hand, more perilous to conduct,
> or more uncertain in its success, than to take the lead in the introduction of
> a new order of things, because the innovator has for enemies all those who have
> done well under the old conditions, and lukewarm defenders in those who may
> do well under the new.
>
> (Machiavelli, 1532)

Machiavelli was writing about political change, but he could equally well have been writing about knowledge management (KM).

For many organizations, knowledge management is something new, and implementing KM can be extremely difficult and politically challenging. Recent history is littered with failed attempts to introduce programmes of change into organizations, and KM is no exception. However, despite the challenges some companies have succeeded in introducing KM, embedding it into the way they work, and delivering considerable value as a result. Implementing KM can be done, and has been done.

This book is intended as a practical guide for the working knowledge management professional, and for anyone else who wishes to get an overview of what is involved in introducing knowledge management to an organization in a sustainable, value-adding way. This is not an academic treatise on KM – there are very many of these on the market already – it is instead a roadmap, based on the experience of the authors and on numerous examples of successful, and some less successful, KM implementation.

The book contains several sections, as shown in Figure 0.1. You can either start from the beginning, or jump to the implementation step most relevant for you.

The first part of the book, Chapters 1 through 3, deals with some **introductory material**, including a discussion of KM and what it covers, an overview of the implementation steps, outlining our recommended approach, and the top 12 barriers and pitfalls you will face.

This is followed by Part Two on **preparation** (Chapters 4 through 10), covering the resources you need to have in place before you begin – the strategy, the people, the budget, the objectives, the partners.

The longest section of the book (Chapters 11 through 20) covers **assessment and planning**, as this is where most of the critical decisions are made. We introduce the audit process, and the concept and potential components of a KM framework, then address the issues of stakeholder management, communication, culture and detailed planning.

**FIGURE 0.1** The structure of this book

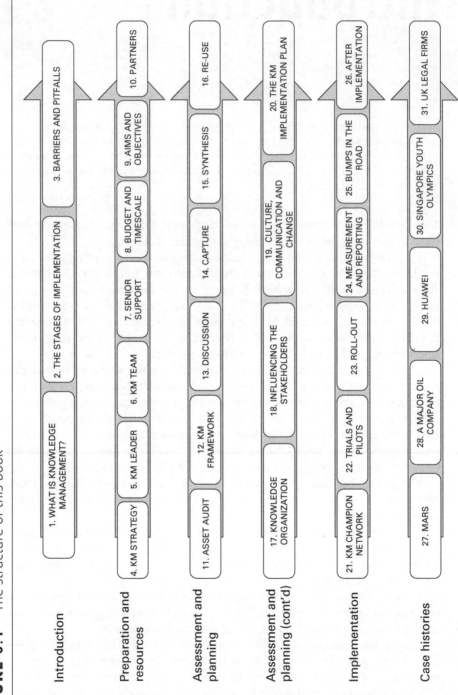

Introduction

1. WHAT IS KNOWLEDGE MANAGEMENT? | 2. THE STAGES OF IMPLEMENTATION | 3. BARRIERS AND PITFALLS

Preparation and resources

4. KM STRATEGY | 5. KM LEADER | 6. KM TEAM | 7. SENIOR SUPPORT | 8. BUDGET AND TIMESCALE | 9. AIMS AND OBJECTIVES | 10. PARTNERS

Assessment and planning

11. ASSET AUDIT | 12. KM FRAMEWORK | 13. DISCUSSION | 14. CAPTURE | 15. SYNTHESIS | 16. RE-USE

Assessment and planning (cont'd)

17. KNOWLEDGE ORGANIZATION | 18. INFLUENCING THE STAKEHOLDERS | 19. CULTURE, COMMUNICATION AND CHANGE | 20. THE KM IMPLEMENTATION PLAN

Implementation

21. KM CHAMPION NETWORK | 22. TRIALS AND PILOTS | 23. ROLL-OUT | 24. MEASUREMENT AND REPORTING | 25. BUMPS IN THE ROAD | 26. AFTER IMPLEMENTATION

Case histories

27. MARS | 28. A MAJOR OIL COMPANY | 29. HUAWEI | 30. SINGAPORE YOUTH OLYMPICS | 31. UK LEGAL FIRMS

Part Four (Chapters 21 through 26) covers the **process of implementation** itself; the creation of the KM champions network, the 'trials and pilots' stage, the roll-out programme, the system of metrics and reporting, the 'roadbumps' you may encounter, and the final handover to a KM operational support organization.

We round off the book with a series of **case studies** describing how KM was implemented in a multinational branded goods company, an oil major, a Chinese telecoms giant, a public sector sports organization, and a UK legal firm.

We hope this book will prove a reliable and valuable guide to your KM implementation journey. In many ways, this is the book we wish had been available when we began our own KM journeys over 20 years ago; it might have saved us a few pitfalls along the way!

May it do so for you.

# PART ONE
# Orientation to knowledge management implementation

## Executive summary

Chapter 1 will give you a rapid overview of how to define KM in practical terms for your organization. It stresses the importance of taking a holistic, balanced approach to KM, and will help you figure out when the KM implementation is out of balance. Chapter 2 sketches out the pros and cons of different KM approaches, and identifies the main phases of KM implementation. This chapter provides a roadmap to the rest of this book. Chapter 3 identifies the most common implementation pitfalls to avoid.

# What is knowledge management?

## 01

## Introduction

This chapter tackles, as best it can, the thorny topic of what knowledge management (KM) actually is, and what it entails. It contains the following elements:

- a definition of KM, and a comparison with other disciplines;
- the six main components of KM;
- a translation of KM into business terms;
- the supply chain as an analogy for KM;
- the essential elements of KM;
- KM as orchestration.

## Definition

There's a saying that if you put five knowledge managers in a room, they will come up with seven definitions of what KM is. This is apocryphal, but it reflects reality. There is a lot of debate and confusion about the nature of KM, none of which is helpful to you as you attempt to implement it within your organization. Hence, your first step, together with your line manager and the steering group for the KM implementation programme, should be to come to a common definition and understanding of what 'knowledge management' means in your organizational context.

Our view is that KM is the latest in a range of management disciplines, and is the discipline with knowledge as its focus. 'Knowledge management' (or KM) represents a way of managing work, paying due attention to the value and effect of an intangible asset, namely, knowledge.

Knowledge is one organizational asset among many. For centuries, organizations have managed their visible assets, such as money, people, property and equipment. More recently organizations have been addressing their intangible assets, such as their reputation, their IP, their customer base, the diversity and talent of their staff, their ability to work safely and sustainably, and how they manage their knowledge.

Knowledge management is therefore just the latest management discipline dealing with intangibles. Risk management, quality management, customer relationship management, brand management, reputation management, talent management and safety management all also deal with intangibles and the implementation programmes for these analogous disciplines can all provide a model for implementing KM. Look at the closest discipline that is already embedded in your organization, and ask, 'How did we implement this? How are we sustaining this? What lessons are there for the KM programme?'

In the industrial sector, probably the closest analogue disciplines for KM are safety management and risk management. Neither of these disciplines are about the management of tangibles – neither safety nor risk are things you can pick up, weigh and put in your pocket. They are about how you manage your organization so that safety and risk are given priority, and so that people's safety behaviours and risk behaviours change. This is exactly what we are looking for from KM. So if your organization has, in the past, successfully introduced risk management and safety management, then you should be greatly encouraged, as KM can then follow a proven implementation path.

KM can also be placed within the same governance framework as the other disciplines. You can position it within the same structures and expectations, and you can review it using the same review processes; the stage reviews of the project management framework, for example. In other words, you can (and should) embed KM within 'normal work'. How are the other disciplines sustained? Do they have a company policy? Support staff? Roles embedded in the business? KM will probably need something similar. This does not mean that you reproduce the frameworks from other disciplines, but it means you can learn from them. Any analogue that has successfully been embedded is a learning opportunity for your KM implementation.

---

**Tip**

Find the people who were responsible for implementing the latest new management framework in your organization (eg risk management, quality management, diversity management, or safety management) and conduct a learning session with them. Probe for the things they did that were successful, and ask for their advice. Find out the things they tried that did not work, work out why they did not work, and discuss how you might avoid these pitfalls yourself. Focus on what was needed to fully embed the framework.

# The six main components of knowledge management

Looking at KM as 'intangible asset management with knowledge as a focus' may help us align it with other management disciplines, but does not particularly help us understand what KM entails, and what it could look like in your organization.

A 2014 survey of knowledge managers from around the world explored this issue by asking the respondents to prioritize, from a list of 11 potential KM approaches, the ones that they focused on as part of their KM implementation (Knoco, 2014). Table 1.1 shows which elements were given highest priority.

**TABLE 1.1**   Survey results showing the priority given to different elements of KM

| Knowledge management element | Percentage of respondents that judged this element to be the highest priority |
| --- | --- |
| Connecting people through communities and networks | 22.2% |
| Learning from experience | 17% |
| Improved access to documents (including search and portals) | 15.3% |
| Knowledge retention | 13.5% |
| Creation and provision of best practices | 9.4% |
| Innovation | 8.7% |
| Improved management of documents | 4.8% |
| Training and development | 3.1% |
| Accessing external knowledge and intelligence | 2.4% |
| Knowledge-based engineering | 2.4% |
| Big data | 1% |

**SOURCE**: Knoco Ltd

The big percentage jump between the 6th and 7th items suggests that the top six are perhaps the core components to KM. These six include:

- connecting people;
- learning from experience;
- improved access to documents;
- retention of knowledge;
- creation of best practices;
- innovation.

Different industries and markets may favour different components, and priorities will shift depending on circumstance and need, but in combination they seem to pretty much map out the mainstream field of KM as it is currently understood.

> **Tip**
>
> Use Table 1.1 on page 9 as a discussion point with your manager. Decide how you will, in your organization, prioritize the six core components of KM. Avoid the temptation to ignore any of these six completely, but they will not all be of equal priority. When you have to rank them, you will find yourself discussing important distinctions for your business.

# Translating KM into business terms

All of the six KM components above are expressed in KM terms. When we communicate to the business about KM, we need to avoid using KM terminology and instead talk about business issues. We need to identify the business problems or issues that the KM solutions will address, and talk about KM in business language.

We can think of an organization as a large-scale entity that needs to solve three broad types of business problem in order to function effectively. Each of these problem types generates specific business problems that KM solutions can address.

## Coordination

The different parts of the organization need to be able to coordinate their activities, maintain shared objectives, avoid mistakes in handoffs, and keep track of how they are making progress on common tasks. Business issues here include:

Collaboration – bringing together knowledge from different parts of the business to develop better ways of working, using the knowledge you already have, but which is scattered and siloed. Here you use KM approaches from the 'connecting people' component, such as communities of practice.

Hand-offs and situation awareness – ensuring effective communication of knowledge between teams and workgroups. Here you can use taskflows, shared calendars, shared knowledge bases and standard templates, as well as the processes and policies that guide their use.

Document and information management – making sure that important shared documents and other information content are made easily accessible to those who need them, regardless of which part of the organization produces them. Here you would use knowledge asset audits to identify high-priority information for sharing, and taxonomies and information architecture to ensure they are easily findable. You may also need to align your knowledge sharing and information security policies to ensure that this information is actually accessible to those who need it.

## Memory

The organization needs to be able to retain key capabilities such as skills, stakeholder/partner relationships, experience and expertise as people come and go, and to keep track of its plans, decisions, activities and commitments. Business issues here include:

Recordkeeping – ensuring that critical decisions, plans and activities are documented and made easily accessible to anyone who needs to refer to them. Here you use records management approaches, alongside the use of standard templates for capturing key information in a predictable and easy-to-use format.

Maintaining capabilities over time – addressing the risk of loss of critical knowledge and capability as people retire, and ensuring that this knowledge is retained, made available to, and used by the remaining and replacing workforce. Here you use approaches from the knowledge retention component.

## Learning

The organization needs to be able to internalize learning from changes in its external environment and adapt its practices accordingly. Business issues here include:

**Speeding up the learning curve** – making sure your employees get up to speed quickly in new jobs or when dealing with new areas of work (new projects, new markets, new products, new geographies). This is of particular importance for organizations seeking to grow, diversify or explore new frontiers, or organizations with rapid turnover of staff. This can use a combination of many of the KM approaches above.

**Continuous improvement** – involves ensuring your projects and business activities do not repeat the mistakes of the past. Learning is built into the organization's memory so that it can build on its solutions and successes. This is the whole area of project-based learning, which KM will address through processes from the learning from experience component.

**Standardization** – comparing and learning from the disparate practices across the organization, to find the ones that work best in given circumstances. Here you use approaches from the 'best practices' component. This may also include arming your customer-facing staff with the knowledge they need to close the deal, or delight the customer, or providing self-help material for your users and customers.

**Business intelligence and decision support** – systematically collecting, analysing and disseminating information about your organization's external and internal environment, to support decision-making, strategies and plans. Here, dashboards, data visualization and analytical tools may help.

**Development of breakthrough products and services** – is a business problem which requires bringing together the knowledge of all relevant staff, as well as external knowledge, to build new ways of doing things, new products, and new lines of business. Here you use KM processes from the innovation component.

---

Tip

Take your prioritized list of KM initiatives from the previous exercise. See if you can translate them into business terms by explaining how they support your fundamental business needs.

---

# The supply chain analogy

A particularly useful analogy for KM is to liken it to a supply chain. We generally think of a supply chain as giving a worker the supplies they need to do their work. When they are constructing an airplane or selling tins of beans in a supermarket, the materials they need have to be sourced, assembled and supplied. For a knowledge worker, the raw material of their work is knowledge. Knowledge management can provide the supply chain by which that raw material is sourced, assembled and supplied.

The analogy of the supply chain has the benefit of thinking about KM from the point of view of the knowledge user. What knowledge do the knowledge workers in your organization need to be able to make the right decisions and take the right actions? How can that knowledge be supplied to them both efficiently and effectively? How can it be sourced (the source often being the experience of others), how can it be packaged in support of their work, and how can it be transported to the user?

John Browne, the CEO of British Petroleum, was quoted in Prokesch (1997) as saying that 'anyone in the organization who is not directly accountable for making a profit should be involved in creating and distributing knowledge that the company can use to make a profit'. This is a vision of the organization as a knowledge supply chain, with the profit-makers as the users.

> **Tip**
>
> It may be too soon to map out the knowledge supply chain in full as we haven't yet covered the knowledge assets audit, but try this simple exercise. Choose a key knowledge user in a critical role, in an activity you are familiar with. Map out the knowledge they need to do their job, their knowledge sources, and the knowledge assets they produce. Determine who the key knowledge users for those assets will be. Note that sometimes the supply chain is a loop – the same group of people may create the knowledge, and use it.

## The essential elements of knowledge management

We will discuss the elements of a KM framework in greater detail in Chapter 12, but underpinning any KM Framework are three core principles. They are as follows:

## Principle 1. KM must address roles, processes, technologies and governance

There are four enablers that support KM, like four legs that support a table. These are the factors that enable the flow and storage of knowledge:

- the technology elements, such as portals, collaboration tools, search engines, lesson management systems, etc;
- the elements of roles and accountabilities, such as CoP leaders, knowledge managers, and knowledge owners;
- the process elements, such as after action review, lessons capture, knowledge asset creation, etc;
- the governance elements, such as KM expectations and policy, metrics and incentives, formats and protocols, taxonomies, and support.

Each of these elements should be mutually supportive and closely interconnected. Like the four legs on a table, the four elements of KM are all equally important. No single element is dominant – they all support each other, they all support KM, and they all support KM in supporting the business. For example, technology needs to integrate with other technology, and with processes, roles and governance. Through the integrated elements the two ingredients of KM – content and conversation – begin to build and flow, and the supply chain begins to deliver.

## Principle 2. KM must cover both the elements of connecting people through conversation and collecting and organizing content for access

This is one of the earliest models in the history of KM, but one that sometimes seems to get forgotten. It identifies two routes for knowledge transfer between knowledge suppliers and knowledge users.

The connect route supports knowledge transfer through connecting people and has particular strengths in tacit knowledge sharing. During the connect approach we facilitate the transfer of knowledge through conversations, whether these are electronically moderated or face to face.

The collect route supports knowledge transfer through collecting knowledge into content and focuses on codified knowledge. During the collect approach we facilitate the transfer of knowledge through captured and codified content in the form of documents, files, text, pictures and video.

Connect and collect are not alternative strategies. They are complementary components of a single framework and a single strategy, which work in parallel. Any complete KM framework needs to enable, promote, facilitate and otherwise support both conversation and content. Your organization will contain critical knowledge of very many kinds. Some of it needs to be managed as content, and some as conversations. Conversations are a far richer medium than content, while content is more scalable, can reach far more people, and has a longer life-span. Knowledge can be transferred effectively through conversations and efficiently through content.

Managing conversation without content leaves no traces, other than in the minds of the people involved. Unless new knowledge becomes embedded and documented in process, or guidance, or recommendations and new ways of working, it is never truly 'learned', and without this we find knowledge has to be relearned many times, with errors being repeated, wheels reinvented and so on.

Managing content without conversation leads KM towards the already established fields of content management and information management. A focus on content without conversation results in a focus on creation of knowledge bases, blogs and wikis as a proxy for the transfer of knowledge, but unless people can question and interrogate knowledge in order to internalize it, learning can be very ineffective. No matter how smart your systems, content does not know who you are or understand your contextual needs in the way that a colleague can, and it does not know how to tune itself to your needs and current knowledge level in the way a good mentor can.

When connect and collect work in unison, you will be supporting four knowledge 'transactions' – discuss, document, synthesize, find/review – as shown in Figure 1.1 below. This mirrors the four modes of conversion of knowledge described by Nonaka and Takeuchi (1995) – socialization, externalization, combination and internalization.

**FIGURE 1.1**    The four knowledge transactions

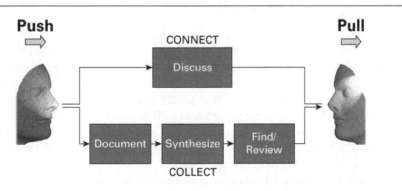

As Table 1.2 shows, the four transactions occur when knowledge is transferred between or within the realms of tacit knowledge ('knowledge in the head') and codified knowledge ('knowledge captured in digital or written form').

**TABLE 1.2**    The four transactions of knowledge as interfaces between tacit knowledge and codified knowledge

|  | To tacit knowledge | To codified knowledge |
|---|---|---|
| **From tacit knowledge** | Discuss | Document |
| **From codified knowledge** | Find and review | Synthesize |

Connect and collect therefore can be seen as representing the four transactions below:

- discussion of knowledge, the means by which conversations on the 'connect' route are conducted;
- documentation of knowledge, the means by which content on the 'collect' route is created;
- synthesis of knowledge, the means by which content on the 'collect' route is combined into new updated and structured knowledge, and old knowledge removed;
- search and review of knowledge, the means by which content on the 'collect' route is accessed and internalized.

## Principle 3. KM must address push and pull (aka supply and demand)

Look back at Figure 1.1. The four knowledge transactions support both push and pull, which represent knowledge supply and demand. Push is the transfer of knowledge driven by supply (publishing, blogging, tweeting or loading material to a database or wiki), and pull is the transfer of knowledge driven by demand (asking a question on a forum, or searching an intranet). The ideal KM framework runs push and pull in parallel, as both supply and demand are valid ways of instigating knowledge flow. A KM supply chain, as described earlier, will require demand (pull) for knowledge at one end of the chain, and supply (push) at the other.

As in economics, push without pull (supply without demand) leads to knowledge over-supply and overload, and ultimately to destruction of knowledge value. Pull without push creates a market, but any market needs to be supplied. Knowledge management, whether you view it as an internal knowledge market or as a knowledge supply chain, needs both push and pull to function.

>
> Review the current balance within your organization between connect and collect, and between push and pull. Which of these is dominant? It is common to have systematic biases in the way knowledge is addressed: a bias towards content push for example, or a bias towards connection through technology. These will need to be balanced with other elements as you develop your framework. If you find such a bias, consider how you can rebalance.

# Knowledge management as orchestration

Earlier in this chapter we talked about analogue disciplines to KM. These are disciplines that you can learn from in implementing KM in your organization. There are also partner disciplines that you will need to work with. These include:

- human resource – especially human resource development;
- organization development;
- information and data management;
- information security;
- risk management and governance;
- records management;
- IT management;
- internal communications teams and corporate communications teams;
- internet, intranet, portal and extranet management.

These disciplines may already have some responsibility for some of the business issues and related KM solutions we described above. In some cases, there may be grey areas or fuzzy boundaries between your territory and theirs. It is extremely important that you are able to:

**a** identify and recognize what they are currently doing;

**b** work with them to adapt what they are doing where there are KM gaps;

**c** negotiate the boundaries, integration and coordination points between your work and theirs;

**d** scope KM projects and programmes collaboratively not competitively.

Later in this book, we will cover stakeholder management and working with partners, either in the direct lines of business, or in these partner (or competitor) disciplines. When you clarify what KM means for your organization, you will also need to clarify how KM integrates with the work of these other disciplines. In short, you will need to become an orchestrator of KM activities as much as an implementer.

---

**Tip**

List out the partner disciplines that exist in your organization. Visit them and learn how they see their main responsibilities, and what their current priorities and projects are. Take notes on where these priorities and projects meet KM needs that you have identified. Ask them for feedback where they think the KM function could integrate with what they are doing, and on where they think you could offer help. To avoid raising unrealistic expectations, explain that you can't take on everything and will have to prioritize. Promise to consult them as your implementation planning progresses.

---

## Summary

Although knowledge management is a fuzzy and poorly defined topic, you have many analogue disciplines such as safety management or risk management which you can use as models for KM implementation, and you can be guided by the experience of other knowledge managers in choosing what to include within your KM implementation. Analogues like the KM supply chain, or KM orchestration, give you alternative views of your task, which you must remember to translate into terms that the organization will easily understand.

Ensure that you take a complete view of KM, including the elements of people, process, technology and governance, the four transactions of discussion, capture, synthesis and finding/reusing, and the two drivers of push and pull.

However you finally define KM for your organization, make sure your definition is shared with your manager and your steering committee and broadly accepted within the organization. Then you can proceed to the next step of developing your implementation approach, which we will cover in the next chapter.

# The stages of KM implementation

## 02

**T**his chapter takes a high-level overview to KM implementation, and identifies the various options and stages. It contains the following elements:

- a comparison of six approaches to implementing KM, with the advantages and disadvantages of each;
- the five phases of the recommended 'trials and pilots' approach;
- the parallel opportunity-led programme of quick wins;
- the escalating levels of management decision.

## The different implementation approaches

There are many different approaches to KM implementation, but in this book we intend to focus on the implementation method that we have found most successful. The main implementation approaches we have seen applied are listed below, with the arguments for and against. The approach we present in this book is an 'agile' combination of a 'trials and pilots' approach with opportunistic delivery of quick wins. This is not to say that the other approaches cannot work; given the right conditions, they sometimes do.

However, the odds are weighted against you, for the reasons explained in Table 2.1 overleaf.

## Our recommended approach

Our recommended approach is a combination of three of the approaches in Table 2.1. The core strategy is a 'trials and pilots' approach (6) to develop the long-term KM framework, combined with an opportunistic approach (3) to deliver short-term wins. Once the KM framework has been proven to be robust, then you move to a roll-out approach (4).

**TABLE 2.1** Advantages and disadvantages of different KM implementation approaches

| Approach | Description | Pros | Cons |
| --- | --- | --- | --- |
| 1. Grass roots/ bottom up | KM starts low in the organization, without management support. | Attractive concept: people do KM because they recognize its value and importance. | Unlikely to work when KM is up against urgent activity – KM gets deprioritized. Multiple diverse and competing KM approaches likely to emerge. Often fails to reach the tipping point, unless early success is deliberately converted into management support. |
| 2. Top down | Management just tell people to do KM. | Quick. May appeal to autocratic management cultures. | May create a 'tick in the box' ethic. Multiple diverse KM approaches likely to emerge as people interpret the management edict in different ways. KM may suddenly go out of favour with changes in senior leadership. |
| 3. Opportunistic | KM is introduced by looking for business opportunities and addressing these one by one. | A low energy approach – you go where the appeal is. | The KM team can be rapidly swamped with some KM activities, while other components of the KM system are not addressed. However this is a useful secondary implementation style, as described in this chapter. |
| 4. Roll out a pre-designed KM framework | Design a KM framework and roll it out to the entire organization with senior management support. | Fast. An approach often advocated by large consultancies, who will help with the framework design. | There is no reliable 'one size fits all' KM approach, and if you get it wrong you get it wrong for everyone. This is a risky one-shot approach. |

**TABLE 2.1**  *Continued*

| Approach | Description | Pros | Cons |
|---|---|---|---|
| **5. Roll out individual KM processes or tools** | Roll out components of the framework one by one (eg search engine, communities of practice, etc). | Allows testing of each component of the KM system. Spreads the investment. | Usually a recipe for failure. Individual KM components are unlikely to deliver value on their own. The organization will need to take the value proposition on faith until roll-out of every element is complete, and they are properly connected and integrated. |
| **6. Trials and pilots** | Pilot a minimum version of the KM framework in one or more business areas. Review, improve, expand, repeat. This could be termed an 'agile' approach. | Secure, robust, allows advancement by discrete steps and decisions. | Slow. Management may be impatient. Risk of being undermined by organizational changes, unless you deliver quick wins, eg through use of the opportunistic approach. |

> **Tip**
>
> Stick with the implementation approach outlined here, and resist the alternatives unless you really have no choice. Particularly resist the pressure to 'just roll out a technology and see what happens'. What usually happens is that the technology reaches 10–20 per cent penetration and then grows no further.

In this recommended approach, your KM implementation programme will go through several phases as shown in Figure 2.1 below.

## 1. Strategy phase

Before implementation, you need a strategy phase, to confirm the need for KM implementation, and to create the business case and the budget for

**FIGURE 2.1**    The five phases of the recommended KM
implementation approach

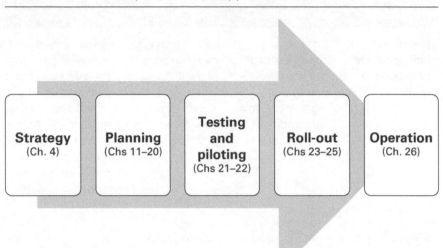

Strategy
(Ch. 4)

Planning
(Chs 11–20)

Testing
and
piloting
(Chs 21–22)

Roll-out
(Chs 23–25)

Operation
(Ch. 26)

setting up an implementation team. We provide a high-level overview of KM strategy development in Chapter 4. For more detail on KM strategy we refer you to *Designing a Successful KM Strategy: A guide for the professional knowledge manager* by Stephanie Barnes and Nick Milton (2015). The strategy phase ends with a decision from senior management to move to detailed planning.

## 2. Planning phase

The detailed planning stage involves a lot of investigation, for example:

- a knowledge assets audit (Chapter 11);
- assessing the elements of a draft KM framework (Chapters 12–16);
- a culture assessment (Chapter 19).

In this stage you will also conduct your stakeholder analysis (Chapter 18), and your communication plan (Chapter 19). Finally you will put together a detailed implementation plan that covers the testing and piloting phase, with a higher-level plan to cover roll-out (Chapter 20).

## 3. Testing and piloting phase

The testing and piloting stage (described in detail in Chapter 22) is when you begin to look for the small 'proof of concept' exercises where you can apply a single KM element to a single business issue – for example a peer assist to help a new project team before they start a project, or a lessons-capture exercise to draw out knowledge from a completed piece of work. You also begin to look for the larger-scale pilot projects. The components of your draft KM framework can be tested in the proof of concept exercises, and the whole framework will be tested and improved in a succession of pilots. This is similar to the agile software methodology which relies on multiple cycles of development with learning from each cycle incorporated into the next. Choose your pilots wisely – they should have a high chance of success, be able to demonstrate clear business value, and deliver lessons and evidence to improve the framework.

By the time you have got to the end of the piloting stage, you should have evidence of value delivery through the application of KM, and you should be able to finalize your KM framework so that it can be effectively embedded into the working structures of the organization.

## 4. Roll-out phase

The roll-out phase (described in detail in Chapter 23) is when the KM framework is applied across the rest of the organization (those parts of the business that were not involved in the piloting). The roll-out decision is a crucial one that needs to be made at the highest level, as this is the decision to commit the entire organization to use of the revised KM framework. Take your evidence of pilot value to your steering committee, and ask them to make this decision, or to recommend the decision to senior management.

The roll-out will involve:

- documenting the framework;
- training people in their new roles;
- training people in new processes;
- training people in the use of new technology;
- finalization of the governance system and the KM policy;
- starting to gather and report metrics;
- coaching people with KM roles and accountabilities, including the KM champions.

Roll-out continues until the whole organization has been trained, and is able to comply with the expectations in the KM policy. At the end of this stage, the decision will be made to close the KM implementation programme and hand responsibility for KM over to a KM operational support team.

## 5. Operational phase

From the operational phase onwards, KM is treated as 'part of the way we work'. There should still be a KM team, but their role is to support and monitor KM activity in the business. Operational activity continues until a decision is made at some future date to refresh KM, in which case a new task force will be set up for this purpose.

## *Exceptions to the rule*

You may meet a situation where our recommended approach is not immediately possible. The case study below is an example where a bottom-up KM implementation was needed in order to gain enough support for the recommended implementation approach to begin.

## CASE STUDY

One of the authors was approached by the IT department of a small international business matchmaking agency with a large headquarters and many small offices around the world. They had identified significant problems with access to information, knowledge flows, and trust between the different departments, and they had recognized that an IT solution alone was not going to help. They wanted to conduct a knowledge audit, and identify useful KM interventions that could help. However, they had minimal support from their senior management, who believed that every department was different. Consequently they felt there was no strong priority for a common KM strategy and framework. Because of this the IT team also had a very small budget. We had misgivings, but we were impressed by the team's commitment. We trained them and supported them through a knowledge audit exercise, and they identified three initiatives – (1) the audit uncovered a core set of information resources from various department silos that were in wide demand across the organization, and they moved them to the shared intranet; (2) they placed a micro-blogging tool on the intranet front page to enable day-to-day sharing of activities and meetings (this became a wild hit with the country teams, who had previously felt isolated from the HQ, and appreciated the chance to improve the visibility of their work); (3) they instituted knowledge transfer interviews with country managers on their trips through HQ, and published these as regular 'need to know' profiles about different countries and markets. Three years later, these initiatives had changed perceptions and culture so significantly that the senior management team commissioned a second audit and an organization-wide KM strategy and framework. While the bottom-up approach is a risky one, with strong commitment and stamina from a core team and judicious, well-grounded choice of projects, it can work to convince senior management that KM has value.

# The parallel opportunity-led programme

What we have described above is a strategic long-term programme of change, based on thorough assessment and analysis, and on trialling and piloting to iteratively test and refine the framework. This gives a robust solution, but can be slow. To many parts of the organization it might appear that nothing much is happening – particularly to those not involved with pilots, or at the end of the queue for roll-out. The cynics start to whisper that KM is promising much but delivering nothing. As well as the long-term strategic development approach, you therefore need to work on visible short-term progress and providing immediate tangible results, so that people will see KM in action and understand the value it brings. You should be looking for opportunities to deliver quick wins at any stage in the programme (potential quick win opportunities are discussed in Chapter 22).

## Tip

To avoid the risk of losing focus on your core trials and pilots approach, consider making one or two team members responsible for the opportunistic 'proof of concept' activity stream, so that the opportunistic work plan can be well bounded and does not consume all your resources. Make sure that you have regular liaison across the two activity streams so that cross-connections and lessons can be exploited.

# Escalating levels of management decision

As you work through these phases you will be working at escalating levels of management decision. The evidence gathered at each stage will support the decisions for the next level of activity.

During the planning phase, the first few 'proof of concept' exercises will be applied to specific activities within a project or department, often involving the application of individual KM techniques and tools. Perhaps you will try a knowledge-exchange workshop, a retention interview from a departing expert, or a lessons-capture meeting from a project (more guidance on these proof of concept exercises is provided in Chapter 22). The decision to conduct a KM proof of concept can be made at team leader level or project manager level, and little investment of time or money is needed.

Proof of concept exercises have limitations: it is hard to scale them up and the application of a single tool means that the rest of the KM framework will be missing. However, you can often demonstrate the delivery of local temporary value and gather feedback and user endorsements from the people involved. This evidence of value can be used to influence the next level of management, whose support will be needed for the KM pilots. This is a low-risk way of building common understanding and support.

Piloting, on the other hand, involves introducing a complete KM framework into one part of the business, in order to impact business results. It might involve, for example, the development of a community of practice in a particular topic, or gathering and sharing knowledge between a number of projects all working in the same sort of area. This is the level at which real value can be delivered to the business. The pilot needs some full-time resource from the business and may last for a few months. The decision to support a pilot will be taken by a programme manager, a divisional manager or the manager of a business line or product line. Because the commitment is greater, the success of your proof of concept exercises will be important in making the case for the piloting stage.

Even in the pilot projects, KM may still find itself hampered by a lack of senior management support, and by corporate policies and structures such as internal competition, reward mechanisms, inadequate technical career paths, lack of accountability for knowledge, and so on. To introduce KM to the whole organization will require the wholehearted support of the senior managers. It requires them to support KM as a necessary component of business activity, to endorse the KM policy, and to develop the conditions that support a knowledge-focused culture. Support is not just saying 'yes' at a management meeting, or endorsing a budget request. It has to go beyond that, and permeate the everyday actions, decisions and resource allocations that senior leaders enact, as described in Chapter 7. The success of your KM pilots will be important in gathering this kind of senior level support and in making the case for the roll-out stage.

## Summary

There are several approaches to implementing KM, and all have advantages and disadvantages. The approach we recommend is a combination of a staged approach involving piloting and roll-out, together with a set of opportunistic 'proof of concept' exercises to solve or alleviate business issues. This process continues until the framework is robust enough for roll-out. This ensures that the necessary long-term strategic change is combined with regular demonstration of the value of KM, and also allows a steady escalation of KM support.

We will explore in detail the issues associated with each of the implementation phases in later chapters, and in our next chapter will look at some of the main pitfalls and barriers you may meet along the way.

# Barriers and pitfalls

## 03

This chapter looks at the things that can go wrong in KM implementation. KM initiatives are complex and multi-faceted. They touch on many different parts of the business, have many dependencies, and offer many opportunities for surprises (unpleasant or otherwise). To identify the pitfalls we draw on evidence from multiple sources – an online survey, a literature review, our own experience, and case studies from others. These give several perspectives on the pitfalls and barriers that may face you – and on how this book can help you avoid them or mitigate them. This chapter covers:

- a review of survey evidence;
- a review of lessons from the field, within which we identify 12 main pitfalls:
    1 KM is not introduced with a business focus;
    2 KM is never embedded into the business;
    3 you fail to secure senior management support;
    4 you don't focus on high-value knowledge;
    5 you fail to show measurable benefits;
    6 the four enablers of KM are not given equal attention;
    7 only parts of the KM solution are implemented;
    8 you make KM too difficult for people;
    9 KM is not implemented as a change programme;
    10 the KM team 'preaches only to the converted';
    11 the KM team fails to engage with key stakeholders;
    12 the KM team have the wrong competence.

## Survey evidence

As part of a global 2014 survey, answered by nearly 400 KM professionals, we asked respondents to rank a number of barriers in order of the impact they had had on their KM programme, ranking these from 1 to 8. The results are shown in Table 3.1 overleaf, with high numbers representing high ranking and therefore high impact.

**TABLE 3.1**  Survey responses identifying the biggest barriers to KM implementation

| Barrier | Average ranking by impact |
| --- | --- |
| Lack of prioritization and support from leadership | 6.0 |
| Cultural issues | 5.8 |
| Lack of KM roles and accountabilities | 4.9 |
| Lack of KM incentives | 4.7 |
| Lack of a defined KM approach | 4.6 |
| Incentives for the wrong behaviours (focus on billable activities, rewards for internal competition, etc) | 4.2 |
| Lack of support from departments such as IT, HR, etc | 4.1 |
| Insufficient technology | 3.8 |

**SOURCE:** Knoco Ltd

Respondents were also asked to prioritize the main enablers for KM which had proved powerful in supporting them in their KM implementation programme, ranking these enablers from 1 to 9. The resulting figures are shown in Table 3.2 (high numbers being high ranking).

The number one barrier and the number one enabler are the same – support from senior management. Without this, you will struggle. With this, assuming it goes beyond lip service and is sustained, you should succeed. The implementation approach described in this book is designed to build the evidence needed to convince senior management to give you their support.

Although culture, roles and incentives are seen as major barriers, they are at the bottom of the enablers table. This is interesting. It suggests some things can be perceived as strong barriers, but weak enablers. Culture, roles and incentives all relate to the engrained habits of an organization. When your KM initiative is aligned with them, everything goes smoothly, and their role as enablers is barely perceived. When your KM initiative is not aligned with them, they immediately produce obvious – and multiple – points of friction. This is why all three of these need to be addressed as part of your KM implementation.

**TABLE 3.2**   Survey responses identifying the biggest enablers of KM implementation

| Enabler | Average ranking by impact |
| --- | --- |
| Support from senior management | 7.8 |
| Evidence of value from KM | 6.8 |
| Championship and support from KM team/champions | 6.5 |
| Effective KM processes | 5.9 |
| Personal benefit for staff from KM | 5.5 |
| Easy-to-use technology | 5.0 |
| A supportive company culture | 4.7 |
| Clear KM accountabilities and roles | 3.7 |
| Incentive systems for KM | 3.0 |

**SOURCE:** Knoco Ltd

The second and fifth biggest enablers relate to the value demonstrated by KM, whether it is value to the organization, or value to employees. Evidence of value from KM is crucial (and incidentally is also closely connected to delivering support from senior management). In Chapter 2 we described an incremental 'value snowball' approach involving KM proof of concept projects, KM pilots and an opportunity-led programme of KM initiatives. This approach is geared towards delivering quick wins and also demonstrating long-term value. It is critical for building management and employee support for KM at ever increasing levels of seniority and influence.

Technology is seldom a barrier, nor is it near the top of the enabler list. Anyone thinking that the solution to effective KM is technology alone, is ignoring the lessons from the past two decades of successful KM! And yet it continues to be a distractor because it is much easier to buy a piece of technology than to 'buy' a piece of KM practice, and this ease of purchase can still be a fatal attraction for decision-makers who know no better.

# Lessons from the field

In this section, drawing from the KM literature, a number of case studies, and our own experience, we identify 12 main areas to watch out for if you want to avoid KM failure. Where we have used external references they are given in the text; otherwise, these are factors that we have encountered in our own experience of working with organizations on KM implementations.

## Pitfall 1. KM is not introduced with a business focus

The best way to embed an initiative into the DNA of a business is to have it driven constantly by a business focus, and the failure to introduce KM with a business focus is one of the most common reasons for failure. KM should not be introduced for its own sake; it should be introduced because it solves business problems and helps people make better decisions, and so work better, faster and/or cheaper. You won't sell KM to anyone, let alone the doubters, the cynics or the high-level sponsors, by assuming that KM has self-evident benefits. You won't get anywhere by saying 'we need to improve knowledge sharing', unless you can clearly demonstrate how improved knowledge sharing will help the business.

### CASE STUDY

One of our clients took a KM strategy to the executive team of their organization. It was a good strategy, but lacked business focus. Luckily, rather than kicking it out, they said 'yes, you can go ahead with KM, so long as you focus it entirely on the growth agenda. If it can help us grow, then go ahead'. That's what the team did, and now, many years later, they have a wealth of stories showing massive growth and many hundreds of millions of dollars of value created, through the help of KM.

Once you have a business focus you have to maintain it. KM often involves a complex set of diverse activities. It is easy to get distracted by the details of implementation and forget the reason why you are doing KM in the first place. In their case study of a failed KM initiative in a pharmaceutical company, Braganza and Möllenkramer (2002) pointed to a tendency to support localized KM practices within distinct functional areas, and so the company built a number of functional knowledge silos, never reaping the full benefits of what they were doing at an organizational level. Once you have a business focus, and remain guided by it, then it is much easier to identify, understand and support the knowledge interdependencies across the business.

Business focus will be a common theme of this book, but we will give it special attention in Chapter 22 which covers pilot projects and proof of concept exercises.

## Pitfall 2. KM is never embedded into the business

Lots of KM programmes do not survive in the longer term because they have never been embedded in normal business activities. They may be delivered by a strong team and a charismatic leader, but they are delivered as something separate – not fully integrated into the work structure and management framework of the company. Once the charismatic leader leaves, KM withers and dies.

Rosina Weber says that implementation needs to be 'inside the process context' (Weber, 2007), and in analysing a KM failure within a pharmaceutical company, Braganza and Möllenkramer (2002) talk about the need to contextualize KM 'within natural activity areas'.

The goal of your implementation programme is to embed a self-sustaining approach to KM in all elements of the business, with clear governance and good support, and clear evidence of sustainable culture change and sustainable business value. Don't stop your implementation until you have got to this point, and even then, plan for a handover period, until embedded operational KM is up and running. Stopping a KM programme before this point is a common reason for failure, and given that it may take many years to reach this point, you need to ensure that your high-level sponsor (see point 3 below) is in it for the long run.

Chapter 23 will cover what is involved in embedding KM.

## Pitfall 3. You fail to secure effective senior management support

In order to embed KM in the business, changes to the business need to be made. You may have to change the incentives policy, perhaps removing the 'factory of the year' award that drives so much internal competition, or the accountabilities of the heads of different corporate functions to include accountability for the maintenance of certain knowledge areas. If managers in the business lines do not accept responsibility for the quality of the knowledge assets under their care, and the quality of the knowledge processes that drive their core activities, then you are in trouble (Weber 2007).

You may have to persuade high-level groups to respond to the output of knowledge-capture sessions, whenever these uncover organizational improvements that can be made. You may need to introduce a new technology across the entire organization. For all of these changes you need support at the highest level. This is why senior management support is both the biggest enabler to KM implementation (if present) and the biggest barrier (if absent).

Note the word 'effective' in the heading to this section. Sponsorship and support cannot simply be lip service. They need to be followed up by political cover while the KM programme is getting under way and before it shows results, by appropriate resource allocations, by changes in policy and process, by clearly defined deliverables, and by properly enforced accountabilities. Steve Barth identifies a failure to follow through with sufficient investment and resources as a common failure point (Barth, 2000) which may well be an outcome of insufficient senior support. We explore the role of senior management in Chapter 7.

## CASE STUDY

In a study of KM implementation challenges in Singapore, Lambe and Tan (2003) found that a superficial understanding of KM among the sponsors and steering group led to over-optimistic assumptions about what could be achieved with limited manpower and resources, and an under-appreciation of the resources, effort and time that were actually needed to show results. This clearly implies the need for a constant process of engagement, communication and education with your sponsor and steering group, to ensure that their support remains well-informed and effective.

## Pitfall 4. You don't focus on high-value knowledge

In her review of factors influencing failure in KM implementations, Rosina Weber talks about overambitious attempts 'to develop a monolithic organizational memory for the whole enterprise'. The knowledge that was captured and stored was generalized and non-specific because it was meant to be accessible for everybody (Weber, 2007). However, all real work in enterprises is highly specific and context dependent. Over-abstraction reduces the utility of the knowledge. If you forget this fact you have forgotten as important a factor as your business focus. The quality of knowledge in the shared knowledge base depends on how relevant and valuable it is for the work of your colleagues in the organization.

The drift towards inappropriate forms of knowledge happens all too easily. In their study of a failed initiative in a pharmaceutical company, Braganza and Möllenkramer (2002) describe how a team in charge of building a knowledge base, once they had started, became obsessed with completing all the elements that could be captured (eg customer data, competitor intelligence, sales data, staff details), without considering the natural working patterns of the end users. Because the content analysis was conducted without an understanding of the end user's everyday activities, the team was unable to prioritize what knowledge was to be collected. They did not focus it on supporting the work that people actually did. It was then hard for users to filter through the 'noise' and identify what would be useful for specific tasks.

Instead your KM should focus on the knowledge of high value – both to the organization (the 'strategic knowledge areas' described in Chapter 4) and to the knowledge workers (the knowledge assets audit described in Chapter 11).

## Pitfall 5. You fail to show measurable benefits

Rosina Weber cites the failure to show measurable benefits to the business as one of the major risks to a KM implementation (Weber, 2007). If you have completed a robust KM strategy development process and identified where your business focus should be, and if you maintain that business focus, then you can mitigate this risk (Barnes and Milton, 2015). However, you also have to show value and benefits on the ground, as well as to your sponsoring organization. The knowledge workers you impact with your KM initiatives need to see benefits too, or they will not participate, contribute, or share (Weber, 2007).

In a set of lessons learned from implementing KM at Siemens, Gibbert *et al* identify two pitfalls they encountered as part of the KM implementation there.

The first, which they call 'the customer trap', is the need to balance the expectations of the business, in terms of value to be delivered by the KM programme, with the expectations of the end users. You will need to show clear benefits to both of these stakeholder groupings (Gibbert *et al*, 2011). Steve Barth, in an analysis of the early failure of KM efforts at the food manufacturer Pillsbury, calls this the 'field of dreams trap'. Pillsbury had identified a clear business focus, and successfully sold it to the top management – to create a knowledge-sharing system around batter manufacture across the different product groups. However, they failed to consider or make clear what the benefits to the teams in the different product groups would be. In fact, some of the vice presidents actively discouraged spending time in sharing knowledge across groups. As Steve Barth puts it:

> The batter effort failed to rise because the originator of the idea focused on the perceived benefits to the organization without considering what incentives would have to be offered to get people to contribute; the IT staff focused solely on delivering a quality technology solution. In short, both wanted to solve a problem but didn't ask if it was the right problem to solve (Barth, 2000).

Balancing these two sets of value perceptions also means gearing your communication campaign to both constituencies. We have seen KM initiatives falter where top management were the main focus of KM communications, or where end users were the main target, to the exclusion of the other party. Both constituencies need to be kept on board, and they need to be alerted regularly to progress and made aware of benefits that make sense to them. We cover communications in Chapter 19.

## Pitfall 6. The four enablers of KM are not given equal attention

In Chapter 1 we introduced the idea of the four enablers for KM, which we likened to the four legs on a table. If you find one of these enablers becomes too dominant during KM implementation, then your table is at risk of becoming wobbly and unstable. If any of these elements is missing completely, your table will fall.

- If there are no **roles and accountabilities,** then KM is nobody's job or it's 'the KM team's job' in which case the team will quickly collapse from being over-extended.
- If there are no **processes** for KM, then nobody knows what to do, or how to do it.
- If there is no **technology** for KM, then nobody has the tools, and KM can never extend beyond the immediate and local context.
- If there is no **governance,** then nobody sees the point. KM remains an optional activity, and nobody has time for optional activity.

Over the years, we have seen that two of these 'table legs' – ie roles and governance – get far less attention than the other two. This is often a contributing factor to the challenges that KM programmes face (Weber, 2007). It is easy to see this in the frequency of Google searches on the four elements, as a proxy measure of where the attention typically lies. A search for 'knowledge management process' gave 330,000 results, for example; 'knowledge management technology' yielded 264,000 results, 'knowledge management roles' 68,000 results and 'knowledge management governance' 34,700 results. If these are the four legs on the KM table, then in the wider KM world the longest leg seems to get nearly ten times the attention than the shortest leg. Do not fall into this trap. Chapter 12 describes an approach to building a balanced KM framework.

## Pitfall 7. Only parts of the KM solution are implemented

All too often, KM implementations take only one element of knowledge management, or one tool or technology, and assume that it will work in isolation. A common assumption is that knowledge has to be captured and published, so people go down a route of collecting documents rather than connecting people, ending with content graveyards that nobody ever visits or uses. An alternative but equally common assumption is that all you have to do is 'let people talk and knowledge will share itself'. So people go down a route of connecting people through social media technology. In reality, knowledge doesn't just 'share itself' without structure or focus. Taking a small element of KM and assuming it will work in isolation is like taking one culinary ingredient and assuming it will create the whole recipe, or like taking one small element of a central heating system and assuming it will heat the house.

## CASE STUDY

A client asked us to come into their organization and capture knowledge from major successful bids. We held a series of retrospects, and found some really good success factors which should be repeated in future, and a whole set of opportunities for improving the bid process, including some things that were really frustrating the bid teams (mostly related to inappropriate company policies). We documented the lessons and the opportunities for improvement, trained the client in the retrospect process, and moved on.

A few months later the client called and said, 'That retrospect process is rubbish'. On further questioning, he said, 'Those issues that were frustrating the team when we started, are still there. They have come up again in the latest retrospects. Nothing has been changed'.

Of course nothing had changed, as all they had done was introduce one element of KM — a knowledge-capture process. Retrospects are great for identifying team learning, but there needs to be a follow-on process to take action on the issue, and for this particular company, those actions needed to be taken at a high level in the organization. They had not implemented a process or workflow for addressing the actions, and had no engagement from senior managers in the learning process.

## *Pitfall 8. You make KM too difficult for people*

Knowledge management is hard enough to implement, without asking people to radically change their work habits as well. You will find the KM implementation journey easier if you can (at least at first) work with the habits and tools that people already have and already use. For example, if people need to regularly log onto a new community of practice website to share knowledge with their peers, this is a new habit and people forget, or don't bother, and the community dies. Better to link the community to established work habits such as e-mail, and ensure members are alerted to new community discussions through their e-mail.

Here is a recommendation from the IDEO Chief Technology Officer Doug Solomon (Solomon, 2010):

> If a tool requires people to go out of their way to use it, adoption will always be a challenge, no matter how wonderfully designed. Wherever possible, strive to integrate tools into existing work processes – bring the system to the user rather than the other way around. For example, the IDEO blogging system didn't take off until the team added a program that sends digest e-mails with new content from the blogs each employee has subscribed to.

In their study of a failed KM initiative in a global bank, Chua and Lam found that the IT team behind the planned global knowledge network had failed to consult the end users in the project development phase, and had little understanding of how they actually worked. When the system was launched the users naturally had little understanding of the rationale for the system or how it was supposed to fit into their work, and little incentive to share knowledge using the system (Chua and Lam, 2005). You need to reduce the barrier to entry to KM whenever you introduce new tools and new processes. Make them as simple as you can, and then simplify them again. Build them into existing work habits, such as e-mail. Don't expect people to learn new tricks, or make new clicks. Chapter 17 describes how to build evidence of user habits into the design of knowledge systems.

## Pitfall 9. KM is not implemented as a change programme

KM is a programme of organizational change. It's not about buying and rolling out technology and it's not about adding another task into the project framework – it's about changing the way people think. It involves changing personal and organizational priorities, routines and habits. KM needs to be introduced as an organizational change programme; with high-level sponsorship, a communication strategy, a desired end-state, and step-wise implementation rather than 'everyone change at once'. Change needs to reach a tipping point, and hearts and minds need to be changed one at a time (see Chapter 18). Organizational change is a well-established field, and KM needs to learn from this field.

Part of the change process is to understand the current impediments to knowledge transfer in your organization, whether they be inappropriate incentives, conflicting processes, or the capacity of employees to communicate, absorb or apply the target knowledge. This is why a knowledge assets audit is a useful exercise in planning a KM implementation (see Chapter 11), and why a culture assessment is important (see Chapter 19).

## Pitfall 10. The KM team 'preaches only to the converted'

The KM team are enthusiasts. They see the value in KM; they 'catch the vision', and they assume everyone else will catch the vision. As they go out into the organization conducting the change programme, they begin to meet other enthusiasts, and will be engaged in exciting discussions. However, they eventually need to move beyond the enthusiasts and engage the rest of the organization. Experience shows that maybe 20 per cent of people are enthusiasts, maybe 60 per cent don't care about KM one way or another (they will do it if their job requires it, but it's not a big deal either way), and 20 per cent hate the idea, and find it threatening. Even though it's much more fun to work with the enthusiasts, pretty soon you will have to move beyond them and start the hard work of engaging the other 80 per cent – the tough nuts, the cynics and the don't-cares. We provide methods of influencing these three KM 'market segments' in Chapter 18.

## Pitfall 11. The KM team fail to engage with key stakeholders

You need to be practical and systematic about who you involve and engage with. One of the key steps in your initial KM strategy building process should be a systematic mapping of key stakeholder groups (Barnes and Milton, 2015). Likely stakeholders include:

- the senior management team;
- the CEO;
- prominent senior sceptics;
- key department heads;
- the sponsors of pilot projects;
- the knowledge workers in the organization;
- the KM community of practice;
- external bodies you share knowledge or information with.

At the implementation stage, stakeholders may also include, as we saw in Chapter 1, partner disciplines or functions in the organization with whom we need to coordinate. The initial engagement with stakeholders at the strategy building stage needs to be sustained and even extended throughout KM implementation. Rosina Weber notes that failure to engage with all the key stakeholder groups is a common failure factor in KM implementations (Weber, 2007). Since different stakeholders may have different needs and demands, this does not mean doing everything they ask, but it does mean systematic engagement, communication and – where possible – alignment.

## Pitfall 12. The KM team have the wrong competence

If KM is a programme of organizational change, then the KM team needs to be made up of change agents and change leaders. The team leader, first and foremost, needs to be a change agent, a visionary leader, capable of working at the highest levels in the organization as well as the lowest, and with the ability, mandate and authority to make change happen.

All too often, the KM teams we come across in organizations are not like this at all. They are the wrong people – back-room men and women, more at home managing databases than inspiring change. They prefer working with computers to working with people. They do not inspire, and they are not visionary. They are uncomfortable in the boardroom. We have also pointed out that KM implementation is, at least partly, an orchestration function. Partner disciplines and functions need to be brought on board and coordinated with. Working with all four enablers of KM requires facility with business process analysis, and sufficient knowledge of technology capabilities to be able to work with the IT team without being either unrealistic or brushed off by 'it can't be done'.

Finding the right people for the KM team is not easy, but changing the culture of an organization is not easy either. We cover the role of the KM leader and the KM team in greater depth Chapters 5 and 6.

# Summary

As Chua and Lam point out, 'KM projects attract an alarmingly high level of risk. Nonetheless, many KM project pitfalls can be avoided if they [are] identified and discussed before the project commences or better managed during the project itself' (Chua and Lam, 2005). This chapter provides an alternative way of navigating the contents of this book, by potential pitfalls and their solutions.

Rest assured that all pitfalls are avoidable or can be largely mitigated with sufficient preparation. Despite the many barriers and the many failed KM projects, there are also many that have succeeded, and these have shown us the way to overcome the barriers. You'll learn about both sides of the coin in the rest of this book.

# PART TWO
# Preparation and resources

## Executive summary

This section of *The Knowledge Manager's Handbook* will help you scope and resource your KM implementation. Chapter 4 reviews the components of a good KM strategy, with illustrative examples. Chapters 5–7 describe the human capital requirements behind KM implementation, namely the KM leader, the KM team, and the role of senior management. Chapters 8–10 cover what you need to prepare in budget and time allocation, setting aims and objectives, and finding partners to work with you.

# Knowledge management strategy

## 04

Knowledge management implementation without a guiding strategy would not be sensible. In this chapter we describe some of the work that you need to complete as the strategic foundation for your KM implementation (for a fuller and more detailed introduction to KM strategy development, see Barnes and Milton, 2015). This chapter covers the following elements:

- deciding the strategic principles;
- identifying the business drivers;
- defining the KM vision;
- agreeing the KM scope;
- defining the strategic knowledge areas;
- assessing the current state of KM;
- creating a draft KM framework;
- deciding how to handle change management;
- creating a business case.

Each of these tasks is outlined below.

## Deciding the strategic principles

Discuss with your sponsor and steering committee the strategic principles that you will apply to your KM programme. Barnes and Milton (2015) suggest the following 10 principles, which are echoed throughout *The Knowledge Manager's Handbook*:

- KM implementation should be led by the organization and should support the organizational strategy.
- KM needs to be delivered where the critical knowledge lies and where the high-value decisions are made.

- KM implementation should be treated as a behaviour change management exercise.
- The endgame will be to introduce a completed management framework for KM.
- The framework must be embedded into the organizational structures.
- The framework will need to include governance if it is to be sustainable.
- The framework will be structured rather than emergent.
- A KM implementation should be a staged process with regular decision points.
- A KM implementation should contain a piloting stage.
- A KM implementation should be run as a project.

These principles are based on sound practical experience from a large number of KM implementation programmes. Do your best to convince your sponsor and steering group that these principles should be followed.

# Identifying the business drivers

Interview a wide range of senior managers to understand the core business drivers for KM. This will help you understand why KM is important to the organization. The four main business drivers include:

- **Operational excellence** – improving the internal practices and processes of the organization so that it operates better, faster, cheaper, safer and cleaner. For companies facing the risk of knowledge loss as an ageing workforce approaches retirement age, KM may focus on maintaining the existing capabilities expressed in practices and processes. Chapter 30 describes how the Singapore Youth Olympics had just one chance to build a strategic capability for running major events.
- **Customer knowledge** – building a better understanding of customers' wants and needs, and how to satisfy them. In Chapter 31 Jessica Magnusson describes how UK law firms use KM to deliver better services to their customers.
- **Innovation** – creation of new knowledge in order to create new products and services. In Chapter 29 Tan Xinde describes how Huawei Technologies worked at using KM to accelerate the rate at which employees could translate knowledge into action.
- **Growth and change** – replicating existing success in new markets or with new staff, or developing the knowledge to enter new markets. Chapter 27 tells the story of KM at Mars, and how the senior managers helped redirect the Mars KM strategy to be completely focused on the company 'bottom line' and the growth strategy that was in place at the time.

# Defining the knowledge management vision

This involves working with your key stakeholders to develop a brief and engaging statement of what KM will bring to the organization.

## CASE STUDY

Suurlu *et al* (2002) describe the development of KM in the Finnish Parliament, and the collaborative process used to develop the parliamentary KM vision with the help of the Members of Parliament. The team carried out a series of interviews with parliamentary civil servants and MPs in 2000–2001 in order to understand the current state of parliamentary KM, the critical knowledge areas related to daily work, the knowledge requirements and problems, and the central changes affecting KM activities, in order to establish a vision of reliable and efficient KM for the Parliament. This is a typical strategic-level data-gathering programme aimed at senior stakeholders.

The final KM vision, which spoke directly to the culture of the institution, was, 'The Parliament is an open and competent knowledge organization with a cooperation-oriented work culture and the capacity and will to learn'.

# Agreeing the knowledge management scope

This involves working with your key stakeholders to understand the limits of your KM implementation programme, and to define those parts of the business and business activity that are in scope, and those that are out of scope.

## CASE STUDY

We were working recently with a financial institution, developing their KM strategy. Although we agreed that the whole scope of operations should be included in the KM strategy, including the Head Office and all branch offices, we decided to make it clear in the strategy document that the KM scope would exclude customer relationship management, business intelligence, enterprise content management and learning and development. Although these areas had high potential value, and had natural affinities and interdependencies with KM, all were considered separate issues already under investigation by other groups, and therefore out of the scope of the KM strategy.

# Defining the strategic knowledge areas

This step involves working with senior management to identify the knowledge of greatest strategic impact for the organization, which is therefore of highest priority to be addressed by the KM programme. This strategic knowledge assessment is a high-level assessment specifically for the strategy stage. During KM implementation it will be reinforced and extended by a more comprehensive and more granular knowledge assets audit.

## CASE STUDY

When Martin Ihrig of the I-Space Institute worked with a group of decision makers at ATLAS, the major particle physics experiment at the European Organization for Nuclear Research (CERN), he interviewed many stakeholders to understand the critical knowledge for the organization, or 'the knowledge underpinning its success' (Ihrig and MacMillan, 2015). Ultimately only a portion of the ATLAS knowledge base was mapped, but the list of 26 knowledge domains was prioritized to identify the eight that were deemed most important to organizational outcomes, and which should be addressed by KM.

# Assessing the current state of knowledge management

The strategic stage of KM implementation often includes a current state assessment, in order to gauge the scale of the task. Barnes and Milton (2015) recommend using the structure of the KM framework as a template for assessment. The framework ensures that you cover all the major components that need to be in place for effective KM, and that will support a realistic gap analysis.

## CASE STUDY

We recently conducted a current state assessment of a company's lesson-learning capability (a subset of KM). The company successfully captured many lessons, and stored them in a custom-made lessons management system. We found however that a lack of governance and quality control meant that many of the lessons were of very poor quality, leading to a lack of trust in the system. There was also no company-wide approach to common practices, which meant that each operating unit had developed its own way of operating and countered the re-use of lessons from elsewhere with a strong 'not invented here' culture. The KM framework helped to identify governance and the development of common practice as two areas that the company would need to address in its renewed KM programme.

# Creating a draft knowledge management framework

An outline KM framework is often created at the strategy stage, to give some idea of what the final outcome may look like. However, the framework will be refined and fleshed out several times during implementation, specifically during proof of concept exercises and pilots.

# Deciding how to handle change management

One of the recurrent themes of this book is that KM needs to be introduced as a change management exercise. This begins with the KM strategy phase. The KM strategy document should contain an outline of how the KM project will employ change management techniques.

## CASE STUDY

The KM strategy for the Food and Agriculture Organization of the United Nations makes an explicit mention of change management, recognizing from the experience of other organizations that promoting constructive change was essential to KM implementation. They proposed a four-step culture change approach (FAO, 2011):

- Step 1: Assess needs and establish the case for change.

- Step 2: Build the required coalitions for change, in which sponsors within technical departments and decentralized offices form their own change initiatives but work collectively towards a shared vision.

- Step 3: Share and enhance the vision through an outreach programme.

- Step 4: Secure short-term wins – concrete, achievable targets to gain confidence and buy-in.

# Creating a business case

In some organizations, you may need to create an outline business case for KM at the strategy stage in order to secure further funding. This is not an easy thing to do at such an early stage. Your strategic business case does not need to be an exact mathematical and logical case; it just needs to demonstrate that KM will bring more value than it costs.

## CASE STUDY

Gorelick *et al* (2004) explain how a task force was set up to create a business case for KM in BP in 1997.

*A task force was formed with 5–10 executives... charged with assessing the state of KM in BP and making recommendations. The task force concluded that the BP environment had many factors conducive for KM, but that a major effort was needed to accelerate the pace and benefits of BP's transformation to a learning organization, and to maintain the momentum of existing knowledge efforts. A half billion dollars annual saving was the anticipated 'big prize' for BP, if they found a way to better leverage know-how. The steering committee approved all the task force recommendations... (and) within a week a decision was made to establish a central KM team reporting to a corporate Managing Director.*

## Summary

The KM strategy is a crucial guidance document for KM implementation. The vision sets the direction for KM, the scope provides the limits for the implementation programme, the business drivers and strategic knowledge areas provide prioritization and focus, the principles explain how implementation will progress, the current state analysis and draft framework define the start state and end state (and therefore the amount of work to be done), while the change management section begins to explore how the change will be introduced. Finally, the business case provides the rationale. In the rest of this book, we will be looking at how your KM strategy is actualized in practice.

# The role, skills and characteristics of the knowledge management leader

## 05

If your KM leader is not yet in place, this chapter will provide some guidance on who to hire, and what she or he will do. Alternatively you may already have been appointed to lead the KM implementation programme, and you can use this chapter to identify the skills you already have, and the skills you will need to develop to perform your role.

The chapter contains the following elements:

- a description of the role of the KM leader, and a list of recommended accountabilities;
- a discussion of whether the KM leader should be an internal or external appointment (we recommend internal);
- the most important characteristic for an external appointment, namely practical experience;
- the important competencies for the KM leader;
- a warning about the 'personality trap' for the KM leader;
- a useful metaphor for the KM leader – that of a gardener.

## The role of the knowledge management leader

Also known as the KM programme manager, the director of KM or the chief knowledge officer, this person is in charge of KM implementation. They are accountable for designing and introducing a working KM framework within the business, which delivers business value and is seen by staff and management as supporting effective business practice. The KM leader will act as project manager for the framework implementation project, and will represent KM at the senior level of management.

The accountabilities of the KM leader during the implementation programme are as follows:

- Develop, together with the leadership of the organization, the vision, objectives, metrics and deliverables of the KM implementation programme. This is done during the KM strategy phase, which precedes KM implementation. Full details of the KM strategy phase can be found in the book *Designing a Successful KM Strategy* (Barnes and Milton, 2015).
- Deliver the implementation project objectives, within the agreed time frame and to the agreed cost and performance metrics. The KM leader manages the implementation project. They are accountable for delivery, for the budget, for managing the members of the KM implementation team, and for managing progress and activity (the standard accountabilities of a project manager).
- Define and test the KM framework through the testing and piloting phase, and ensure that the KM framework operates effectively and efficiently. 'Effectively' means that the desired objectives are met, and 'efficiently' means within a reasonable range of effort and cost. At the end of the piloting stage, the KM leader is accountable for delivering a tested and validated framework.
- Ensure that the KM framework delivers business value. Delivering the framework is not an end in itself; the framework only exists to deliver business value and the KM leader must keep this value objective constantly in mind. Very often the success of the pilots, for example, will be measured in business terms: money saved, time saved, or value created.
- Act as champion for the corporate vision of KM. The KM leader is the figurehead and champion for KM within the organization. She or he is responsible for ensuring that knowledge management, as applied within the organization, is understood, and seen as an important and valuable activity by all of the main stakeholders.

Once the implementation programme is over, the KM leader role changes to a more operational one, concerned with maintaining KM activity, monitoring and reporting on the application of KM, and looking for enhancements to the KM framework.

Tip

Use this section of *The Knowledge Manager's Handbook* to check and update your job description. Is anything missing? Is there any part of your job description that is surplus to requirements? Update your job description accordingly, and if there are any significant changes, be sure to discuss them with your manager.

# Should the knowledge management leader be an internal or external appointment?

Should the KM leader be an internal appointment (and often therefore with little experience in KM), or should you should recruit a KM expert to take this post? Our advice is that it should be an internal appointment. KM is a simple idea to grasp, but very difficult to do in practice. The idea that people should share knowledge with each other and learn from each other is not complicated; the challenge is getting it to actually happen. Implementing KM is about culture change, and culture change is both difficult and politically charged, and best handled by an 'insider'.

The KM leader should therefore ideally be an existing respected senior member of the organization, with a history of leading change, who knows the internal politics and knows how to get things done in the organization. Learning enough knowledge management to lead a KM programme can be done quickly, with the right mentoring and coaching from specialists. Learning the politics of an organization can take years, if not an entire career.

## CASE STUDY

One of us worked with an organization where one of the elements of the KM framework called for stronger governance in the shape of corporate policies around the management of records, and clearer guidance about balancing the need for information security against the need to share knowledge across silos. With the KM leader, we went to the senior leadership team to ask them for endorsement to develop clear policies to this effect. Their reaction was unenthusiastic, and instead of endorsement we got lots of conflicting responses as disagreements emerged around the table about how to handle the issue. Several senior leaders thought that KM should be entirely voluntary, and should not be governed by policy. We were concerned that this would be a roadblock, but the KM leader was not disheartened. He told his team to go ahead anyway – 'When they see what the policy looks like, they will understand why it's important.' And indeed, the policies were eventually adopted. The KM leader knew when he could sidestep the formal approval process and get things done a different way, because he knew how his colleagues thought and operated.

# The most important characteristic for an external appointment

If there is no suitable and willing internal candidate and you end up appointing an external KM expert to lead an internal KM programme, the first thing you should look for on their CV is practical experience. There is no point in hiring a KM expert who doesn't have a track record of implementation delivery. This point was made forcefully to us by a knowledge manager in a large engineering firm:

> I would (hire) somebody with a practical background – somebody who maybe likes the academic side and likes to research, but somebody who has put that research back into delivery. If I was recruiting somebody and I had an interview and I asked 'do you think you were successful (in your last KM implementation)' and they said 'yes we were absolutely successful' I would instantly be suspicious, because knowledge management is not straightforward. I want practical evidence that it is painful. I want to see the blood and the guts. I want to know that they have been there and they have struggled with KM.

# What competencies does the knowledge management leader need?

First and foremost, you need a proven 'change agent' to lead your KM implementation. Leading change is different from leading other types of projects, and requires distinct approaches and skillsets. People with a proven history of change leadership are difficult to find in any organization, but the ability of the KM leader to deliver change is a crucial success factor for the implementation project.

Secondly, the leader needs influencing skills. Influencing management, stakeholders and knowledge workers is a big part of the leader's role. The KM leader needs to have strong communication and influencing skills, and if they are a proven change leader they will already have these. We cover influencing techniques in more detail in Chapter 18.

The KM leader needs to know the company, the company structure and strategy, the company terminology and the stories that circulate around the organization, and they also need to be widely known. Ideally they should have history and credibility in more than one division, rather than having spent their whole career in marketing, or in research, or in finance. They should know the important people, and be very well networked.

The KM leader needs the ability to take a long-term view. They need to be in KM for the long haul, as an implementation project can take several years before the framework is fully embedded. They need to focus on the long-term change programme, while still moving KM forward through a series of quick wins.

Above all, the leader needs to be able to translate KM into the day-to-day working language of the organization. KM jargon and theory should be kept within the KM team and their immediate circle of knowledge champions, while to the business, the KM leader should be able to speak in business language. This is another reason why the KM leader should be someone with wide experience within the business divisions.

> **Tip**
>
> Assess yourself against these competences, and also ask your team and your manager to assess you as well. If you are lacking in any of these areas, see what you can do to strengthen your competence. Build your network, go on an 'influencing skills' course, or take training in change management. If you aspire to a KM leadership role in the future, actively seek out diverse roles within the business (not just in KM), and get involved in change programmes. Find a mentor who has the qualities and competences that you aspire to, and observe how they handle tricky situations and roadblocks.

## The personality trap

A strong, passionate leader is essential for an effective KM implementation team. However, the risk in relying on the personality of a strong leader to drive transformation is that when the leader moves on, transformation can falter.

For example, a project manager working in a major project in South East Asia took the lead in implementing KM in his part of the business. He set up a knowledge network of project managers who would meet, exchange documents, and swap lessons learned for further re-use. And it worked – in his area he cut costs, shortened timelines and improved safety statistics. He acted as champion, thought leader, and role model for KM within the wider business.

Then he left – moving on to another part of the business. The community stopped functioning. Knowledge capture ceased. Many people in the business claimed that they were unaware of what he had been doing. Knowledge management in the South East Asia division dwindled away and died. The culture reverted to where it had been before.

No matter how strong the leader's personality, and no matter how much they can get done by personally driving change, there comes a time when they have to pass over the reins – not to another strong personality, but to an embedded framework that is going to function no matter who is driving it.

# A metaphor

People often think of knowledge as being organic. An ecosystem or a garden is a pretty good metaphor for the world of knowledge in an organization. Knowledge is something that grows and develops. It can be replicated and seeded. It is not something solid and static like a car or a factory or a coin that can be grasped and controlled and physically managed. Instead it needs to be nurtured and tended.

The KM leader, in this metaphor, is the head gardener. If you want to produce flowers or vegetables, there is hard work involved. Gardens require a lot of management to bear fruit.

Let's assume you are tending the knowledge garden for your organization, driven by a desire to create value for the key stakeholders – the knowledge workers, the management, and your external customers. If you want to create value from a garden, you don't just 'create the conditions so anything can grow', because all you will get is nettles, brambles and other weeds. Gardening is extremely active.

## Tilling and preparing the ground

For gardening and for KM, you need to get the conditions right for growth. This is the culture change element of your role – the communication strategy and the hearts and minds campaign described in Chapters 18 and 19. You also need to provide the supporting infrastructure. Just as a gardener puts in place the canes, cloches and trellises to support the new seedlings, so you need to ensure there is sufficient technology to support emergent KM activities (recognizing, of course, that technology alone will not create KM, any more than trellises alone will create a garden).

## Planting the seeds

These are the proof of concept events and the KM pilot projects (Chapter 22); the early knowledge assets, KM practices and trial communities of practice that you might set up where there is greatest demand and greatest value.

## *Watering and fertilizing the growing seeds*

As a knowledge manager, the early seeds in your KM garden will need your supervision and your support. You will need to work with the community of practice leaders, the knowledge owners and the project staff to ensure the early KM work does not wither and die through lack of care.

## *Propagating growth*

Some of the plants in your KM garden will thrive. Learn from these, find out the secrets of their success, and seek to reproduce these elsewhere. Just as a gardener will take cuttings, runners and seeds from their prize-winning plants, you too can propagate success from the best performers.

## *Removing the weeds and pests*

If there are any things that hamper the growth in your KM garden – be these incentives that backfire, loud sceptics, or misbehaviour in the community of practice discussions – then you need to address them, and see if you can remove them before they start to spread. For example, incentives that drive internal competition may need removal before they stunt the growth of KM or kill your tender plants.

This is all very hard work, but the rewards for successful KM are the same as those for a successful gardener – a thriving ecosystem and a mountain of produce.

---

**Tip**

If the head gardener metaphor doesn't appeal to you, find another one. Perhaps you are the knowledge supply chain manager, or the conductor of the KM orchestra. A good metaphor can often help you keep your role in context.

---

# Summary

The role of the KM leader is crucial for the success of KM implementation. In this chapter we have explored the role in detail, discussing the account-abilities, background and competence that an effective KM leader (or head knowledge gardener) requires. In the next two chapters we will look at the people who will support the KM leader: the KM team members and your organization's senior management.

# The KM team members

## 06

One of the first decisions a KM leader will need to make is 'who's on the KM team?' This includes deciding how big the KM team needs to be, the skills and competences you will need on the team, and the sort of personalities you need to look for.

In this chapter we cover:

- the size of the KM team;
- the skillsets you will need on the team;
- the attitudes and values the KM team needs to share; and
- the roles you will need on the KM team.

## How big should your KM team be?

How big is the average KM team? The answer depends on a) how big your organization is, and b) what you mean by average. The results from the Knoco 2014 global survey of KM practitioners show that the mean size for a KM team is nine people, while the most common (modal) size is four people. However, this figure represents answers from both small and large companies, so it makes more sense to look at the mean KM team size for different company sizes, as shown in Figure 6.1.

Although KM team size depends on organizational size, with team size growing progressively with larger companies, this is not a linear relationship. Increasing the organizational size by 10 does not result in a 10-fold increase in KM team size. Also, even in the smallest companies, there seems to be a minimum number for an effective team – three people.

The non-linear relationship represents the two elements of building a minimal capacity, and economies of scale. There are many tasks which all KM teams perform irrespective of the size of the organization: creating the KM strategy, designing the KM framework, piloting the KM framework, etc. However, a successful KM activity can scale rapidly with relatively little support. Time can also be traded off against team size. When the framework is rolled out, during the later implementation stages, it may take more people to roll out KM across a large organization, or it may take a smaller team

**FIGURE 6.1**    A graph of KM team size for a variety of organizational size ranges

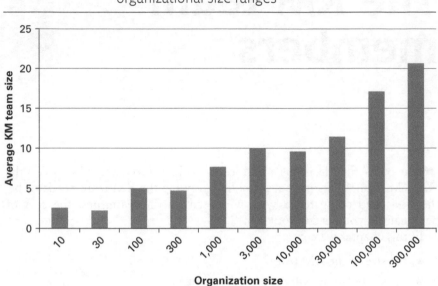

**SOURCE**: Knoco Limited

a longer time. An implementation team of three in a 30-person organization can sort out KM in a few months. An implementation team of 12 in a 30,000-person organization may take a few years to do the same job.

> Tip
>
> Build a bottom-up estimate of the size of the team you will need to deliver your KM programme, and then use the statistics here as a benchmark. Are your figures realistic?

## What skillsets will you need on your team?

There seem to be seven core skillsets people look for in a KM team, although the balance of these skillsets varies from one sector to another. You will never find people who have all seven of these skills, so you need to think about selecting a mix of people with a mix of skills. Here are the seven core skillsets:

- business skills;
- facilitation skills;
- knowledge organization skills;
- change management skills;
- writing skills;
- IT skills;
- project management skills.

## Business skills

The most important skillset to have on the team is functional experience in the work of your organization. If you work in a legal firm, you need lawyers on the KM team. If you work in an aeronautical firm, you need aeronautical engineers on the team, and so on. KM team members need these skills and background to translate KM into the working language and working practices of the business. When members of the team are working with KM pilot projects in the business, they want to be seen as 'part of the business', not 'specialists from HQ who know nothing about our work'. The larger the organization and the more types of work the organization does, the greater the number of these business skills you will need, and ideally the KM team will contain people with solid backgrounds in each major organizational function.

## Facilitation skills

Next you need people with facilitation skills. Many of the processes in your KM framework take the form of facilitated meetings, and much of KM is concerned with conversation. Your KM team will need to facilitate the meetings and the conversations. Look for the natural facilitators, and provide facilitation training for the other team members as soon as you can.

## The skills of knowledge organization

Then you need people with skills related to the organization of explicit knowledge. KM covers content as well as conversations, so you need people on the team with information management, content management and library skills. The areas of metadata, taxonomy and document lifecycle management will all need to be addressed, and you will need some awareness of records management as well, since records management forms one important aspect of organizational memory.

### Change management skills

Also important are change management skills. The KM implementation team has a tough job ahead of them, changing the culture of the organization. The 'soft skills' of influencing and communication are absolutely core, and the team will need to be skilled in training, coaching and mentoring. The early stages of implementing KM are all about raising awareness, and 'selling' the idea. The team needs at least one person who can support the KM leader in presenting and marketing. This person may also help to raise the profile of the organization's KM achievements and activities at external conferences.

### Writing and journalism skills

You will need people with good writing skills. The processes of knowledge capture and packaging are in some ways very akin to journalism. Interviewing, capturing discussions, analysis, summary, write-up, presentation, are all part of the stock-in-trade of knowledge capture. Make sure there is at least one person on the team with journalistic or writing skills.

### IT skills

The team needs at least one person with IT skills, who is aware of the details of the current in-house technology, and the potential of technology as an enabler of KM. This person should be able to liaise effectively with your IT department, and help define the most appropriate technologies to introduce to the organization. When the IT team say something 'can't be done', you need someone who knows enough to be able to suggest an approach or strategy to get it done.

### Project management skills

Finally, since much of KM implementation is project and programme driven, you need strong project management skills on the team. This includes experience in developing project plans with clearly defined major deliverables, monitoring progress and managing scope, and adjusting the plans based on lessons learned during the project.

## Attitude and values

In addition to the core skillsets, you also need the right attitude and values. The members of the team need to be passionate and knowledgeable about KM. They need training in the skills and theories of KM and best practice transfer, and access to books, conferences and forums on the topic. They should participate in KM communities of practice. They must be enthusiastic about applying KM tools and techniques to enhance the quality of their own work.

**Tip**

Create a skills matrix. Use the seven core skills here as the horizontal rows, and your candidate KM team members as the vertical columns. Tick off the skills each candidate team member has, and ensure each of the core skills is present in the team. Don't forget to include yourself on the matrix. If you find some skillsets are missing, think what you can do in terms of training or recruitment to meet the gaps.

# Team roles

The skills and competences may translate to specific roles on the team (note that sometimes one person can hold more than one of these roles). Here are some of the roles you will probably need.

## Project manager

For a large team, you may want to appoint a project manager to look after the administrative aspects of the project; maintaining the project plan, managing the budget, and creating the reports for the steering group. Having a separate project manager will free up the KM leader to concentrate on the change management aspects of their role.

## Knowledge manager

The team will almost certainly need a knowledge manager, to maintain and document the knowledge of the team, to build and coordinate a KM community of practice (including all KM champions), and to start to build the corporate knowledge base on KM. This person will play the role of subject matter expert for KM within the organization.

## Communications lead

You will need somebody in charge of communications for the team, who can manage and deliver the communication strategy and plan. In a larger team, tasked with implementing KM across a large and complex organization, this is often a full-time role, and may even involve more than one person. Make sure this person is a skilled communicator, perhaps with a marketing or internal communications background.

## KM workers and coaches

You will need people to go out and support KM activities in the organization. These people deliver the 'proof of concept' exercises, and work with the business implementing the pilots. This is the primary role for the business people within the team.

Finally you may need people to take accountability for specific components or projects within the KM programme. Your IT specialist may take accountability for the development of supporting tools, your knowledge organization specialist may take accountability for developing the enterprise taxonomy, and so on. However make sure that all of the roles work as a coordinated team and not in isolation, otherwise the KM framework that you develop and deploy may not work as a complete system.

# Summary

The KM team has an important and varied set of tasks. They need to help develop new ways of working and new knowledge-friendly behaviours across the organization, and to do this the team needs to contain the correct mix of skills embodied in a clear set of roles. Establishing the team is a key step in the implementation programme. With the right team, you can accomplish anything. With the wrong team, your implementation will be much more difficult. Even the best team, working with the best KM leader, will need support from senior management. This support is the subject of our next chapter.

# The role of senior management

## 07

In addition to the KM leader and team, senior management also have a key role to play. Besides understanding their role, you may also need to coach them in supporting KM implementation. This chapter covers the following topics:

- the role of the sponsor;
- the risks to effective sponsorship;
- the KM steering team; and
- working with the other senior managers.

## The role of the sponsor

The sponsor is the person who commissioned the KM implementation. They act as your internal client for the implementation project and your representative at high levels, so the higher the level of your sponsorship, the easier your job will be. Ideally you would want a C-level sponsor. At the World Bank, for example, the president of the bank acted as sponsor for a KM programme to deliver his vision of 'a knowledge bank' – using KM to increase employee effectiveness and efficiency across the organization. You would be very lucky if you had such high-level sponsorship. It is more common for sponsorship to be delegated down to a functional head or divisional head.

The main elements of the sponsor role during KM implementation are as follows:

- To agree, with the KM leader and team, the aims and objectives of the implementation programme and how these will be measured. The sponsor is the primary client for the programme and will be the person who judges the success or failure of the implementation programme, so make sure you agree clear objectives which can be measured easily and unambiguously.
- To challenge the KM team over these objectives. It is not the job of the sponsor to give the KM team an easy ride. To show value to the business, your KM objectives should be tough, and it is the sponsor's role to add some challenge.

- To provide the required resources to deliver those objectives. The sponsor provides the budget for the KM programme, which pays for the salaries of the KM team and any travel that may be needed. They also provide the legitimacy. They are the figurehead for the programme.

- To provide the business view to the KM team, and represent the needs of the business to the programme. The sponsor should help the team understand what knowledge is strategic to the organization, so that KM activities can fully support the strategic agenda for the business. To this end, the sponsor often appoints and chairs a steering team (described later in this chapter).

- To regularly review progress. The sponsor chairs the review meetings that ensure the implementation project remains on track.

- To make commitments to proceed. This is an important point. The KM team will deliver results, but they expect the sponsor to make decisions based on those results. The expectations might be expressed like this:

  - 'If we deliver an effective plan to deliver KM, and demonstrate that the key processes can work in the organizational context, we expect you to give us approval to move to piloting.'

  - 'If the KM pilots fully deliver against the agreed objectives, we expect you to endorse and support KM roll-out.'

  - 'Once roll-out has started, we expect your support in removing the organizational barriers.'

- To champion KM at a senior level. KM will not be the sole priority for the organization, and there will be many issues competing for management attention. The role of the sponsor is to talk and lobby on behalf of KM, to ensure the resources are protected, and to broker alliances and remove conflicts with other initiatives which may be going on. The sponsor is also expected to provide political cover for KM in the early stages, before results begin to show.

- To remove barriers. Once implementation reaches the roll-out phase, there may need to be changes to the way the organization operates in order to allow KM to deliver its value; changes to the project management framework, the reward and recognition system, or the accountability of subject matter experts, to name but a few (see Chapter 23 for more details). The sponsor may need to press for these changes in order that the value from embedded KM can be fully delivered.

## The risks to effective sponsorship

There are a few ways in which your sponsorship can be sub-optimal, and you should be aware of these, and prepared to redress the balance wherever possible. Here are the top three:

**A sponsor with a one-sided view.** In Chapter 10 we describe how an HR sponsor could be too interested in the KM roles, an operational sponsor could be too interested in the KM processes, and so on. In each case you need to ensure the sponsor's view is balanced with other views through the use of a KM steering team, as discussed later in this chapter.

**A sponsor who is too low in the organization.** Many of the roles of the sponsor mentioned earlier – lobbying, removing barriers, brokering deals – require the sponsor to have power and influence, which requires a level of sponsor seniority.

**A sponsor who is uninterested in KM.** Where a sponsor has been appointed with no real motivation or interest in KM, you will have real problems in driving KM forward and getting it embedded into the business. See if you can use your organizational connections to negotiate an interested and committed sponsor. If not, then ask your sponsor 'what would you need to see, in order to be fully enthusiastic about KM?'

---

**Tip**

How good is your sponsor? Do they pass the tests above? If they fall short, what can you do to improve the situation? Use your peer networks in the wider KM community to source ideas and strategies.

---

# The knowledge management steering team

One of the critical elements in delivering change is the steering committee, known in change management terms as the 'guiding coalition'. This is an active team of diverse leaders who drive the change effort by providing guidance, resources and decision-making authority. A successful steering committee is powerful in terms of its composition (titles, expertise, reputations, relationships, leadership skills, access to support and resources), their mutual level of trust and their shared objectives.

KM will usually need such a team to drive the change and steer the programme, particularly in large and complex organizations. The steering team can also ensure that the business is fully represented in the planning and decision making within the KM implementation. Team members should represent the main functions (IT, HR, quality, etc) and the main lines of business (marketing, sales, production, etc) in order to represent all primary stakeholders. They are not a decision-making board, but an advisory board to the sponsor and so to the KM leader. They give decision-making authority in the sense that decisions will be well informed, relevant to the business, and likely to garner support.

The steering team members do not have to be KM converts. In fact, it is probably useful if some of them have some level of scepticism. This adds a level of real business challenge to the programme, and can ensure that objections are met and resolved early on. The steering team can also act as ambassadors for the KM programme in their own part of the business. The head of IT, for example, can ensure that the needs of the KM programme are honoured by the IT department, the head of HR can help ensure KM expectations are included in the annual appraisal system, and the head of operations can help identify and facilitate KM pilots in the operational departments.

The steering team should meet on a regular basis, for example quarterly, chaired by the KM sponsor. They meet to review the progress and performance of the KM programme, and to advise on next steps.

---

### Tip

Try to ensure that HR, IT, Projects, Strategy and R&D (if you have these departments) are represented on your steering team. Try to ensure that it is the head of department who attends, and ask your sponsor to make it clear that this is what he or she expects.

---

# Working with the other senior managers

As you move into the later stages of KM implementation, the involvement of all senior managers becomes increasingly important. Managers are among the most powerful influencers of culture, so a manager who has not bought into KM can create significant drag on the behavioural change that is needed. The senior managers are some of the most important stakeholders and 'selling' KM to them will require many of the influencing techniques described in Chapter 18. By introducing KM into the manager's business, you can help improve delivery, save money, increase customer satisfaction and reduce risk. In return, you will need several things from them:

- You need them to invest in KM resources and roles within their part of the business, for example the knowledge managers, subject matter experts and KM champions. Help them to see that this is an investment rather than a cost.

- You need them to help steer the KM programme in their part of the business. They should help the KM team understand which knowledge is strategic for that specific business unit or business group, so your KM activities can fully support the manager's business agenda.

- You need them to lead by example. KM is not something that will only be done by the junior grades – the managers need to be involved as well, so you would expect them to take part in KM events, and to contribute their own knowledge.

- Managers need to take the lead in setting an expectation for managing knowledge in their part of the business. They need to make it clear what they expect to see from their staff, asking questions like 'Who have you learned from?' and 'Who will you share this knowledge with?' They need to challenge their direct reports to continuously improve performance through applying knowledge from others.

- It is not enough to set expectations. They need to follow up on these expectations. The organization will be watching closely how senior managers deal with people who shirk their KM responsibilities, and who refuse to learn and share. It will send a very negative message if senior management ignore non-compliance, or reward and recognize the wrong behaviours. This includes fostering internal competition that discourages open sharing, rewarding the lone hero who 'doesn't need to learn', or the knowledge hoarders who keep it all 'in their heads'. Ask the managers to recognize instead those who learn before doing, those who share hard-won lessons, and those who show bravery in admitting to mistakes from which others can learn.

> **Tip**
>
> Use the guidance given in this section to write a one-page brief for your senior management on 'Your Role in Supporting KM'. Discuss this brief, and their role, with them at the next steering team meeting.

# Summary

Support from senior managers is generally recognized as the single most important enabler for KM success, and where it is absent is the single biggest challenge (see Chapter 3). Ensure that you have an engaged, influential and supportive sponsor, a representative and high-level steering team, and an approach to engaging other management-level stakeholders as your implementation progresses.

# Budget and timescale

## 08

One of the big early decisions to be made in your KM implementation is to decide the size of the budget and the timespan of the KM implementation project. In this chapter we give you some guidance and some benchmark figures from other organizations. The chapter covers:

- the need for a budget;
- the size of the budget;
- assigning your budget among the four KM enablers;
- benchmarking your budget;
- the duration of your KM programme; and
- the self-funding trap.

## The need for a budget

One of our colleagues was in a KM workshop recently with a client, and raised the issue of KM budget. One of the people in the room asked 'What? Does KM need a budget?'

Yes, KM needs a budget. All KM programmes should have a budget. You need a budget to pay the team who will plan and drive the change, bring in people to help draft your strategy and framework, buy any new software, and pay the trainers who will train staff in new processes and new roles. For a global company you will need a travel budget for the KM team to visit and work with the regions and divisions, perhaps to support the face-to-face meetings of global communities of practice, or to facilitate knowledge transfer between globally separated projects.

For a large multinational company, the KM budget can easily run into millions of dollars. This is not a cost, but an investment. When focused on business value and framed well, the value that KM will deliver can be 10 or 100 times the cost. Even if you lack initial senior support and are attempting a bottom-up approach to KM, you need to be clear about your costs and your returns if you are going to translate any success you have into senior management support. All KM programmes need a budget, no matter what their size or scale.

# How big will the budget need to be?

You should first try to calculate the size of the budget from the bottom up, by listing out your effort and resources required. You can then benchmark this figure against global statistics. In the later stages of the KM programme the bottom-up budget can be built from a detailed activity plan, as described in detail in Chapter 20. However, in the early stages your plan will be poorly defined and the budget will be based on estimates of the cost of the KM team over the length of the programme, plus allowances for travel, technology spend and consultancy support. This initial budget therefore contains a lot of uncertainty. However the costs will clarify over time, and your budget will be a living document. The budget for the roll-out phase, for example, will be much clearer at the end of the piloting phase than it will be at the beginning. The best approach, as used at Mars (Chapter 27) is to create a plan and budget with a broad three-year time horizon and a more detailed one-year plan.

---

**Tip**

Work with your team to brainstorm all the tasks you think you will need to perform during implementation, and write each of these on a Post-it note. Use the tasks listed in Chapter 20 as a rough guide, even though more work may be needed to confirm these later. This will give you the cost of internal resources to complete the tasks. You then need to include external spend on technology, travel, and any assistance from experienced consultants to support your implementation.

---

# Assigning your budget among the four KM enablers

There is no magic formula for allocating your KM budget, but there is a sense check you should apply to ensure you have covered all the angles. The four KM enablers of roles and accountabilities, processes, technology and governance were introduced in Chapter 1, and it is worth ensuring that each of the enablers gets a significant share of the budget.

- The spend on KM **roles** includes defining the roles that will be needed, as well as coaching, training and support for the knowledge manager, KM champions and community of practice leaders in the business.

- The spend on KM **processes** includes facilitating those processes, documenting them, and introducing them to the business through pilots and training.
- The spend on KM **technology** includes user requirements analysis, acquisition of new technology, integrating it into your infrastructure, maintenance, and training the users.
- The spend on KM **governance** includes monitoring, reporting, value tracking, creation of guidance and reference material, engaging with the business to embed KM into existing workflows, accountabilities and structures, and the negotiation and drafting of the KM policy.

Most of the time, we find that the companies we speak with spend far more on technology than on the other elements, and most of the time we find that their KM programme suffers as a result. Technology alone will not deliver KM, and an overspend on technology is usually a signal of a poorly balanced KM implementation approach.

---

**Tip**

Identify the elements within your budget which relate directly to the four enablers of Roles, Processes, Technology and Governance. Bear in mind there will be many other elements of the budget related to managing the KM programme itself, for example change management, communication, etc, which are not directly related to any single enabler. Are these elements of the budget roughly comparable, or within the same order of magnitude as each other? If not, what have you missed? Which elements have you underestimated?

---

## Benchmarking your budget

Once you have the bottom-up budget, you can then benchmark it. There are a few sources of benchmark data, the first of which is the global KM survey conducted by Knoco in 2014 (Knoco, 2014). As part of this survey participants were asked to specify the scale of their annual KM budget in order-of-magnitude terms. Twenty per cent of the participants did not know how much their budget was, and 10 per cent preferred not to share their budget figure. The mean KM budget of the remainder of the respondents was $950,000 per annum.

Obviously the budget will vary according to the size of the organization. The relationship between budget and company size is non-linear, as shown in Table 8.1.

**TABLE 8.1** The mean annual KM budget against staff size

| Organization size (number of staff) | Annual KM budget |
| --- | --- |
| Tens of staff | $110,000 |
| Hundreds of staff | $125,000 |
| Thousands of staff | $950,000 |
| Tens of thousands of staff | $1.6 million |

**SOURCE:** Knoco Ltd

This non-linear relationship is linked to the same economy of scale in relation to KM team size. The bigger the company, the smaller the ratio between KM team size and company size, and the smaller the ratio between KM budget and company size. KM team size and budget are more closely correlated, with an average budget per KM team member of $130,000, reflecting the salaries of the KM team and the uplift for travel and external spend. This is probably another good benchmark figure for you to use.

# How long will it take to implement knowledge management?

One of the most important questions affecting budget is how long the KM implementation programme will take. KM can take a long time until it becomes embedded, but this time can be shortened with a well-organized, supported and funded implementation programme. To benchmark how long KM takes to embed, we can again refer to the results of the 2014 KM survey (Knoco, 2014). Survey participants described the level of maturity of KM in the organizations in two ways; firstly with an estimate of the number of years that KM had been a focus for them, and secondly with a verbal description of maturity, by choosing whether KM was 'in the early stages', 'well under way' or 'fully embedded'.

You can see the distribution of maturity levels in the graph in Figure 8.1. More organizations surveyed were in the early stages than at any other active stage. The vertical axis shows the number of respondents.

Looking at maturity levels by how long the organizations had been doing KM is also instructive. The figures below demonstrate the long timescales involved in KM implementation.

**FIGURE 8.1**    Organizational KM maturity levels from a 2014 KM survey

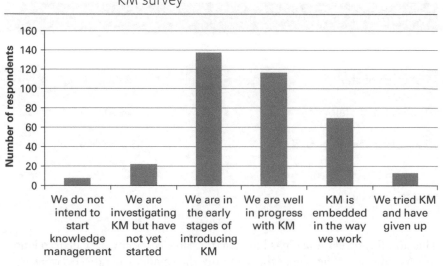

SOURCE: Knoco Ltd

- Organizations which self-assessed as 'in the early stages of introducing KM' had been doing KM, on average, for 3.5 years.
- Organizations which were 'well in progress with KM' had been doing KM, on average, for 8.2 years.
- Organizations that said 'KM is embedded in the way we work' had been doing KM, on average, for 11.8 years.

These figures are borne out by the experience of the Information and Knowledge Management Society's 'KM Excellence Awards' between 2008 and 2012 in Singapore. In these, silver awards showed significant business impact in parts of the organization, and gold awards showed pervasive business impact across the organization. In line with the figures above, silver and gold award winners had typically been implementing KM systematically and methodically for eight or more years.

If the early stage lasts more than 3.5 years, and embedding takes place somewhere after 8 years and before 12 years, then KM is a long-term affair. This does not mean that it takes 8–12 years to show business value, or return on investment. With well-chosen pilots, you can show value very early on. But it does mean that it takes a long time for KM to become fully sustainable and embedded in the organization. KM implementation takes longer for large organizations, as you might expect. Figure 8.2 below shows that for small organizations of fewer than 300 staff, the average number of years at which they judged they were 'well under way' was just over five, compared to nearly 10 years for the organizations with over 100,000 staff.

**FIGURE 8.2**  KM maturity levels by organization size (number of staff)

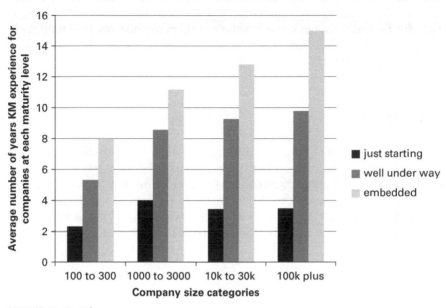

SOURCE: Knoco Ltd

---

Tip

Use these figures to sense check the timeline for your KM implementation and your budget. Allow for the size of your organization and your starting point – whether you have a supportive culture, or have any elements of KM in place already. If your budget and timescale are radically different from the global benchmarks, then seek external advice.

# Beware the self-funding trap

We have seen more than one organization where the KM team was told they had to become 'self-funding'. In other words, they would receive no centrally funded money, but instead would generate funds to cover their own operating costs by charging the business for their services. This is not a valid model for KM implementation for the primary reason that it causes the team to become tactical rather than strategic. In Chapter 2 we discussed the dual implementation approach of delivering short-term business wins while at the same time driving long-term organizational change. If the KM team becomes self-funding then they will be motivated to deliver the quick wins for the business, but nobody will fund them to undertake the long-term cultural and behavioural change. You should resist this pressure, and avoid the self-funding trap!

## Summary

Implementing KM is a lengthy process requiring a substantial budget. You can use benchmarking to build early estimates, but be prepared to refine this as you progress. The message that 'KM is long term' may arouse concerns that KM might not be able to show returns to the business in the short and medium term. In the next chapter we address this, by looking at how to set business aims, metrics and SMART objectives for the programme.

# Aims and objectives for the KM implementation programme

## 09

In this chapter we address the aims and objectives that you set for your KM programme. We assume that you have already developed a KM strategy, and that you have a shared vision with your sponsor about what KM can achieve. Now you need to get much more specific, and begin to define what your KM programme will deliver, in measurable terms.

This chapter covers the following topics:

- benefits mapping;
- setting interim objectives;
- making your objectives measurable;
- choosing the key business metrics;
- setting your targets;
- dealing with imposed targets;
- what to do if you cannot measure value in monetary terms; and
- the risk of confusing measures with targets.

## Benefits mapping

The aims and objectives of your KM programme need to be expressed in terms of organizational outcomes. It is tempting to write objectives such as 'deliver better access to knowledge', or 'improve innovation and the retention of knowledge', but neither of these is a helpful objective in business terms. Your organization does not exist to retain knowledge or deliver access to knowledge, but to make money, deliver services, or sell products. The KM objectives need to be linked to these organizational objectives, so that everybody is clear that what you are doing is supporting the core business of the organization. We use a technique called benefits mapping as a graphical way to link your planned KM interventions to the objectives of the business. The template for the benefits map is shown below.

**FIGURE 9.1**   Benefits map template

| KM interventions | Business changes | Measurable outcome | Strategic goals |
| --- | --- | --- | --- |
|  |  |  |  |

There is a column on the left where you put your planned KM interventions; in the column on the far right you put the main strategic goals for the organization; then, to the left of this, identify a number of measurable outcomes relating to those strategic goals. The space in between is where you create your benefits map.

Let's imagine that you are working for a sales and marketing organization. Your main strategic goals are growth, profit and sustainability, so you begin by entering these in the right-hand column.

You have decided with your team that suitable KM interventions might include the creation of a new markets community of practice, a sales wiki, a marketing knowledge base and a consumer forum. You enter these down the left-hand column. Then, starting from the left, you map what each of the KM interventions makes possible. These go in the 'business changes' area, on the left, with an arrow coming from the relevant intervention, as shown in Figure 9.2.

This is the first round of mapping. The second round is to ask what the changes you have just identified will make possible, and add these as new boxes moving always to the right, and joined by arrows (for example, sharing sales tips and hints may make it possible to develop sales best practices). Then you repeat the process a third time, and possibly a fourth or fifth time, until the business changes become measurable using standard business metrics, in which case you put them into the 'measurable outcomes' column,

**FIGURE 9.2**    The first round of populating the benefits map

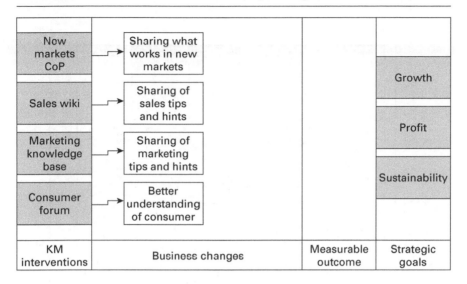

| KM interventions | Business changes | Measurable outcome | Strategic goals |

linked to the relevant strategic goals. If you are not able to work your way through to the measurable outcomes on the right, then this is a sign that the proposed KM intervention may not be appropriate to the business goals. An example of a completed benefits map is shown in Figure 9.3.

This map establishes a clear relationship between the KM interventions and the strategic goals. For example, Figure 9.3 suggests that by introducing the KM interventions, we should be able to deliver faster growth in new markets, an improved share in existing markets, more sales, and better customer and staff retention. Each of these is measurable and each could be a potential business objective for the KM programme. The map can be expressed as a statement, eg 'through the introduction of a sales and marketing KM framework, we will increase sales in existing markets and deliver faster growth in new markets'. Note that you do not have to list every single objective. Just select the ones that you are most confident about and in which your sponsor and steering team are most interested.

---

**Tip**

Create the benefits map in a workshop with your team, and with your sponsor if possible, using a large whiteboard and Post-it notes. The workshop format allows you to access a wider range of ideas, and can unite your team behind the potential business objectives. If you involve your sponsor it will also reinforce in his or her mind that KM really will help deliver better business performance.

**FIGURE 9.3** A completed benefits map

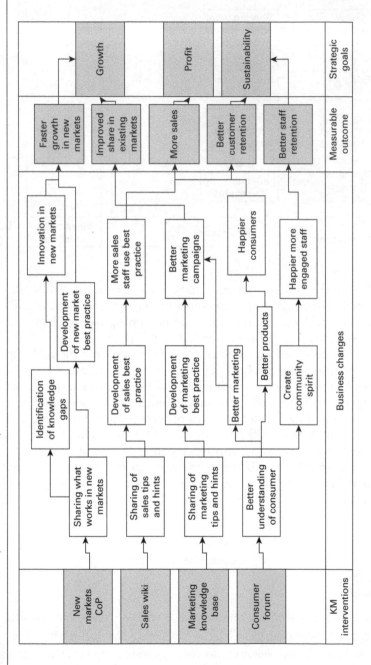

# The interim objectives

The benefits map you have created here represents a long-term view of what KM will deliver to the organization. However as we described in Chapter 2, the implementation project will be delivered in a series of steps, and the pre roll-out phases also have specific objectives.

## The planning stage

The objectives of the planning stage will be to deliver a credible KM implementation plan, and an agreed number of completed proof of concept exercises which have been judged by the people in the business to have been valuable exercises in their own right. The credibility of the implementation plan will be judged by the steering team, and the evaluations of the business people involved in the proof of concept exercises will be captured as a series of success stories.

## The testing and piloting stage

The objectives of the piloting stage will be to deliver an agreed number of KM pilots, and through these pilots to deliver an agreed set of business outcomes. The level of business outcome needs to be high enough to convince the steering committee, at the end of the piloting stage, to approve a systematic roll out of KM across the organization. In fact when you are setting the objectives for the piloting stage, you should agree in advance with the steering committee that if those objectives are delivered, they will accept this as sufficient evidence to warrant general KM roll out.

## Tip

As we showed in Chapter 8, implementing KM is a long-term process which can take years to become sustainable and embedded. Rather than try too hard to develop objectives for the complete project, concentrate on creating objectives for each stage, or even for each year. If you are too rigid in your forward planning, then your plan will be unable to adapt to the changing circumstances of your business. As you progress you will be able to better understand what KM can deliver to your organization, and each year you will be able to set objectives with greater confidence.

# Making the objectives smart

Reaching this level of agreement with the steering committee will be far easier if you make sure that the objectives are specific, measurable, action-oriented, realistic and time-bound (SMART). SMART objectives are particularly important in the piloting phase, as this phase provides the evidence to support the major decision to roll out KM. As an example, during the piloting stage of the BP KM implementation in the late 1990s, the objective was 'to deliver $100 million in benefit to the business through KM pilots in 1998', to be measured through reduced budget submissions from the business in the following year. The objective was very specific, measurable and time-bound, and although at the time the team didn't feel it was very realistic, in practice it proved to be achievable.

To create SMART objectives such as this, you need to know:

- what business metrics your KM programme will address (these will have been defined through the benefits mapping exercise, and example metrics are covered in the next section);
- the approximate impact your KM efforts will deliver; and
- some way of measuring the improvements in the metrics (which implies that you already have a baseline measure).

# Impact metrics for knowledge management

The metrics that you use to define your KM programme objectives should be business metrics related to the type of business that you do (other KM metrics are covered in Chapter 24). Some of the common business metrics that will be impacted by KM are listed below, with the most commonly used metrics at the top of the list, as reported in the Knoco 2014 KM survey (Knoco, 2014).

## *Time to find information*

Your KM framework will almost certainly include components related to improved accessibility of critical knowledge and information, making it easier for people to find the knowledge and information they need, and so improving operational efficiency. To demonstrate these efficiency gains, you will need to measure how long people spend searching for information before and after KM implementation. This is a very commonly used metric, but saving costs through reducing the time to find information is seldom a significant concern for senior managers, and is not always where the major value of KM lies. Managers tend to be more interested in big topics such as project cost overruns or the failure to secure large bids. However, in a large company, and in environments where time is a critical factor (such as law firms, consulting businesses, fast-moving technology companies), this measure may be important.

## Time to competence for new staff

This metric is important for organizations that are growing rapidly, or have a high turnover of staff. The more rapidly you can bring new staff to competence, the more efficiently they will work, and the less you will experience productivity dips while staff get up to speed. As an example, the US Nuclear Regulatory Commission, a rapidly growing organization, focused their KM efforts on knowledge transfer. Setting up communities of practice for new inspectors and providing links to training resources reduced by 25 per cent the time it took new employees to qualify, from two years down to a year and a half. Those employees are able to 'go solo' sooner instead of having to be paired with more experienced workers for longer (Johnson, 2011).

## Project or operational costs

By capturing and reusing lessons and best practices from projects and operations, organizations can improve the way they work, eliminate repeat mistakes, reproduce process improvements, and so reduce cost. The more expensive the projects and operations, the greater the value that KM can bring. This is the primary KM impact metric for all organizations involved in major projects in the oil and gas sector, the construction sector, and in major engineering companies. For example (Ajimoko, 2007) reported a 40 per cent reduction in time and cost to drill a well on the Saih Rawl field in Oman, through the application of lesson learning.

## Project or activity cycle time

As well as doing things more cheaply, KM can help projects do things more quickly. For construction projects and other projects with large penalties for delay, speed is of the essence. Taylor (2014) describes how Crossrail (a massive European railway construction project in London) delivered significant time savings by sharing lessons and best practices through an 'innovation portal'.

> At the Pudding Mill Lane site in Stratford, East London, the contractors had struggled with erecting a reinforced earth wall. They tried a new technique, which had mostly worked, but there were a few problems. So they captured the lessons learned and logged the new construction technique on the innovation portal. A year later, contractors at the Plumstead site, also in East London, were having difficulties with a reinforced earth wall of their own, while battling severe time constraints. Fortunately, the innovation team was able to point them in the direction of the innovation portal and the lessons learned from Pudding Mill Lane. These were taken and developed further in order to devise a frame in front of the wall. [This]... took three weeks off production and they delivered the wall on time.

## Product and service quality

For manufacturing companies creating products, for organizations such as legal firms and consulting companies delivering services, or for government departments that generate policies and support citizen services, product or service quality is a very important business measure. Poor-quality products and services can result in rework, waste, product recall, unhappy customers, and even lost customers. For such organizations, product or service quality can be the most important measure KM can impact; even more important than cost or time.

Steve Wieneke of General Motors used an existing taxonomy, 138 best practice teams and a set of subject matter experts to populate and maintain 'Technical Memory', a database of explicit knowledge and best practice designed to standardize product quality (Weineke, 2007). According to Ash (2007a), early outcome metrics demonstrated the value of this KM initiative.

> During the 36 months in service, for vehicles sold during 2000 through 2003, actual warranty costs dropped by almost 20 per cent below forecasts. The catalogue of engineering solutions, technical memory and the closed-loop learning are three of the current 10 activities identified as the engineering enablers driving the warranty cost down.

## Sales volume and market share

For sales organizations, cost, time and quality may be insignificant compared to the impact of increased sales. Firms such as Mars (Chapter 27), Kraft Foods, Coca Cola and Heineken all deploy at least part of their KM activities in service of sales. KM can also impact the success of bids and competitive tenders, as shown in the example below from AON insurance (Adams, 2004).

### CASE STUDY

Aon Australia's Melbourne office received an invitation to tender for the insurance business of a leading Australasian toll-road company, which was held by one of Aon's major competitors. The timeframe for the tender submission was very tight, allowing for little time to gather data and statistics. The Australian account director sent an e-mail to the Property GPG [global practice group, a knowledge-sharing forum similar to a community of practice] requesting urgent benchmarking information that would demonstrate Aon's global expertise in the field of toll roads, tunnels and bridges.

Information on the insurance cover of similar companies was quickly collected from across the globe... Property experts from China, Hong Kong, Canada, Brazil and Belgium sent details regarding their clients' cover, which were anonymized to protect their identities – a good data protection policy.

The practice group was able to visibly demonstrate exactly what the toll company's international peers were paying for property cover and provide details about limits and deductibles. Within 24 hours, Aon's Melbourne office received the information; two days later the presentation was made to the company and less than two weeks after that Aon Melbourne was appointed as the new broker.

## Customer satisfaction

For many customer-facing organizations, the critical business metric is not cost or time, but customer satisfaction. Satisfied customers mean loyal customers, with high levels of customer retention leading to a stable or growing market share. An example of KM impacting customer satisfaction is provided by Lawley (2006) who describes how a combination of coaching and communities of practice improved the operation of call centres at the telecoms operator Orange.

> KM practitioners are often criticized for running initiatives that cannot easily be assessed in traditional business terms, such as return on investment. However, in this case the results were almost immediate and quantifiable. The KM team could point to a steady increase in the customer satisfaction figures in the months after the community [of practice] system was put in place, increasing from 69 per cent to 76 per cent. This was a remarkable achievement in such a short space of time and primarily attributed, in the company, to the change in coaching style.

Tip

When choosing metrics to measure the impact of your KM programme, it is best to select from the standard set of business metrics already being collected and reported in your organization. These metrics have been chosen because they are important to senior managers, and will already have a baseline to allow you to recognize the poor performers whom KM can help, and to measure progress against. If instead you create your own set of metrics, then firstly you have to create your own baseline, secondly you have to create your own measurement system, and thirdly you need to convince your senior management that these metrics are significant to the business.

# Setting the value targets and estimating ROI

All of the metrics described in this chapter can be positively impacted by KM, as the stories show. Your benefits map will help you identify which metrics are most likely to be impacted by the KM initiatives you are proposing. These metrics will allow you to measure success, and will help you determine the value targets you will aim for. Value targets are most important for the piloting stage of KM implementation, as the value delivered from the KM pilot projects will create the business case for KM roll-out, as we discussed in Chapter 2.

The best way to set your value targets is to sit with people from the business and work back through the benefits map to see where the leverage points are for KM, and to estimate how much difference KM can make. For example Figure 9.3 above suggests that a 'new markets' CoP can drive the development and application of best practices in new market development, leading to faster growth. You may have selected this area as one of your pilot projects, and need to estimate the value a KM pilot may deliver.

In this example, you would work with people in the new markets area to discuss the following:

- The current growth rates of the new markets (measured in income growth, sales growth, or whatever the standard business metric is). This forms your baseline.

- The current limits on growth, whether any of these might be related to knowledge, and whether the business will support your assertion that developing and deploying best practice will accelerate growth.

- How much impact knowledge sharing might have – for example, if the slowest-growing markets were to learn the secrets of success from the fastest, what impact might this have? Could they grow 10 per cent faster? Twenty per cent faster?

- The overall growth rate improvement in the new markets that KM could therefore deliver.

This growth rate improvement will inform your target for the new markets pilot.

Usually each of the targets for your pilot projects can be converted into monetary terms. Imagine you agreed that KM could realistically help deliver a 3 per cent improvement in new market growth. You should be able to convert this figure into improved sales and improved profit. You can then sum up the monetary targets to create an overall target figure for the piloting phase.

It is worth saying at this stage that it is better to under-promise and over-deliver. If you feel you could realistically deliver $20 million in benefit from your KM pilot projects, then perhaps it is safest to set $10 million as your official target. The road to value delivery is complex, and one or more of your pilot projects may be withdrawn, or fail to deliver the expected value (this is less likely if you select the pilots wisely, following our advice in Chapter 22).

Tip

As part of your pilot project planning, create separate benefit maps for each of your pilot projects, in conjunction with the pilot project sponsor. These benefit maps will be very helpful in determining pilot-specific targets, as well as providing a valuable framework for discussing KM value with the sponsor.

# Dealing with imposed targets

Sometimes you do not have the luxury of choosing your own targets. The BP $100 million value target in 1998 mentioned earlier in this chapter was not calculated by the KM project team, but imposed from above by the steering committee. In a circumstance such as this, you may have little ability to negotiate. If this is the value they need to see to be convinced of the importance of KM, then that is the value you need to deliver.

Here again working through the benefits map with the relevant business leaders can help you to identify ways of extracting greater value from the pilots. For example, if the benefits from the KM interventions in the left-hand column do not look like they can deliver the expected benefits, then you go back to your team and ask 'what else should we be doing to increase the value'? Working through the benefits map is an iterative process, from left to right, and from right to left, until all the stakeholders are comfortable that it represents a practical and feasible representation.

# What if you can't measure value in monetary terms?

Not every organization will measure value in monetary terms. A fire and rescue department, for example, does not measure its success in terms of money. Neither does a hospital. Both are much more likely to focus on measures of quality, where quality can mean the difference between life and death (reduction of mistakes, adverse outcomes, accident and injury rates, improved recovery rates). Time measures may also come into play – time to competence for new staff, time to effective response to an emergency situation, waiting time for patients.

There is always a way of measuring the value that KM brings. The important thing is to find an outcome that is valued by the knowledge workers and the management, that KM can impact, and that you can measure in some way.

## Not all measures should be targets

It is worth adding a cautionary word here. While effective KM planning depends on rigorous approaches to measurement and setting targets, it is sometimes easy to get distracted by the measures we use, and to confuse value measures and outcome targets with activity measures (see Chapter 24). It is tempting, before you achieve your desired outcome targets, to seek some indicators of progress, especially if your targets are ambitious. For example, if you establish a community of practice, you may want to measure participation rates to be assured that you are on track. This is an activity measure, and participation rates in a community of practice do not actually tell you whether you are moving towards your desired value outcomes.

Not all measures work well as targets, and turning them into targets can have unintended consequences. Take this example from IBM's efforts to build a repository of best practices in the 1990s (Barth, 2000):

> Contributions [to a knowledge base] were reflected in performance evaluations and/or bonuses. Everyone submitted. But we were on a calendar year, so 90 per cent of our submissions came in between December 15th and 31st. Worse, there was no process to monitor the quality of the written contributions. Not only did they all come in at one time, but they were incredibly long and unintelligible. Forced to improve the method, IBM eventually created a community submission process involving a network of experts that on a rotating basis review, comment on and request contributions to the knowledge base.

By turning the metric of submission quantity into a target, IBM was actually compromising the quality of its knowledge base, and subverting its original intent.

## Summary

This chapter covers one of the most difficult areas in KM: the area of setting objectives and targets, and of demonstrating value. The benefits map approach that we described here is a tool to help you and your internal customers to work through how and where KM can add value, which leaves you with the tricky last step of estimating exactly how much value you think you may be able to deliver. Notice this is an iterative and collaborative activity, undertaken with your business customers.

Despite its difficulty, this step is crucially important. Throughout this book we have linked KM and business value, and when you come to set your KM programme objectives you have to make this link not only explicit, but also something against which your performance will be measured. Luckily the amount of value which KM can create is often far greater than we realize. Be bold, set your targets, and have faith that you will reach them.

# Finding partners to help you

## 10

In Chapter 1 we said that one of the functions of the KM team is to orchestrate KM-related activities among partner disciplines. We also said that to be sustainable, KM has to be embedded in the everyday workings of the organization. This means that KM is not 'done' by the KM team 'to' the rest of the organization; the organization needs to be facilitated to do KM through a process of adopting and embedding KM technologies, roles, processes, and governance elements. These enablers usually have distinct functional units that need to be consulted with and coordinated: IT for technology, HR for people and some elements of governance, Strategic Planning for other elements of governance, and Operations for process.

In this chapter we look at the orchestration role that the KM team has to play in KM implementation to ensure that the four enablers are properly coordinated and addressed. We cover the following topics:

- who should be responsible for KM?
- KM as partnering;
- initiating strong partnerships;
- transitioning partnerships through your KM journey; and
- identifying non-obvious partners.

## Who should be responsible for KM?

We are often asked 'Who should be responsible for KM: IT or HR?' In fact, we have worked with KM teams led by many different corporate functions, from IT to HR to organization development, organization excellence, quality management, corporate planning, information management, even corporate communications. We've also worked on KM initiatives that were run out of specific 'line of business' operations such as marketing, drilling or R&D.

The 2014 KM survey (Knoco, 2014) identified a wide range of reporting lines for KM teams, shown in Table 10.1.

**TABLE 10.1**    Reporting lines for KM teams

| Reporting line | Percentage of responses |
|---|---|
| Separate reporting line to senior management | 19% |
| HR | 11% |
| Operations | 9% |
| IT | 8% |
| Strategy | 8% |
| Learning and development | 7% |
| R&D | 4% |
| Projects | 4% |
| Business improvement | 4% |
| Sales and marketing | 2% |
| Quality | 2% |
| Innovation | 2% |
| Engineering | 1% |
| Technology | 1% |
| Internal communications | 1% |
| Legal | 1% |
| Information management | 1% |
| 'Other' | 17% |

**SOURCE:** Knoco Ltd

The short answer to this question is that what matters more than the reporting line for the KM team, is whether:

  **a** The KM team has the high-level sponsorship described in Chapter 7, a KM leader with the right qualities and influencing skills (Chapter 5) and a KM team with the right competences (Chapter 6); and

  **b** The team is able to ensure balance between the four KM enablers.

Each of the corporate functions we have mentioned previously is likely to have a bias towards specific enablers or elements of KM:

- IT has a bias towards technology and finds that easier to deal with, so may neglect the other enablers.
- HR has a bias towards areas like corporate culture, roles and responsibilities and learning and development, and may not have the capability to influence the other enablers with any authority.
- Corporate functions like organization excellence, quality management and corporate planning may have insight into the operational areas of the business, but may not have the background to deal with the cultural and technology aspects.
- Information Management is likely to have a bias towards the explicit aspects of KM.
- Corporate Communications is likely to have a bias towards ensuring good information flows and situation awareness, but may have weaknesses in dealing with areas like learning, expertise, knowledge retention, and KM technologies.

This functional bias is a risk, but if treated carefully this risk can be managed. For example, one of us worked with an IT team that developed and implemented a balanced and effective KM strategy covering both tacit and explicit knowledge needs. They started small, focused on getting good results for the business, solved some pain points, attracted the attention of HR who came on board to support them on the people side of the equation, and also involved corporate planning, who helped to integrate KM planning into the annual work planning process. They were able to manage the risk because the KM leader had the qualities (and the patience) we described in Chapter 5, and because the sponsor (the CIO) was willing to step outside her comfort zone and try some small experiments.

However we have also worked with an enlightened IT team that also came up with a balanced KM strategy, but then met with an antagonistic response from the HR team, who refused to cooperate because 'IT is intruding on our turf'. The technology aspects of the initiative were able to proceed, but the people, process and governance aspects were stymied by the refusal of HR to treat KM needs as a priority in their work plan. It turned out that the IT director and the HR director did not get along, and although HR attended meetings during the strategy development process, they were uncommitted, and bided their time until action was required, at which point they refused to acknowledge KM as a priority in their agenda.

If you have influence over the decision on where KM should reside, then the ideal is that the KM team exists as a separate small department on its own with a separate reporting line to senior management (the most popular option in Table 10.1). They can then develop ways of working with the other key departments.

There are three structural ways of working with these key functions:

1 If several of these functions are clustered together in a 'corporate support' cluster, then the KM department can be located within this cluster, under the same boss.

2 Select your project sponsor based on their oversight or influence over the corporate functions you will need to work with.

3 Ensure that the other functions are represented (ideally by the heads of function) on your KM steering team.

At the end of the day, however, there is no 'one size fits all' answer. You will need to read the culture and politics of your organization, to understand where the influence and capabilities needed to implement KM reside.

---

Tip

If you have not yet identified the reporting line of the KM team, consider the balance of needs listed above, including the sphere of influence of your KM leader and sponsor, the key functions that will need to be involved in KM implementation, and the accountability to the business. Where should KM be placed?

---

# KM as partnering

'Partnering' is a concept most highly developed in the world of non-profits, NGOs and commercial joint ventures, but it is a useful one for KM implementation. Partnership is more structured than collaboration, but it is less formal than a set of delegated responsibilities. Partnership expresses a voluntary coalition, developed and agreed upon as equals, where the different partners bring different resources and capabilities to a commonly agreed agenda. It recognizes that the partners have differing priorities and agendas outside the partnership agenda, and that they need to negotiate the benefits of partnering with their other needs as well. Hence it stresses 'complementary objectives' over 'common objectives', 'agreements' over 'contracts' or 'mandates', and 'participation' over 'consultation' (Tennyson, 2003).

This is a useful model for KM, because all of KM's likely partners (HR, IT, IM, etc) have responsibilities and priorities that go beyond KM. KM may be at the centre of your universe but it is not at the centre of theirs. In a partnering approach, this is explicitly recognized and transparent to everybody involved, and the approach is one of respectful negotiation. The implications of the partnering approach are very clear. From the KM strategy phase onwards you will need to identify your potential partners and engage with them so that they can participate in the planning for the next stage.

**FIGURE 10.1**   Resource mapping template

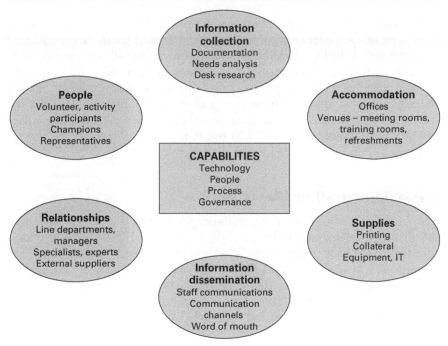

**Information collection**
Documentation
Needs analysis
Desk research

**People**
Volunteer, activity
participants
Champions
Representatives

**Accommodation**
Offices
Venues – meeting rooms,
training rooms,
refreshments

**CAPABILITIES**
Technology
People
Process
Governance

**Relationships**
Line departments,
managers
Specialists, experts
External suppliers

**Supplies**
Printing
Collateral
Equipment, IT

**Information dissemination**
Staff communications
Communication
channels
Word of mouth

**SOURCE**: Adapted from Tennyson (2003)

Your KM steering team is the mechanism for enacting the partnership. The partnering approach makes it clear that the KM steering team is not a group of 'to be consulted' stakeholders, but a 'to be engaged' group of stakeholders, actively involved in planning, resourcing and reviewing each cycle of activity. The resource mapping technique is a useful tool for identifying and engaging potential partners. Figure 10.1 shows a resource map template for a typical KM project.

This template can be used within your team to brainstorm potential partners to join your KM steering team. Use it to think about what resources you will need for your next stage of activity, in each of the capability areas of technology, people, process and governance, and in each of the likely resource needs, from information collection, to accommodation and supplies, to information dissemination, people, relationships and expertise. Identify the partners who can give you access to those resources and capabilities.

**Tip**

Together with your team look at your outline KM strategy, and use the resource mapping framework to brainstorm who you should engage as partners in the implementation stage.

# Initiating a partnership

The resource mapping template is also a powerful engagement tool at the beginning of each partnering stage, when the invited partners are gathered to a partnering initiation meeting. When partners attend this meeting they will have differing perceptions and expectations, and probably differing levels of motivation as well. The purpose of the initiation meeting is to create a shared agreement that will form the basis of your activity throughout the next phase, whether it be identifying proof of concept projects, expanding to pilots, or implementing a full KM roll out.

An initiation meeting has four distinct stages.

## 1. Assessment of need

The partners need to have a shared understanding of the current situation, the major problems or challenges to be overcome, and a common understanding of the root causes to be addressed. Depending on where you are in the process, your needs analysis for the KM strategy, or the knowledge assets audit findings (described in the following chapter), will provide valuable input. Your partners will have their own perspectives on this, and these perspectives need to be heard and acknowledged.

## 2. Shared vision

If you have developed a KM strategy you should already have a vision statement for what KM should achieve for the organization. This needs to be accepted, internalized, and/or adapted by the partners in terms that they are comfortable with. The shared vision is what helps the partners to identify and agree on an over-arching goal for the next phase of activity.

## 3. Benefits and costs of partnering

At this stage, before you move to firm commitments, the partners need to have a frank and open discussion about the benefits and costs to them of participating. Thus far, you have been speaking in terms of the benefits to the organization as a whole. However, partners also need to be clear about what concrete benefits they will receive for their own functions as a result of the KM initiative. They also need to be open about their constraints and challenges, and the potential cost of participation.

Maybe HR has an intensive competency framework consultancy about to start. Maybe the IT department is in the middle of implementing a CRM project and it is not going well. Maybe Corporate Communications is tied up with getting the Annual Report out, and is currently under-staffed.

It is important that these constraints and commitments are surfaced, because if they are not surfaced they cannot be addressed, and three things can happen: (1) your plan ends up being too ambitious and impractical; (2) you lose the opportunity to clarify the benefits to participation to key partners; or (3) you lose the opportunity to leverage parallel projects and activities by exploiting their needs analysis and information-gathering activities, or by aligning KM projects to support other corporate initiatives.

If your organization culture is not very open and transparent, and you do not feel that participants in the meeting will be open about these hesitations and concerns, then you will need to do significant pre-work before the initiation meeting to gather this insight in one-on-one meetings, and then you will have to skilfully facilitate the meeting to elicit these factors of concern. It's not sufficient that you are aware of these constraints. In effective partnering, all the partners need to have this sense of transparency about benefits and costs.

## 4. Agreed objectives and contributions

Once there is a strong common understanding of benefits, costs and constraints, the partners need to agree what the objectives are for the next stage of KM implementation activity. As part of this, they need to agree how they will contribute to these objectives, and what the expectations will be about roles, responsibilities and accountabilities. This is where the 'respectful negotiation' begins, as they seek to balance this initiative with their other priorities and other demands on their time and resources.

The resource map template shown above can be useful here. Post a large version of it up on the wall, and working from the agreed objectives, ask the partners to brainstorm contributions into each section, using Post-it notes. Continue until everybody agrees that the resource commitments match the agreed objectives.

At this stage, in the spirit of respectful negotiation, your partners may wish to go back and check with colleagues before any hard commitments are entered into. Hence we would normally separate this initiation meeting from an action-planning meeting, at which firm commitments, timelines, and accountability procedures are agreed.

# Transitioning the partnerships

Partnering implies repeated cycles of activity. Your partnering needs should be reviewed at every transition you make, from KM strategy to identifying proof of concept, from proof of concept to pilots, from pilots to full roll-out. This is to ensure that you have the appropriate resources and support you need for each stage of activity, as it spreads and as it scales up.

Some partners will stay with you for the long haul, but their contributions will change. Some partners will come in early and drop out for a while if they are not actively needed, then rejoin later on. Sometimes the role of a

KM partner becomes institutionalized, and a formal part of their functional responsibilities. This is more and more likely to happen as the KM implementation matures, and as you start transitioning from implementation to steady state (Chapter 26).

At each stage, you (and your partners) should review the partnering requirements for the next phase. Healthy partnerships are continually reviewed and renewed as the environment matures. These transitional stages need to be celebrated. Tell the story of the partnership up to that point, what it has achieved, the challenges it has faced and overcome. Celebrate the contributions of the different partners. They become a model for partnership in your successive phase.

# Identifying non-obvious partners

Some partners are obvious. They are the corporate functions that bear significant responsibility for one of the four enablers of KM. We have already identified several of them. Some partners are less obvious. They are functions or disciplines with whom you have overlapping and sometimes competing interests.

## Policy owners

Because one of your enablers is governance, any owners of corporate policies are potential candidates for engagement as partners because their policies might compete or conflict with yours (the creation of a corporate KM policy is discussed in Chapter 23).

We worked with an organization whose CEO and senior management enthusiastically endorsed a policy statement that said 'it is our policy that we increase our organizational efficiency and effectiveness through knowledge sharing and reuse'. Some time later we came across the same organization's information security policy that said 'sharing of information is on a need-to-know basis only'. Here we had two policies that were, if not in conflict, at the very least in tension with each other. The role of a corporate policy is to clarify what is expected of employees, but we had muddied the water by not resolving an important inconsistency. The KM team worked with the information security department to develop a set of compatible policies giving much clearer guidance on what information and knowledge could be openly shared, and what information needed greater protection.

Policy owners may be constrained by legislation, regulation, contractual or external compliance requirements, in areas such as privacy, confidentiality, intellectual property rights, commercial risk, or compliance against audited standards. All of these may have some bearing on how knowledge pertaining to that policy domain is captured, stored, protected and shared.

## Information and data management functions

'Neighbouring' disciplines are also potential flashpoints for discord if not identified early. These include records managers, data managers (and owners of data-based business applications), information managers and corporate librarians.

Records managers deal with the capture and preservation of documentary records of the organization's decisions and activities. While accessibility and usability of records is within their remit, as a profession they have tended to place greater emphasis on preserving the integrity and reliability of records more than ensuring that they are easily accessible for everyday use.

Data managers deal with data in structured form, often in line of business applications, to support specific activities and transactions, and also to support decision making through the use of analytics and reporting tools.

Information managers deal with information support to the business and the management of information in documents and structured or unstructured web content.

Corporate librarians typically look after published information resources made available to the organization, both electronic and hard copy, manage subscriptions to databases and other types of content, and may do selective dissemination of information to specific functions in the organization.

All of these functions deal with the more explicit forms of knowledge, but taken together they already present a confusing spectacle to the average knowledge worker, before we even add an additional layer of KM.

## Learning-oriented functions

There are some professional functions that span internal organizational boundaries even though they may have central coordinating functions. These include project management, quality management, risk management, and health, safety and environmental (HSE) management.

These functions have two things in common with each other, one of which makes them particularly amenable to KM, and the other which makes them formidable resisters if not engaged early in the process.

1 They all have a strong interest in learning. In project management, project effectiveness, cost, cycle time, and efficiency are all affected by the ability to learn before, during and after a project so that repeated types of projects can be completed cheaper, faster and better than their predecessors. In quality management, quality is often improved, and these improvements shared, using processes very similar to KM processes. In risk management, known risks need to be identified and assessed at the start of a project or activity cycle (which often requires experience as well as access to past lessons), effective strategies for avoidance, mitigation or recovery identified, and triggers identified to alert the team to the emergence of any risks. In HSE, lessons from previous incidents improve safety awareness and education, as well as providing a base for avoiding such incidents in future. The capture

of minor incident and 'near miss' reports and their analysis can go a long way to improving the safety culture of an organization.

2 These functions are highly constrained by set procedures, standards and in some cases, external regulatory compliance requirements or standards. The way they conduct their work is highly governed, and changes in how they work need to be consistent with their pre-existing operating models. It's all very well for KM to come in and propose learning processes and models for knowledge capture and re-use, but if these models are not consistent with the operating models of the discipline, and do not 'speak the language' of the discipline, they will not be adopted. If these are functions that are likely to be targets of KM projects, then they need to be identified, engaged and partnered with at a very early stage.

---

**Tips**

1 Make a list of the corporate policies that might have some impact on how knowledge is managed in your organization, and identify their policy owners as potential stakeholders and partners.

2 Your business focus will sharpen as soon as you start identifying candidates for proof of concept and pilot projects. Look at the potential stakeholders in those business areas from the data, information and records point of view. Do they need to be engaged as partners?

3 Are there any other major corporate initiatives rolling out information platforms, data-based business applications, or records management systems? Do they need to be engaged as partners?

4 Which functions in your organization have a strong interest in learning? Are they highly constrained in the way that they operate? Are they likely to be targets for KM initiatives, and do they need to be engaged as partners?

---

# Partnering with external companies

This may be the first KM implementation programme you have led. You may lack experience and knowledge in this area, and you might feel you would benefit from learning more about KM. Buying this book is a good first step. A second step is to partner with trusted consultants and with other KM professionals.

## *Partnering with trusted consultants*

Many people have a suspicion of management consultants, but the best management consultants should be considered as knowledge resources. An experienced KM consultant will have been involved with dozens of KM programmes, and can make this experience available to you to help you avoid the pitfalls and maximize your chances of success. If it accelerates your KM implementation or improves its effectiveness this will be money well invested. Trusted KM consultants can make excellent mentors. Select a consultant based on their breadth of experience. It does not need to be experience in your precise industry, as there are many factors other than industry segment that affect KM implementation. Better to find someone who a) you personally get on well with, b) who shares knowledge openly, c) has a very wide KM experience base, and d) has wide professional networks.

## *Partnering with other KM professionals*

The best way to partner with other KM professionals is to join either a paid KM consortium, or to join a local KM professional grouping. The consortia are more professionally run, while the local groupings are less expensive but are often run by volunteers. In each case you will probably find that the group is comprised of professionals just like you, and their KM programmes are at a similar state as yours, ie still in progress. So while the bulk of the membership may not exactly be experts in KM implementation – few of them having reached the end of the journey yet – they can often act as a support group for each other, and can exchange tactical advice.

Wherever possible, find a more experienced KM professional to filter and make sense of advice you get from peers in a consortium or group; either a trusted consultant to help you or a very experienced mentor in the community.

# Summary

The KM reporting line can affect delivery, and if KM reports through a pre-existing corporate function it may face challenges in reaching beyond that function's core capability. Given a choice, we recommend an independent reporting line for the KM implementation programme. More important than the 'ownership' question, however, is the need to engage in active partnering with the other functions in the organization whose help you will need, and with external experienced KM practitioners. In this chapter we have covered the elements of successful partnering. We will complement this later on in Chapter 18 with some advice on influencing the wider pool of stakeholders.

# PART THREE
# Assessment and planning

## Executive summary

Part Three covers the critical foundation work for any KM implementation. Chapter 11 covers the knowledge assets audit, which provides the evidence you will need for detailed planning. Chapter 12 introduces the concept of a KM framework, and defines its elements. Chapters 13–16 will help you assess your needs against the major elements of the KM framework to ensure that your KM implementation remains balanced and integrated. Chapter 17 explains how the discipline of knowledge organization supports the goals of the KM framework. Chapters 18–19 take you through the steps involved in mobilizing others through the implementation process, and Chapter 20 will help you turn your assessment findings into a detailed implementation plan.

# Conducting the knowledge assets audit

## 11

At this point, you have completed your preparation for KM implementation, you have your KM strategy to guide you, and you should have the resources to start delivering, embodied in your sponsor, team, leader, budget and partners. It's now time to start looking at potential areas where KM may add value. You may already have conducted some form of strategic audit or assessment as part of your strategy-building phase, and now can conduct a detailed, more granular analysis to help you identify specific potential KM initiatives at the operational level in your organization. This is called a knowledge assets audit. By 'knowledge asset' we mean an identifiable area of knowledge or competence owned by the organization, and which may or may not be well managed.

The chapter covers the following areas:

- a definition of knowledge assets audit and how it relates to other forms of knowledge audit;
- an explanation of why the knowledge assets audit is useful for KM implementation, and how it helps to avoid common pitfalls;
- what it is that we are auditing when we audit operational knowledge assets;
- the steps in a knowledge assets audit;
- analysing the results from a knowledge assets audit.

## What is a knowledge assets audit?

We use the term 'knowledge assets audit' to distinguish it from the more generic term 'knowledge audit'. We need this distinction because the term 'knowledge audit' can mean a number of quite diverse activities:

- assessment of KM practices or KM capabilities (mentioned in Chapter 4);

- a culture audit in relation to knowledge sharing behaviours (Chapter 19);
- assessment against a KM standard when one exists;
- evaluation of existing KM programmes and their effectiveness; or
- creating a baseline inventory of knowledge assets and gaps.

This latter activity is the one we are focused on in this chapter.

If you have developed your KM strategy in a robust way, you will probably already have conducted a KM assessment and identified strategic knowledge assets that need to be protected, preserved, scaled up or created (Barnes and Milton 2015). Strategic knowledge assets are high-level capabilities of an organization. To be able to work towards implementation and help you define practical KM projects, they may need to be broken down to more operational-level components through a knowledge assets audit.

For example, in a tax authority, a strategic knowledge asset might be the capability to detect tax fraud. To be able to figure out what to do about protecting this capability, we need to break this down to how the capability works out at operational level. For example, knowledge embedded in algorithms that analyse tax payment patterns, segmentation of taxpayers and benchmarking them to detect anomalous behaviours, the experience of seasoned tax officers in spotting anomalies that the algorithms don't catch, investigation skills, forensic analysis of tax records, explicit knowledge embedded in guidelines and check lists, case studies and lessons learned from past investigations, and so on. We need to understand how well these knowledge assets are managed for each major tax type such as income tax, property tax, and corporate tax. We need to be able to understand the knowledge flows that feed the strategic capability, and to detect gaps in the operational knowledge assets, or blockages in the knowledge flows. This is what an operational knowledge assets audit does.

The typical output of a knowledge assets audit includes:

- an inventory of knowledge assets associated with each key business activity or strategic capability – in diagrammatic form this is often called a knowledge map;
- a representation of knowledge flows (confusingly, this can also be called a knowledge map); and
- an analysis of knowledge risks, knowledge accessibility issues, and knowledge asset gaps.

# How does the audit help a KM implementation?

In Chapter 2 we recommended a trials and pilots approach to KM implementation, supplemented by a readiness to be opportunistic in responding quickly to pressing business needs. In such a dual strategy, the knowledge assets audit helps you to link opportunistic projects to the overall strategy by giving you a clear connection between the strategic knowledge areas and the specific operational changes that you are making in the proof of concept and pilot projects. It also gives you a detailed understanding of how knowledge works at the operational level, and where your leverage points are in the implementation phase.

If your strategy were compared to building a house, the knowledge assets audit functions like a site survey, to understand the characteristics of the ground on which you want to build. With a site survey you can make better decisions about how to build, how high you can build, and what building materials to use. Similarly, a knowledge assets audit can help you avoid pitfalls in KM implementation, since it will give you a very clear picture of your high-value knowledge, and the current weaknesses in how it is managed.

# What are we auditing?

Knowledge asset audits measure more than just explicit information and documented knowledge carried in documents and databases. In this chapter we use a six-part framework to identify different knowledge asset types, heavily influenced by David Snowden's ASHEN framework (Snowden, 2000). We have supplemented Snowden's framework with an additional knowledge asset type which represents the way we access knowledge in other people through relationships. Here are the six different types of operational knowledge asset that an organization typically uses in order to carry out its various business activities.

## Documented knowledge

This is the only type of asset that represents completely explicit knowledge ie knowledge that has been codified in text, pixels, bytes, etc. This type of knowledge may include printed material such as manuals and standard operating procedures (SOPs), as well as digital information in shared folders, databases, systems and webpages, audio-visual materials and other artefacts.

## Skills

Skills represent knowledge embedded in people's ability to perform a task, usually acquired through training and practice. Skills cannot be communicated through documents, and you must differentiate knowledge gained by reading from knowledge gained by doing. For example, reading a document on how to ride a bicycle including how and where to position the limbs and maintain balance does not equip you with the skills to ride a bicycle, which are gained through practice. Skills-based knowledge is differentiated from experience-based knowledge (described later) in that skills can be trained, whereas experience requires deepening of knowledge through repeated practice over time.

## Methods

Methods represent a form of implicit knowledge, embodied in ways of working, but not completely explicit. Methods can be observed in the ways in which work gets done and can include procedures, processes and workflows, as well as shortcuts and heuristics. We identify knowledge assets as methods if there is a set, routine and habitual way of doing things that employees learn when they enter a work unit, but when not all aspects of these methods are documented in SOPs. If a process is completely documented by SOPs, then it will be represented in the audit as a document. Examples of methods are processing of various applications and permits, conducting study trips to learn best practices from others, benchmarking, regular meetings with customers, and so on.

## Relationships

Human beings do not have sufficient brainpower to store all the knowledge we need for our lives. So we distribute our knowledge socially, meaning that we do not need to know everything, so long as we have relationships with people who know the stuff we are not knowledgeable about. We capture knowledge assets as relationships when the knowledge we need to perform an activity resides within other people, and it is only possible to access this knowledge through relationships. The relationships might include those with vendors and suppliers, governing bodies, partners and collaborators, internal divisions and departments where tight coordination is required, or within a community of practice. Some areas of work are highly dependent on access to knowledge through relationships. It's usually not enough to know who knows what, however. We also need some degree of familiarity with each other (which gives us the ability to understand each other's needs and communicate concisely and effectively) and some degree of trust (which affects somebody's readiness to help us and give us rich replies). This makes relationship knowledge assets much less easy to transfer than, say, documents, methods, or skills.

## Experience

Experience refers to the ability to identify trends and patterns in what's happening around us, and to respond effectively. It is acquired over time and with frequency of observation and reflection. It is valuable and is not easily replicated, and contributes to positive outcomes in business activities. Experience is different from skills because while skills may be trained, experience may not. Skills give us the ability to deal effectively with relatively standard situations. Experience gives us the ability to deal effectively with unusual and challenging situations. Examples of experience knowledge assets are risk planning, responding to emergency or crisis situations, negotiations and so on.

## Natural talent

Natural talent is innate and occurs naturally in people. Some people do certain things better than others because of their natural ability, quite apart from their training or experience, for example in mathematics, interpersonal skills, art and design. This kind of knowledge asset cannot be constructed or replicated. It is difficult to manage but needs to be nurtured nonetheless. The range of work situations where natural talent is important is relatively limited (largely because it constitutes a risk and is difficult to replace).

> **Tip**
>
> Try conducting a knowledge assets audit during the scoping stage of each KM pilot, just focused on that work area, to understand the KM issues, the knowledge gaps and the knowledge flows.

# What are the steps in a knowledge assets audit?

In a knowledge assets audit you first identify the target business activities you are interested in at the operational level. There are two main types of audit, a comprehensive audit, and a targeted audit.

In a comprehensive audit, you work systematically through the departments in the organization, and through all their core business activities as defined by them. The comprehensive audit will be slower, but will likely pick up important insights that you may have missed at the strategy phase.

In a more targeted audit, you focus on those departments and teams that are engaged in the strategic knowledge areas or the organizational capabilities you have already identified as core to your KM strategy. The targeted audit will be more focused and swifter to conduct, but you may miss blind spots not picked up earlier.

It might be worth planning two audits – a targeted one in the early stages of the implementation programme to identify quick wins and pilots, and a comprehensive one later as part of planning for the roll-out phase. The success of the earlier targeted audits can help you justify the effort involved in the comprehensive audit.

Once you have identified the business activities you are interested in, then you need access to two or three people who have experience in those activities (typically middle managers at the operational level), to help you map:

- the knowledge that is currently available and being deployed in those activities;

- knowledge assets that are not currently available but that would help to make those activities more effective (knowledge gaps);
- where the knowledge comes from, how it is accessed, and who has it;
- the knowledge assets that are produced as a result of performing the activity;
- where those knowledge assets go, and who applies them.

The maps you produce with these experienced staff will give you rich insight into the balance between the more explicit and tacit knowledge types, will give you evidence from the knowledge workers themselves of knowledge gaps, and will identify existing knowledge flows.

There is another powerful step you can take, however. If you expose the knowledge maps to the other departments and teams in the organization, and ask them to identify knowledge assets existing in other teams' maps that would be useful to them in their business activities, you can very quickly identify knowledge assets that are not currently being made widely available, but that would be helpful if shared. This enables you to identify high-value, high-demand knowledge assets from the ground up, which can yield unanticipated benefits from the knowledge assets audit exercise. You are more likely to get these unanticipated benefits from a comprehensive knowledge assets audit than from a more targeted one.

---

**Tip**

Review your KM strategy. Which would be more appropriate at the current stage for your organization – a comprehensive knowledge audit or a more targeted one? (Hint: this will depend on how focused or broad your strategic knowledge areas are, and on how important it is for you to improve wide accessibility to knowledge assets.)

---

# Analysing the results of the audit

If you understand the balance of different knowledge types required to perform the key business activities you are interested in, then you immediately have clues about what KM implementation steps would be appropriate or inappropriate to manage this knowledge.

## *Documents and data*

If you have an activity that is heavily dependent on documented knowledge assets, then the classic way to improve the management of documents on any scale is through information management supported by IT systems and content management or document management solutions. There are also processes which can be put in place to support management of this knowledge type, for example using standardized templates to introduce consistency in how documents are presented, developing taxonomies to enhance the findability of information and knowledge, and so on.

## Skills

Skills-dependent activities are most straightforwardly managed through training. Typical activities are training needs analysis, competency mapping, training plans, and e-learning solutions. However, not all skills work is necessarily delivered in training rooms or online. It can also be supported through on-the-job training, job shadowing, apprenticeships, coaching and mentoring.

## Methods

Methods represent unwritten routines and heuristics. Because of this, one of the easiest ways to manage this kind of knowledge is by documenting it in standard operating procedures, operating guidelines, FAQs, quick tips or step-by-step tutorials. However, methods that are quite sophisticated or complex (for example where skills or experience are also involved) might be better managed by giving people access to more experienced colleagues through a help desk, expertise directory, or supervisors.

## Relationships

There are three ways to enhance relationship-based knowledge access. First is allowing staff to find others with relevant knowledge, for example people directories listing areas of expertise or experience. Second is the ability to ask a person for help, and this is not easily done on a 'cold-call' basis. It is much easier if the different parties are already known to each other, and ideally have trust relationships already formed. This is why socialization opportunities, building up the informal social capital among groups who belong to different knowledge domains, is so powerful. Thirdly the development of communities of practice focused on critical knowledge areas encourages the formation of structured and facilitated relationships through which knowledge can flow.

## Experience

Business activities that have a heavy reliance on experience knowledge assets are more vulnerable and trickier to manage. Development of experience can be facilitated through job placement, assignment to specific work areas, career and succession planning programmes, knowledge retention and transfer programmes, mentoring, coaching and job shadowing. KM processes such as knowledge exchanges, peer assists and retrospects provide facilitated opportunities for experience-based knowledge to be identified, discussed and shared. Communities of practice can discuss and share experience through community dialogue processes such as knowledge exchange. While it is a more challenging set of assets to manage, the acquisition and sharing of experience is a core task for knowledge management.

## Natural talent

Natural talent can only be managed by managing the people themselves. Once you are aware that a particular work area is especially dependent on natural talent, then you need to rely very heavily on your HR processes for attracting, motivating and retaining the talent you need. There's very little else you can do in the way of growing or transferring this kind of knowledge.

## RAG analysis

Besides the insight that the balance of knowledge asset types gives you, there are some other specific pieces of analysis that you can undertake, to sharpen the focus and usefulness of your implementation projects. We call this a RAG analysis, standing for:

- **Risk analysis** – the more tacit types of knowledge asset (relationships, experience, natural talent) expose you to greater risk than others because they are harder to acquire, transfer or grow. In a risk analysis of the maps you will look at tacit knowledge asset dependencies, and check whether those knowledge assets are concentrated in just a few people, whether you are at any risk of sudden loss, and whether you have processes in place to identify, capture, transfer, or grow this knowledge.

- **Accessibility analysis** – when you capture the data about the knowledge assets you will also capture data about where they are located and who has them. When you expose the maps to other departments, you pick up information about the latent (currently unmet) demand for knowledge assets. You can put these two pieces of analysis together and identify strategies for making high-value knowledge assets more accessible to those who can benefit from them, either by moving them to a common platform (in the case of documents) or documenting them (in the case of methods) or knowledge retention and transfer programmes in the case of the more tacit knowledge asset types.

- **Gap analysis** – when you conduct the mapping sessions, it is important to ask the representatives if there are any knowledge assets that are not currently available that would make the activity more effective. These 'desired' knowledge assets are your knowledge gaps. Once you know what the gaps are, and have assessed them for criticality, you can identify strategies to meet those gaps.

The analysis from a knowledge assets audit will throw up a lot of insights and ideas that will be candidates for quick-win proof-of-concept projects or KM pilot projects. It is important that you sense check these candidates against the priorities outlined in your KM strategy.

## Summary

The knowledge assets audit is a powerful method for surfacing potential KM interventions that have both strategic and operational benefits. It helps you focus on the knowledge that is in most need of attention, and engages with some of your most important stakeholders – the knowledge workers. In this chapter we have identified the purpose, scope and content of a knowledge assets audit, and described how it connects to the KM strategy, and feeds into the KM implementation planning. In subsequent chapters we look at how you begin to build and test your KM framework, and engage with that other 'ground level' factor, your organizational culture.

# The knowledge management framework

## 12

In this chapter we take a high-level look at the management framework for KM that you plan to implement. An effective embedded KM framework is your final goal, and your implementation programme is a process of designing, testing and refining the framework. This chapter introduces the concept of the framework, and provides a template structure. We cover:

- the concept of a framework;
- why a framework is needed;
- the principles behind the framework;
- a KM framework template;
- different types of framework;
- framework – structured or emergent?

## What is a management framework?

Every management discipline is implemented as a framework, and KM should be no exception. By a 'framework' we refer to a linked and integrated set of roles, processes, technologies and governance which ensures that an asset is properly managed. They are the elements that need to be in place for a sustainable and responsible exercise of the discipline. Let's investigate this concept, by looking at another management framework – the framework for financial management. Although knowledge and money are not the same, both require an organization-wide integrated management framework if they are to flow round the company in an effective and systematic way. Some of the common elements of financial management frameworks are as follows:

- Financial management roles:
  - budget holders – the people accountable for money within projects and operations;

- accountants and cost engineers – the people doing the nuts and bolts of money-tracking;
- central finance team – the people who shuffle money between the projects and operations;
- CFOs and finance directors – the people accountable for the financial management system itself.

● **Financial management processes:**

- financial planning and forecasting;
- budgeting;
- invoicing;
- cost control;
- cost tracking;
- billing;
- financial reporting.

● **Financial management technology:**

- technology for logging and tracking transactions, such as SAP;
- technology for reporting figures, such as Excel;
- technology at point-of-sale, including tills, cash registers and card readers.

● **Financial management governance:**

- financial policies;
- accounting standards;
- legal requirements;
- monitoring and auditing;
- training and support.

All of these elements fit together into a financial management framework, allowing money to be acquired, tracked, spent and reported. The complexity of the framework needs to fit the scale of the operation. The framework listed above has 19 elements. Financial management frameworks in very large organizations can easily have more elements. If any of the elements of the framework were missing the framework would be severely weakened. Imagine how well financial management would perform with no budget holders, or with no financial reporting, or no company-wide financial technology, or no auditing. Each element of the framework protects against risks of failure in the financial management function. Financial management therefore needs a minimum framework consistent with the scale of the business, and if there are holes in that framework, financial management becomes impossible.

# Why we need a framework for KM

A KM framework, like a financial management framework, will contain a mix of roles, processes, technologies and governance, which collectively enable the acquisition, sharing, maintenance and re-use of knowledge. Like financial management, KM needs a minimum number of elements in the framework, and if there are holes in that framework, KM becomes unviable. Here are some examples of the risks:

- If there were no people accountable for KM within projects and operations, then no attention would be paid to KM because it would be 'nobody's job', and it just would not get done.
- If there were no defined process for knowledge capture, the organization would not know what to capture, or when, and each unit would capture knowledge in its own way rather than to a common standard.
- If there was no consistent KM technology, there would be no way of compiling, comparing and communicating knowledge across the organization.
- If there were no KM governance, there would be no way of knowing whether people were doing proper KM, people would cut corners and fudge practices and soon a consistent approach to KM would disappear.

The benefit therefore of applying a management framework to KM is to ensure that all enabling elements are covered and that there are no missing elements. If we return to the concept of KM as a supply chain, as we discussed in Chapter 1, the framework ensures that the supply chain is complete. Every element of the framework is a link in the chain, and a complete framework means there are no links missing.

---

**Tip**

Review some of the existing successful management frameworks in your organization, and map out the roles, processes, technologies and governance that sustain them. Look at quality management for example, or safety management, or HR management. These successful frameworks will give you some idea of the level of scale and complexity your KM framework may need to be viable in your organization.

**TABLE 12.1**    An empty KM framework template

|  | Discuss | Document | Synthesize | Find/review |
|---|---|---|---|---|
| **People** |  |  |  |  |
| **Process** |  |  |  |  |
| **Technology** |  |  |  |  |
| **Governance** |  |  |  |  |

# A template for your KM framework

In Chapter 1 we introduced the four knowledge enablers of roles, processes, technologies and governance, and the four knowledge transactions of discuss, document, synthesize and find/review. Together these can be used to create a 16-cell table which we recommend as a template for building a KM framework. The purpose of using these elements as the axes of the table is two-fold:

- to provide you with a generic template that can apply in any organization of any size in any industry;
- to ensure the framework is as complete as possible and that all enablers and transactions are addressed.

An empty framework template is shown in Table 12.1.

The 16 cells in the template are listed below, and detailed examples of potential roles, processes, technologies and governance to be incorporated in your framework are given in Chapters 13 through 16:

- roles for facilitating or supporting discussion;
- roles for facilitating or supporting documentation of knowledge;
- roles and accountabilities for knowledge synthesis;
- roles for facilitating for supporting finding and reviewing knowledge;
- processes for discussion of knowledge;
- processes for documentation of knowledge;
- processes for knowledge synthesis;
- processes for finding and reviewing knowledge;
- technologies for supporting discussion;
- technologies for supporting documentation of knowledge;
- technologies for knowledge synthesis;
- technologies for supporting finding and reviewing knowledge;
- governance for knowledge discussion;
- governance for documentation of knowledge;

**TABLE 12.2**    An example completed KM framework for an oil company

|  | Discuss | Document | Synthesize | Find/review |
|---|---|---|---|---|
| **People** | Community of practice leaders and facilitators | Lesson capture facilitators | Knowledge owners for each critical knowledge topic | Knowledge managers for projects and departments |
| **Process** | Knowledge exchange, peer assist | Lessons capture meetings, after action review | Distillation and packaging of knowledge, creation of best practice | Before action review, KM plans |
| **Technology** | Discussion forum, Yammer | Lessons database, blogs | Wiki, portal | Search, tags, RSS |
| **Governance** | Defined set of CoPs, community charters and business cases | Expectations for lessons capture, quality standards for lessons | KM policy, taxonomy, metadata, information architecture | Expectations for lessons re-use |

- governance for knowledge synthesis;
- governance for finding and reviewing knowledge.

Please note that some governance elements such as an overall KM policy or a taxonomy may apply across the different knowledge transactions, and some roles may fit in more than one box.

An example of a completed KM framework is shown in Table 12.2, based on a KM framework for an energy company. An example KM framework for a legal firm is shown in Table 12.3.

Other organizations may complete the framework with different roles, processes, technology and governance elements. The next four chapters will help you determine how you populate this table for your own organization.

---

**Tip**

Do you already have some elements of KM in place? You can review your current organization against this template, to see which elements are already in place and working well, which are in place but require improvement, and which are completely missing.

**TABLE 12.3**   An example completed KM framework for a legal firm

| | Discuss | Document | Synthesize | Find/review |
|---|---|---|---|---|
| **People** | Practice area experts Practice-related communities | Professional support lawyers | Practice area experts | Professional support lawyers |
| **Process** | Online discussion | Post-matter reviews Precedent collection | Creation and update of precedent library | Pre-matter research |
| **Technology** | Discussion forum, Yammer | Post-matter review database | Intranet portal | Search |
| **Governance** | Guidelines for practice areas and communities | Expectations and quality standards for precedents filing | Taxonomy, metadata, information architecture | KM policy |

# Summary

The KM framework is the complete management framework for KM. You will design, test, pilot and roll out this framework during your implementation programme. We recommend a framework template which covers the four enablers of KM applied to the four 'knowledge transactions'. A complete KM framework will have something in place for each cell in the framework template, ensuring there are no links missing in your KM supply chain. In the next few chapters we will cover the columns of the framework template one by one and suggest some options for you to populate the cells for your own organization.

# The knowledge discussion elements of the KM framework

## 13

Steven Denning, one-time head of KM at the World Bank, said at the Ontario KM summit in 2006 that 'the learning capacity of an organization is directly related to its ability to hold conversations', and we truly believe he was right. Many management disciplines are based on conversation. Safety management is driven by conversations about safety, in order to drive awareness of safety issues and identify mitigating actions. Risk management is driven by conversations about risk, in order to drive awareness of risks to projects and to identify mitigating actions. KM is similarly driven by conversations about knowledge.

We discussed in Chapter 1 how conversations and content are the dual paths by which knowledge is transmitted, and we said that discussion should form one of the main components of your KM framework. In this chapter we describe some potential framework elements for knowledge transfer through conversation:

- dialogue as the preferred form of discussion;
- roles for knowledge discussion;
- processes for knowledge discussion;
- technologies for knowledge discussion;
- governance for knowledge discussion.

## Dialogue as the preferred form of discussion

Conversation is widely recognized as the most effective KM tool there is. Knowledge and experience can be shared through conversation, but not through every type of conversation. Conversations have many functions, and knowledge sharing is only one of them. Conversations can take the form of:

- **small talk** and social chatter, where the process of communicating is more important than the content;
- **social cohesion,** the purpose of which is to align people through agreement, for example sharing impressions of a football match or a TV episode you have both watched;
- **reporting and debriefing,** which are 'broadcasts' where people state facts and opinions for an audience (many project meetings are like this);
- **argument and debate** are the 'win/lose' conversations where someone has an opinion, and defends it against alternative opinions;
- **dialogue** is conversation with the aim of exploring different perspectives and reaching mutual understanding (though not necessarily agreement).

Dialogue is the kind of conversation we need to promote in order to facilitate knowledge sharing in organizations. The goal of dialogue is not winning or convincing, but reaching a deeper level of collective understanding. Dialogue involves asking questions, seeking clarification, testing understanding, and looking for that 'aha' moment when the knowledge is really transferred. It helps us access and build deep tacit knowledge and it allows us to check whether we have really understood the knowledge. Dialogue requires listening skills as well as debating skills, as people allow their opinions to be challenged, and indeed, welcome that challenge. It requires trust and openness, but it generates trust and openness as well.

Dialogue is a very difficult conversational style to achieve, requiring good facilitation. Without this conversation can easily degenerate into debate and argument, and the opportunity for effective knowledge sharing is lost. The roles and processes we describe below are designed to foster knowledge transfer through dialogue.

# Roles for knowledge discussion

Here we describe two sorts of role: roles related to conversation within communities and networks, and roles related to facilitating conversation.

## Communities and networks

The purpose of communities and networks is to provide access to the tacit knowledge which people hold in their heads. Once the person is connected into a network that transcends the organizational boundaries, their tacit knowledge becomes 'linked into a system' and becomes more accessible to

**FIGURE 13.1**    The average effectiveness rating for communities of practice as community size grows

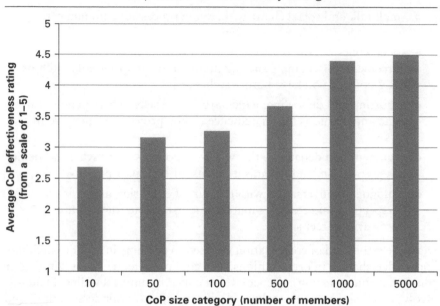

**SOURCE:** Knoco global KM survey 2014 (Knoco, 2014)

others. Much as a piece of explicit knowledge joins the organization's knowledge base when linked, made accessible and searchable, so a piece of tacit knowledge joins the organization's knowledge base when the knowledge holder is linked, made accessible and findable through a network or community of practice.

For any organization's working from multiple offices or in many countries, communities and networks will be an element of your KM framework (see the Oilco case history in Chapter 28, for example). When KM is fully embedded, you would expect to see a community or network associated with every business-critical knowledge topic. Successful communities span organizational boundaries, and are large enough to contain a wealth and diversity of knowledge. Figure 13.1 shows how the effectiveness of communities increases with community size (as rated by community members).

## *Roles within a community or network*

- There are a few distinct roles to be played in a community, the key role being the **community leader** – the person who is accountable for ensuring the community functions as a knowledge-sharing and learning vehicle. This leader is involved in the start-up and growth of the community, and in developing and maintaining the community processes. The choice of a good leader is crucial to the effective operation of the community. The leader often reports to a **community sponsor**.

In some cases, the leader appoints a **facilitator** (in other cases, the leader also takes the facilitator role). The facilitator should be a recognized networker within the community. Their role is to facilitate the linkages and relationships between the members, to facilitate online community discussion, and potentially to steward any community output – for example, through documentation. A good facilitator leads from within, energizes the community, and builds trust and ownership among the community members. The main tasks of the facilitator include:

- building membership and welcoming new members;
- maintaining activity and energy through a rhythm of events;
- setting the behavioural style of the community;
- managing discussions and inviting participation;
- managing relationships; and
- brokering connections between members.

There are often no formal roles in a community of practice apart from the leader and/or facilitator, and there is no single structure that will suit all communities of practice. Communities thrive on the energy and participation of their members, and so build their own identities and characters, much as individuals do. You will undoubtedly see many levels and forms of participation within the community, including:

- core team members, who work with the leader and facilitator to nurture and grow the community;
- subject matter experts, who manage areas of community knowledge (this role is described in more detail in Chapter 15);
- active community members, engaged in asking questions and sharing knowledge;
- community sub-groups which can be set up to work on allocated tasks or specific topics; and
- lurkers – community members who at the moment are just watching and learning.

## Discussion facilitation roles

Good facilitation is essential to effective face-to-face KM processes. Effectively identifying and exchanging knowledge in a meeting requires high-quality interactions between people through the medium of dialogue as discussed earlier. The role of the facilitator is to:

- maintain high-quality dialogue in service of delivering the desired outcomes of the meeting;
- ensure balanced input from many people;
- explore disagreements without descending into argument; and
- allow good discussion while still finishing the meeting on time.

Facilitation is a form of assistance and guidance that makes it easier for a group to effectively deliver the objectives of KM processes such as retrospect, peer assist, or knowledge café. The facilitator manages the process of the meeting (including the quality of the dialogue) while the group itself looks after the content.

Most organizations that value knowledge sharing also value facilitation, simply because good facilitation produces high-quality sharing.

## CASE STUDY

The leader of one KM programme we were involved with trained his entire KM team in facilitation skills and found that this not only enabled them to facilitate KM processes, it also gained them access to many non-KM meetings, where they were able to introduce KM processes into the agenda. Part of your KM implementation may well include the deliberate development of facilitation skills in the organization. In some cases the KM team can provide these resources, you can use KM champions as facilitators (Chapter 21), and you should also build the facilitation skills of community facilitators and knowledge managers.

# Processes for knowledge discussion

For knowledge to be effectively transferred through dialogue, the conversations need structure and process as well as facilitation. These conversations can occur online, or face to face.

## Online Q&A

The most powerful mechanism for online knowledge sharing within a community or network is through question and answer. Q&A-based discussion allows members of a dispersed, sometimes multinational, community to help, teach or advise each other. A community member can raise a question on a specific topic, and anyone in the community with knowledge or advice to share can answer. Some Q&A forums send the questions only to a group of experts (such as the 'Ask Anglo' system in Anglo American, the mining giant). Others send them to the whole community.

A Q&A forum can be a lifeline for individuals who are geographically or organizationally isolated (in a remote branch office, for example), as it allows them to tap into the knowledge of their peers elsewhere in the organization. Part of the role of the community facilitator (discussed earlier) is to support asking and answering within the community forum, through encouraging questions, prompting for answers, requesting clarifications, and summarizing discussion threads.

Question-based knowledge 'pull' seems to be a much more effective mechanism for transferring knowledge within communities than 'just in case' publication 'push' of knowledge articles. Knowledge pull is a question looking for an answer, or a problem looking for a solution, and so there is greater certainty that the shared knowledge will be applied. Grant (2013) says that 'direct requests for help between colleagues drive 75 to 90 per cent of all the help exchanged within organizations'. For the word 'help' we can substitute the word 'knowledge'.

## CASE STUDY

Ash (2007b) shares a story from an employee of the engineering and construction multinational Fluor which described how an online forum was used to gain valuable technical knowledge. A question was posed asking about the design for a piece of refinery equipment called an electrostatic coalescer, which contained a salt-bed drier.

> Within three days, three responses were received, from the Haarlem [Netherlands] and Calgary [Canada] offices. They provided project references and contacts for each of the different design options considered. The information underlined the strong effect of operating temperature on salt-bed efficiency: at too high an operating temperature the efficiency of the salt bed is eliminated by the brine solubility in diesel...
>
> Based on this information and project references, our recommendations to the client were to pre-cool the diesel feed to 60 °F with a chiller before being sent to the coalescer and to eliminate the salt-bed drier... The elimination of the salt-bed drier saved the client money on equipment cost (reduced by €1m) and operational cost. Our client is so pleased that a new work order has been awarded to Fluor: a similar study for the other refinery of the client. This study represents a business value of €700,000.

## *Face-to-face discussion*

Periodic face-to-face meetings for knowledge transfer, despite the associated time and travel cost, are highly effective if well structured and well facilitated, because they allow discussion of knowledge and experience in a high-trust environment. All face-to-face knowledge transfer meeting processes are based on dialogue, and the specific process you select depends on how many teams have the knowledge, and how many teams need the knowledge.

For knowledge transfer from one team to one other team, an appropriate choice may be the **Baton-Passing** process (Keyes, 2012, p 256). This process, invented at Pfizer by Victor Newman when he was their Chief Learning Officer, involves the transfer of knowledge and lessons from one team to another team that is either tackling similar work, or continuing the first team's work. The process involves the following steps:

- the first (knowledge-holding) team maps out the process of the work they have just completed, as a timeline or a mindmap on a large sheet of paper;
- they identify learning points within the map (often using Post-it notes) where they have gained useful new knowledge;
- the second team use a different colour Post-it to identify areas where they want to learn from the first team;
- the two teams explore these learning points through dialogue;
- the second team then creates an action list to decide what they will do with the knowledge they have gained.

For knowledge transfer from one team to many other teams, an appropriate choice is the **Knowledge Handover** process (Milton, 2010, p 126); often held when one team has completed a project and wishes to transfer its lessons to others. The process involves the following steps:

- prior to the meeting, the project team discusses, identifies and documents the lessons and new knowledge they have gained from the project;
- they publish these lessons to people they think might benefit, and invite them to co-create an agenda for the knowledge handover, which will focus on those topics of most interest to others;
- at the meeting these topics are discussed one by one, and a brief presentation from the project team is followed by a much longer period of questions from the visitors;
- where several topics are discussed in parallel sessions, these are followed by a full-group session to summarize the main learning points from the parallel sessions;
- at the end of the meeting the visitors summarize the main things they have learned through the session, and the actions they will take on return to their own projects.

For knowledge transfer from many teams to one team, an appropriate choice is the **Peer Assist** process (Milton, 2005, p 49). A peer assist is often held when one team (the host team) is planning a project and wishes to learn from the experience of others (visiting teams). This process involves the following steps:

- the facilitator sets the ground rules of the Peer Assist – openness and generous listening from the host team, positive advice and feedback from the visitors;
- the host team explains their context, and lists the issues they believe they need to learn about, including options they have already considered;
- the visitors outline their past experience and add other issues that they believe the host team also needs to learn about;
- each issue is discussed through dialogue in small teams;
- the visitors then summarize their advice to the host team, and the host team summarizes the actions they will take as a result of the new knowledge they have gained.

For knowledge transfer between many teams, or involving many diverse members of a community of practice, an appropriate choice is the **Knowledge Exchange** process (Young and Milton, 2011, p 40). A knowledge exchange is often held as a way for people to compare different approaches to a task and decide on a best practice. This process involves the following steps:

- the group divides the topic in question into its main components (tasks within a process, components within a design, etc);
- dialogue sessions are held around each component, and participants share their experiences and the approaches they use, and they attempt to combine their knowledge to develop a 'current best' solution based on existing knowledge, as well as identifying current knowledge gaps;
- where the components are discussed in parallel sessions, the recommended best practice is validated with the rest of the attendees;
- a documented knowledge asset is produced based on the discussions at the knowledge exchange.

# Technologies for knowledge discussion

Software to support discussion of knowledge can include discussion forums to allow online questions and answers, people-finder software to find the relevant people to discuss with, and some forms of discussion-focused enterprise social media.

**Discussion forums and Q&A forums** provide locations where users can post messages for others to read, answer and comment on. Often the discussion is hosted on a website, and users can interact directly on the site or via e-mail. Good facilitation helps the longer-lasting discussions to stay focused and avoid 'topic drift'.

**A people-finder system** is an index of 'who knows what' – a knowledge directory for the organization. It is an easy way to locate anyone working in the business, based on their knowledge and expertise. The system will be based around a knowledge taxonomy, to allow people to categorize their knowledge and experience, and so be searchable and findable. The people-finder system does not create the knowledge flows that come from mutual familiarity and trust, but can help locate knowledgeable people. Your discussion processes are then necessary to build the familiarity and trust needed for knowledge flow.

A range of **enterprise social media** exist for use in organizations. The ones that most strongly support conversation threads, dialogue and people-finding will be those which are most valuable for KM. Others, such as the enterprise equivalents of Twitter, can be useful for promoting awareness of people's ideas and activities, as long as you have other tools and processes to help them develop the conversations. It is very difficult to hold dialogue when limited to 140 characters.

---

**Tip**

Avoid the temptation to have multiple competing conversation channels or technologies in the organization. There should be one technology to support discussion, so people know which technology to use when asking a question, knowing that this will allow them to access all the relevant tacit knowledge. Multiple channels that fulfil the same purpose introduce confusion and duplication, they scatter conversations, reduce the energy and activity that flows in any single channel, and increase the chance that critical knowledge will get lost somewhere between the supplier and the user.

---

## Governance for knowledge discussion

Some of the governance elements to support knowledge discussion might be:

- a defined list of required communities and networks;
- a business case and a charter for each community or network;
- an expectation that every employee should have a profile in the company people-finder;
- training for all community leaders and facilitators;
- training for process facilitators;
- reference materials and guidelines for all discussion processes and technologies;
- success stories from community and network knowledge transfer.

# Summary

Exchange of knowledge through conversation, specifically through dialogue, will be a vital component of your KM framework. This is likely to include communities of practice, with their own specific supporting roles, technologies and governance, and a suite of processes for face-to-face knowledge transfer supported by trained facilitators. You will need to test these KM framework elements in your own context, and select the discussion components that will work in your organization, and that can be embedded into your own procedures and systems.

# The knowledge capture and documentation elements of the KM framework

## 14

In this chapter we focus on the first step in content-based knowledge transfer, namely the documentation of that knowledge. Knowledge capture is a core component in your KM framework, to ensure that new knowledge is recorded on an ongoing basis as a part of operational work. We cover:

- the difference between documented knowledge and information;
- roles for knowledge documentation;
- processes for knowledge documentation;
- technologies for knowledge documentation;
- governance for knowledge documentation.

## The difference between documented knowledge and information

Documenting knowledge is not the same as filing information. In Chapter 1 we discussed the knowledge supply chain, the purpose of which is to provide the knowledge workers with the knowledge they need to make decisions and take actions. Therefore we need to document as knowledge those things which others can learn from and act upon, such as insights, lessons, advice and experience. This is the knowledge that needs to be documented, and it is distinct from normal work-related information products such as reports, budgets, maps and diagrams.

You may also need to collect some of the work products to accompany the documented knowledge in order to illustrate, and give context to the documented knowledge. We can therefore think of four types of output from work activity, of which three are handled as part of KM:

1 undocumented knowledge, still in people's heads, transferred through conversation (Chapter 13);

2 documented knowledge: insights, lessons, advice and experience from which others can learn, transferred as content (this chapter);

3 high-value information which gives context to, and provides examples for, the documented knowledge, also transferred as content (this chapter); and

4 all other kinds of information, which will be handled by an information management framework rather than the KM framework. Your knowledge organization activities (Chapter 17) cover both information and knowledge assets, in order to connect your documented knowledge with related information.

It is the creation of documented knowledge and the capture of high value information which we address in this chapter.

# Roles for knowledge documentation

There needs to be defined accountability for knowledge documentation within the line organization, so that individuals in the projects and departments know whether they are accountable for ensuring that lessons and new knowledge are documented. Sometimes it is seen as 'everyone's job' to capture knowledge, but even then some accountable roles are needed to make sure that 'everyone' is actually doing his or her job. Usually the project manager or department manager is accountable for making sure this happens, and they frequently call on the support of specialist KM roles to help them.

Four such supporting roles are described below: knowledge engineers, lesson-learned facilitators, learning historians and knowledge base publishers.

The **knowledge engineer** (Milton, 2007) is the key knowledge documentation role in any KM approach that focuses on analysing complex decision making applied by experts, turning this analysis into rules and guidance that less experienced people can use, or incorporating this analysis into expert systems. The knowledge engineer might work with a retiring expert as part of a knowledge retention programme, or may work to set up a knowledge base.

Historically the knowledge engineer was focused on creating expert systems, but in reality the major challenge for this role is in eliciting the knowledge in the first place, rather than in creating the subsequent system. The task of the knowledge engineer is as follows:

● Assessing the problem for which the knowledge needs to be acquired and packaged.

● Eliciting the knowledge – the most difficult step, and where the skills of the knowledge engineer are most important. There is a range of techniques for knowledge elicitation with interviews being the primary method, augmented by techniques such as analysed problem solving, card sorting and the creation of concept maps (Milton, 2007).

- The elicited knowledge then needs to be structured into an expert system, a knowledge base or a knowledge asset. The knowledge engineer creates the structure and populates it with the elicited knowledge.

- The structured knowledge needs to be validated, through review by subject matter experts and by validating the knowledge against known outcomes.

---

**Tip**

If your KM framework is likely to include knowledge engineering, or the creation of expert systems, then seek training in knowledge elicitation skills for one or more members of your KM team.

---

**Lesson-learned facilitators** play a similar role to knowledge engineers but in relation to lesson capture and documentation. We discuss lesson-capture meetings such as retrospects later in this chapter. The completeness and quality of the lessons captured at these meetings depends on the quality and objectivity of the dialogue at the meeting, and an external skilled facilitator is crucial to delivering good quality output. The main tasks of the lesson facilitator are as follows:

- to facilitate lesson-capture meetings so that observations are discussed and explored in order to draw out insights and lessons;

- to ensure lessons are fully discussed, with balanced insights from all project team members;

- to ensure the lessons are captured and expressed in a clear and usable way;

- to document the lessons, and (if appropriate) to enter them into the lessons management system; and

- to monitor agreed follow-ups such as changes to procedures and verify that they are actually completed.

A third possible role is that of the **learning historian**. This role is linked to the concept of a learning history, described by Kleiner and Roth (1997) as a written narrative of a company's recent set of critical episodes such as a corporate change event, a new initiative, a challenge met, or even a traumatic event such as a major reduction in the workforce. The learning historian creates a learning history through the following steps:

- interviews and data gathering from participants in a project or activity;
- distillation of knowledge, and establishing key themes and 'plots';
- creation of a learning history in narrative form;
- validation of the contents through reflective feedback;
- dissemination and publication of the learning history, with guidelines on application and learning transfer.

Finally, organizations operating customer-facing knowledge bases often embed the role of **knowledge base publisher** within the support departments. The publisher is authorized to create and modify content on the knowledge base, making articles (which may have been authored by others in their team) visible to partners or customers. The publisher therefore needs to combine good technical knowledge and writing skills with deep understanding of the knowledge base and its use, and knowledge of the various target user groups.

# Processes for knowledge documentation

Knowledge documentation involves extracting tacit knowledge from people's heads and recording it in written, diagram or audio-visual form. The main challenge is that people who are the source of the knowledge do not always 'know what they know' until they discuss it. Sometimes organizations set up a system whereby people voluntarily identify lessons and new knowledge, and add them into a lessons database, wiki or knowledge base. We believe you capture only a small proportion of the knowledge this way, because people are often not aware of what they know, or are not aware of other people's needs and how their knowledge could help.

A much better alternative is to use dialogue-based, questions-based processes to first identify what people know, and then probe for the detail that makes the knowledge re-usable. The question-based approaches use a similar format, where the questioner (the interviewer, knowledge engineer or facilitator):

- identifies learning points;
- explores these learning points to find the root causes for success, or the heuristics used by the expert;
- asks a future-tense question, to require the person or team to analyse the learning and create a recommendation. Questions might include:
  - What would be your advice for someone doing this in future?
  - What mistakes might a novice make?

    – If you were doing this again, what would you do differently?

    – If you could go back in time and give yourself a message, what would you tell yourself?

There are two main approaches for timetabling these questioning processes: reactive, and scheduled. **The reactive approach** triggers documentation of knowledge as a result of a notable operational success, near miss or failure (for example a safety incident, loss of a major client or significant project overruns). Many companies have mandatory processes for reviewing these failures. The successes are often less obvious, though one company we have worked with uses global consultants and technical directors to identify, on their global travels, good practice that needs to be documented. The approach of Appreciative Inquiry (Barrett and Fry, 2010) is often employed when analysing notable successes, and represents a question-based alternative to problem-focused analysis. Appreciative Inquiry looks to analyse the best approaches in order to define an even better future.

    **The scheduled approach,** common within project-based organizations and customer support teams, is to schedule knowledge capture and documentation processes within the activity framework. Some of the more common capture processes are discussed below.

> ### Tip
>
> To build a culture of knowledge capture we recommend the scheduled approach. Once you have tested and piloted knowledge documentation processes, try to get them scheduled into the project cycle or operational cycle as distinct tasks within the normal process flow.

## Interviews

An interview is the most effective way to capture and document knowledge from an individual. Interviewing is a form of dialogue – a question and answer process which continues until the interviewer feels they have reached core knowledge, expressed as future recommendations. The interview may be taking place as part of a knowledge retention programme, because an expert holds knowledge which needs to be incorporated into an expert system, or because they have been through a valuable learning experience which needs to be analysed and documented. The stages of the interview are as follows:

● Identify the main learning points to be discussed. Before the interview, talk with the individual, his or her manager, team mates and community of practice (whichever are appropriate) to identify what topics the interview needs to cover.

- At the interview, explore each topic one by one. Ask about success factors and challenges, and explore the root causes behind each one. For example, you might say 'One of the success factors you mentioned was teamwork. Can you tell me how this good teamwork was achieved?' Explore counterfactuals – other ways that the situation might have unfolded – because this can pick up heuristics the expert themselves may be unaware of, and also help to distinguish the expert's approach from that of less experienced people. Finally you need to ask a question designed to capture advice and recommendations for the future, for example, 'If you were advising someone starting a similar project, what would you advise them to do to ensure good teamwork?'

- As the interview develops, you might find that so do new avenues of questioning. The interview can become a cycle of asking questions, exploring the answers, summarizing and feeding back, and developing new questions. It is often useful to chart out the progress of the interview in something like a mind map, to stay on track.

- Don't be satisfied with vague answers; press for specifics. You are looking, all the time, for recommendations for the next knowledge worker doing similar work. Also listen out for mention of important documents, diagrams and other material which might be useful to collect. Once you have gathered as much knowledge as you can from each topic, summarize and move on to the next.

- End the interview by asking the interviewee to summarize the main lessons. For example, 'As a summary of what we have been discussing, if you were speaking to somebody who was just about to start on a similar project tomorrow, what would your key points of advice be?'

- For a further range of techniques to access 'deep knowledge' from experts, see Milton (2007).

## After action review

The after action review (AAR) is a regular team-based questioning process to get at the ground truth behind the results of an exercise or activity (Milton, 2005, p 59). It is a process both for discussion (and could have been included in the previous chapter) and for knowledge capture. AARs are usually conducted immediately after brief actions where there is learning potential, eg a maintenance team ending a shift at an oil refinery, a fire crew after dealing with a fire, or a nursing team at a shift handover.

In an AAR the team's expectation of an event is compared with what actually happened, and the facilitator leads a questioning process to find the reasons for the difference between the two. Where there is a difference between expectations and reality, there is potential for learning. The process involves dialogue around five questions:

**1** what was supposed to happen (during the activity we are reviewing);

**2** what actually happened;

**3** why was there a difference between 1 and 2 (either a positive or a negative difference);

**4** what have we learned;

**5** what do we need to do to sustain (keep doing) this, or what changes do we need to make to embed this lesson?

The quality of the questioning determines the value of the knowledge derived from an AAR. Superficial questioning gives shallow knowledge of limited use. Deeper questioning, maybe using the technique of 'the five whys' (Bicheno, 2008, p 152), gets at the deeper knowledge, where the real value lies. Where AARs are run by team leaders, you will need to provide training in the skills of AAR questioning, and in particular training on how to probe with sensitivity and without blame, especially where things did not go as well as expected.

## Creation of A3 reports

An A3 report is a process developed by Toyota for reviewing and documenting learning about product failures and product design improvements (Kennedy *et al*, 2008). It looks at one specific problem identified by direct observation or experience, and offers a structure for analysis and resolution, documented on one side of A3 paper. There are up to seven sections in the A3 report, each often recorded graphically with charts, diagrams and photographs.

The steps for creating an A3 report are as follows:

**1** Identify the problem with the current design – what's the background?

**2** Conduct and document research to understand the current situation.

**3** Conduct and document root cause analysis (eg through the five whys).

**4** Develop a 'target state'.

**5** Determine actions or countermeasures to address root causes.

**6** Create an implementation plan with accountable actions and costs, to get from the current state to the target state.

**7** Develop a follow-up plan, including preparation of a follow-up report.

A3s are a reactive process, documenting the knowledge from a solved problem, ideally completed by a focus group of two to three people. They be stored in hard copy in a ring-binder, or online in a lessons management system.

## *Retrospects*

The retrospect is an externally facilitated team meeting, held after the end of a project or project milestone, where the team identifies and analyses learning points through discussion and dialogue, in order to identify and document lessons and actions for the future (Milton, 2005, p 68). Retrospects are used by project-based organizations from every industry, and the use of them is mentioned in the Huawei case study in Chapter 29. Mega-projects may hold many retrospects in a single project; one company we worked with held a series of 30 retrospects to cover different aspects of a multi-billion dollar project.

At the retrospect, the facilitator leads an inclusive discussion to identify what went well and what did not go to plan in the project, why the successful elements succeeded, why the failures and mistakes happened, and how future projects can repeat the success and avoid the failure. The key questions in a retrospect are therefore what, why and how; very open questions which allow full exploration of the lessons learned. Note that there is no 'who' question; like the AAR, the retrospect is a no-blame process.

The process of a retrospect is as follows;

- The learning points for discussion are identified – either beforehand by canvassing views of the project team, or at the meeting. These should include success factors for the project as well as problem areas or areas for change.
- The learning points are prioritized, with priority given to those that had a big impact on the project, and are transferable to other projects.
- Each prioritized learning point is discussed as if it were a single AAR, as described above.

---

**Tip**

A retrospect of a high-profile project forms an excellent proof of concept exercise for KM, since it will certainly surface re-usable knowledge that can produce value elsewhere in the business. Look for successful projects where learning has been gained, and offer to facilitate a retrospect.

---

# Technology for knowledge documentation

In this section we cover two types of technology – recording technology, and knowledge storage technology.

## Recording technology

Traditionally, meeting facilitators stand up at the front of the room and write bullet points on a flip chart. However, when a good dialogue gets going, there is no way that you can write bullet points quickly enough, and in enough detail, to capture the subtleties and the context of the knowledge that is being discussed. You therefore need to record the meeting or interview. Acquire a digital voice recorder, and either transcribe the recording yourself (time consuming, but accurate) or use a transcription service (more economical, but they may not understand the technical context or terminology).

Video recording is also a good way to capture knowledge – not by video recording a whole retrospect or interview (boring and dull to re-watch) but by recording short summaries immediately after the interview or retrospect is over. The human voice and human face give context, humanity, and credibility to the knowledge.

> ### Tip
>
> Buy some good-quality digital audio recorders and video recorders for your KM team. Link the audio and video snippets to the fuller documentation and learning outcomes, so that the audio and video clips function as 'shop windows' to the content. Consider podcasts and video broadcasts.

## Storage technology for newly documented knowledge

It is often possible to place new knowledge directly into your long-term knowledge store, by editing a wiki page or posting an article in a knowledge base. Such long-term knowledge stores are covered in the next chapter. However there are some cases where new knowledge is stored temporarily, on its way to the long-term store, perhaps as provisional knowledge needing later validation or as ideas and observations. Some options for this storage of provisional knowledge are as follows:

### Lessons management systems

If lessons are being learned from many projects, then these lessons need to be captured and stored somewhere where they can be compared, searched, and transferred from one project to another. They need to be captured in a consistent format (for example through form-based entry), and stored with a consistent set of metadata to allow easy retrieval in a single system to which all the projects will have access. This should involve an active workflow system where lessons are pro-actively routed to those who need to see them, and actions associated with lessons are sent to those who need to take action. Usually the actions involve embedding the lessons into process and guidance, and lessons are archived once they have been embedded. A lessons management system also generates a set of metrics that support oversight of the lesson-learning process.

## Blogs

While it is possible to use discussion forums to share learning reflections from operations, blogs are a far better mechanism for sharing new knowledge with a community or network. A blog allows such knowledge to be tagged, people can discuss the knowledge through the comments system, and if you set up a series of topic-specific blogs then individuals can subscribe to topics which interest them, allowing them to be instantly notified of new relevant knowledge. The community then has two tools, with the blog being a 'push' tool for very current documented knowledge, and the discussion forum (Chapter 13) being a 'pull' tool for undocumented knowledge.

# Governance for knowledge documentation

Here are some of the possible governance elements to support knowledge documentation:

- a knowledge retention strategy focusing on identifying the risk of knowledge loss from the departure of key individuals, and actions taken to document or transfer their knowledge;
- defined expectations (and compliance measures) for the process and frequency of lesson capture within projects and work activities, the use of A3 reports during product development, or the creation of knowledge articles as part of normal work;
- a clear definition of the 'knowledge collateral' needed from projects;
- style guides and quality expectations for lessons, A3s and knowledge articles;
- training for interviewers, lessons facilitators and knowledge engineers;
- reference materials for all processes and technologies;
- collection of success stories from the use of lesson learning and A3s.

# Summary

Documentation of new knowledge is another vital component of your KM framework. It will require its own roles and accountabilities, processes, supporting technologies and governance. You will need to test these in your own context, and select the documentation components that will work in your organization, and that can be embedded into your own procedures and systems.

# The knowledge synthesis elements of the KM framework

## 15

Any organization that is successful at documenting knowledge has to address the issue of knowledge synthesis. Effective knowledge documentation will create a rapidly increasing amount of lessons, good practices, blog posts, wiki pages and knowledge articles, and this volume of material means that the same knowledge may be documented many times, knowledge from different places and different times may contradict each other, it may be very difficult to find the knowledge you need among the many tens of thousands of documents, and each individual knowledge worker is required – often in a hurry – to figure out their own answer from this mass of evidence. Knowledge synthesis is required to constantly process this mass of material into integrated, organized and useful guidance.

In this chapter we cover:

- what knowledge synthesis is;
- what synthesized knowledge 'looks like';
- roles for knowledge synthesis;
- processes for knowledge synthesis;
- technologies for knowledge synthesis;
- governance for knowledge synthesis.

## What is knowledge synthesis?

Knowledge synthesis is the summary, collation and integration of multiple sources of documented knowledge into a single set of guidance material, which knowledge workers can use to help guide their business decisions and business activity. Most or all of the KM best practice companies employ a step of knowledge synthesis within their KM framework. For example:

- Shell collate their best practices ('practices worth replicating'), their lessons learned, and the results of community discussions into synthesized guidance within the Shell wiki. ConocoPhillips take the same approach with their community wiki sites.

- Most militaries collate all lessons and observations from the field into guidance documents on all military processes. These are called 'doctrine manuals', which represent synthesized knowledge on these processes.

- General Motors synthesizes its technical knowledge into a set of Approved Best Practices.

# What does synthesized knowledge look like?

Synthesized knowledge is a single set of structured material, validated by a process owner, practice owner or community, collated from many sources, structured in the most useful way for the knowledge user, and containing guidance telling the knowledge worker how to perform or approach a task, design or sell a product, or how to interact with a customer.

Synthesized knowledge may contain some or all of the following:

- process guidelines;
- techniques and methods;
- product design guidelines and principles;
- checklists;
- FAQs, and answers to questions;
- templates;
- exemplars;
- tips and hints.

It is unlikely to include such items as project documents, case histories or individual lessons, unless these are used as illustrative examples.

Synthesized knowledge can also be categorized by the validity or the 'weight' that it carries, as described below.

There is the **'must follow'** knowledge; the company standards which have been signed off by the knowledge owners (with the endorsement of any relevant community of practice) as being the only safe or effective approach. Examples might be the operating procedures for a nuclear plant, or the in-flight checklists for a Boeing 747.

There is the **'should follow'** knowledge; the 'current best practice' which the community and the knowledge owner collectively agree is the best way to do something in a certain circumstance or context, and which should therefore be used as a default unless you have a good reason to do otherwise.

This knowledge can often be found in the community wiki or knowledge base, and there will be generally some form of validation procedure to determine that this really is the best knowledge available at the moment.

Finally there is the **'could follow'** knowledge; the good ideas, good examples, tips and hints, and templates drawn from the community forums and the best of the 'knowledge collateral' we discussed in the previous chapter. It is useful material, but its use is optional.

> ### Tip
>
> Creating synthesized knowledge for a critical knowledge topic is often a good candidate for a pilot or a proof of concept exercise. Choose a single user group where you know there are scattered knowledge assets that would benefit from synthesis. Use this pilot to experiment with the best way to store and structure the knowledge so that it can be easily and effectively used by its target users.

## Roles for knowledge synthesis

The primary role for knowledge synthesis is the role of the **knowledge owner**; the person accountable for managing the contents of the knowledge base for a particular area of knowledge, and ensuring the knowledge is synthesized, findable, up to date and useful. Alternative names for this role are process owner, practice owner, knowledge domain expert or subject matter expert (SME). Each of these acts as the steward for a particular area of knowledge, taking accountability for the quality, completeness and currency of the synthesized knowledge.

Some of the specific responsibilities of the knowledge owner are as follows:

- monitoring the development of knowledge within their specific topic;
- ensuring that a set of synthesized knowledge relating to their specific topic is available, either by writing it themselves or by delegating and coordinating the writing activity to others;
- ensuring the guidance documentation is findable (see Chapter 16);
- updating the synthesized knowledge and standards as new knowledge and new lessons become available;
- monitoring use of the synthesized knowledge, and acting on feedback to improve this;

- liaising with the leader or coordinator of any community of practice that covers the topic; sometimes the knowledge owner and the community leader are the same person, sometimes the community leader reports to the knowledge owner.

The knowledge owner or owners may need the support of a **knowledge base administration team** or **team of online librarians**. Their role is to:

- determine the customers for the knowledge base;
- carry out market research into customer needs;
- work with the knowledge owners to develop and maintain a structure for the knowledge base;
- provide coaching and guidance on content creation and formatting;
- provide technical editing and technical writing support where appropriate;
- monitor content standards;
- develop and monitor processes for refreshing and renewing content and for removing old material;
- provide coaching in the use of online tools, taxonomy and the search engine;
- coordinate and communicate feedback on desired improvements to the taxonomy or supporting software.

---

**Tip**

It can sometimes be difficult to find people willing to act as knowledge owners. Managers often prefer to put their best experts on the most difficult projects (a very old-fashioned approach to knowledge!) and some of the best experts may initially feel that the job is unappealing, as it sounds too much like 'writing down everything I know'. Search long and hard for the few experts who are keen to be involved, and work with them in the early stages so they have an influence on the definition of the role. Give them the support they need (including the help of knowledge engineers) to create appealing and valuable synthesized knowledge for which they can gain kudos and recognition.

# Processes for knowledge synthesis

## Individual creation

A common approach to synthesizing knowledge is to leave this to the individual efforts of the knowledge owners. However, the knowledge owners will almost certainly need guidance, training, templates, and some help in combining multiple viewpoints. The General Motors process for knowledge synthesis (Weineke, 2008) included:

- identification of the knowledge topics, and assignment of knowledge owners to best practice teams covering topics such as front suspension, rear suspension, steering, etc;
- coaching the teams in knowledge synthesis;
- capturing knowledge about individual design attributes from individual engineers (attributes were things like safety, squeak and rattle, and manufacturability);
- facilitated sessions where the individual views were 'balanced' (synthesized) into a best practice overview of the component design.

Siemens developed a five-stage process known as KNAC (knowledge asset creation process) for creating synthesized knowledge about specific topics and products (Freudenthaler *et al*, 2003):

- prepare – defining the scope, key topics, terminology and structure;
- structure – defining and outlining a set of processes, work product and tools;
- consolidate – describing the processes, work product and tools and adding best practices and recommendations;
- illustrate – adding tips, checklists, examples and slides; and
- polish – a final view of layout and formalities.

## Knowledge exchange

This process was described in Chapter 13 as a knowledge discussion process, whose outcome is documented knowledge that is effectively synthesized by a community of practice.

## Wikithons

A wikithon is like a virtual online knowledge exchange, but with more synthesis and less discussion. It is a special event in which content owners, community of practice members and others collaborate intensively on creating and editing wiki content. Wikipedia call this an 'editathon'. A wikithon may last from a couple of hours to a day or more. The event may be co-located or it may be virtual. As a side benefit, the wikithon often introduces many new people to the concept of the wiki.

There are many wikithon examples in the federal sector in the United States, for example the wikithon for creating the mobile gov wiki, held in a coffee shop in Washington (Glick, 2011), or the annual wikithons at Colombia University to create the content for the WikiCU (Leslie-Skye, 2014). The US Army has used wikithons to create online doctrine content (Dixon, 2009).

---

**Tip**

If you are experimenting with using a wiki as a knowledge base, use a wikithon as a way to kick start online content for your wiki, once you have a knowledge owner identified, and the basic structure of the topic worked out.

---

# Technologies for knowledge synthesis

Knowledge synthesis requires a technology where knowledge can be structured, stored and collaboratively synthesized. Some of the main types of technologies are listed below.

## Wikis

A wiki is a website that allows a number of people to create, edit, add and delete content, and can be an excellent platform for creating a synthesized body of knowledge that evolves over time. Wikis are increasingly being used to develop and store synthesized organizational knowledge in a form that allows continual updating. Shell make extensive use of a wiki as a corporate knowledge base to provide access to operational business know-how as well as general knowledge on the Shell organization, and to make available training material from the Shell University (Ligdas, 2009). The content of the wiki was originally created by subject matter experts, but the articles are open to comment by readers, and are updated if these comments identify new lessons or other process improvements.

Wikis are sometimes assumed to involve informal, bottom-up technology, designed to draw on the wisdom of crowds. The often-quoted example is Wikipedia, with no formal content-ownership roles (though the editorial roles are very strong), voluntary ad hoc submission, and edits by the readership.

However, there are major drawbacks to the Wikipedia model. Contribution rates are so low that it requires a huge user base, and the voluntary model results in a skewed distribution of contributors (predominantly young unmarried western males) and a skewed distribution of content (the Wikipedia article on 'knowledge management' for example is half the length of that on the Star Wars character Jabba the Hutt). Successful wikis in commercial firms or public sector organizations instead ensure that each wiki is part of a KM framework, stewarded by a knowledge owner, with clear processes for updating and 'feeding' the wiki, and with clear governance. For example, one training organization we worked with had a client profile wiki, and reasonably regular turnover of new trainers. New trainers joining the organization had an orientation and induction responsibility to interview the more experienced trainers about the company's clients and update the wiki with new insights. The new trainers got a rapid orientation to their colleagues and the clients, and the wiki was kept current.

## Portals

A web portal is a site accessed through a web browser which provides structured access to information and documented knowledge. One problem with early portals was that they were not designed for comments or for collaboration. They were primarily document libraries. For well-established and mature processes, this is not a problem, as content will be only rarely be added or updated. However, for process knowledge that is dynamically evolving, it can be very useful to allow readers to comment on the documentation, or even to edit it as new lessons are learned and new knowledge becomes available. Newer generation portals, some of them working on sophisticated wiki software, have more collaboration capabilities and tools added, and can be valuable tools for communities of practice.

Some of the advantages of portals include:

- intelligent integration and access to enterprise content, applications and processes;
- improved communication and collaboration among customers, partners, and employees;
- unified, real-time access to information held in disparate systems;
- personalized user modification and maintenance of the website presentation; and
- consistent look and feel, headers and footers, colour schemes, etc, which gives the user a feel and sense of consistency, uniformity, and ease of navigation.

### Knowledge bases

Knowledge bases are portal-like technology designed to support:

- customer-facing staff in answering customer questions;
- customers seeking answers to their own questions;
- internal users in very structured knowledge domains seeking solutions to frequently encountered issues.

With powerful search and tagging supported by a defined taxonomy, a user can find existing solutions to customer questions (for example), and does not need to create a new solution. By tracking solution re-use and user ratings of the usefulness of the answer, the knowledge base allows close monitoring of the knowledge base quality and value. Companies such as Salesforce, Oracle and HP are the major players in this field.

# Governance for knowledge synthesis

Governance elements to support knowledge synthesis can include:

- a listing of critical knowledge topics within the organization, often structured into a well-maintained corporate taxonomy (Chapter 17);
- a clear assignment and delegation of accountability for ownership of these topics;
- a defined expectation for what 'knowledge ownership' entails;
- training, coaching and support for knowledge owners;
- a career path for knowledge owners;
- a defined expectation and compliance measures for the quality and update frequency of synthesized knowledge;
- monitoring use and application of the knowledge;
- reference material for all processes and technologies;
- collection of success stories regarding the re-use of synthesized knowledge.

# Summary

Knowledge synthesis also requires its own roles and accountabilities, processes, supporting technologies and governance. You will need to test these in your own context, and select the components that will work in your organization, and that can be embedded into your own procedures and systems.

# The knowledge finding and re-use elements of the KM framework

**16**

All the work of documentation and synthesis described in the previous two chapters will be of no value if people do not re-use and apply that body of knowledge. The 'find and re-use' step includes the issue of 'internalization', which means appreciating and understanding the content of the documented knowledge, getting it 'into your head' and into your internal repertoire. Once knowledge is internalized it can be applied, but first it must be found, reflected upon and discussed.

This chapter flows directly into the topic of the next chapter, knowledge organization, and covers:

- the challenges of knowledge re-use;
- incentivizing knowledge seeking;
- the importance of findability;
- roles for knowledge finding and re-use;
- processes for knowledge finding and re-use;
- technologies for knowledge finding and re-use;
- governance for knowledge finding and re-use.

## The challenges of knowledge re-use

There are many barriers to finding and re-using knowledge. Ghaedian and Chen (2012) identified several barriers in a study of KM at Volvo Trucks in Sweden:

1 'no time' to stop doing the task and search for knowledge;
2 captured knowledge was not consolidated (synthesized);
3 it was not easy to access knowledge;

**4** it was not easy to search for and retrieve knowledge;

**5** it did not occur to some employees that there might be answers for their question somewhere in the organization;

**6** re-using knowledge was not a focus;

**7** there was no supportive culture for reading documents to get knowledge;

**8** there was no clear flow of knowledge from project to the line organization and/or to other projects;

**9** there was no good structure for employees to build up their network.

Some of these barriers are related to an incomplete KM framework (item 2 apples to synthesis, item 9 to discussion, and item 8 to the lack of any defined framework) but others relate specifically to the lack of a 'culture of seeking'. The claim that there is no time to seek knowledge is actually saying that 'seeking knowledge is not prioritized'. Lack of processes, roles, governance and tools for enhancing findability and accessibility of the knowledge is responsible for items 3 and 4.

# Incentivizing knowledge seeking

Many clients ask us, 'how should we incentivize knowledge sharing?' We answer, 'don't incentivize knowledge sharing. Incentivize knowledge seeking, and sharing will follow'. Knowledge sharing in the absence of a defined need usually achieves little, as knowledge needs to be applied (re-used) before any value has been added. Without an appetite for knowledge re-use, knowledge sharing can actually be counter-productive, resulting in unvisited databases full of unwanted knowledge, and the feeling that 'KM is a waste of time'. It is better to create the appetite for knowledge before you create the databases, and creating demand will stimulate supply.

Knowledge seeking can be incentivized in three ways:

- Managers can create a high-performance culture, where people are encouraged to continually push the boundaries of performance. People who are satisfied with current performance have no reason to learn, but if they wish to go beyond the known limits, they will need to seek out new knowledge.

- Managers can set expectations for knowledge seeking. The technical director in one organization mandated that no project would be approved if it could not demonstrate learning from other projects, for example.

- Managers can set stretch targets to stimulate knowledge seeking. John Browne, the CEO of BP, set the expectation that 'every time we do something, we should do it better than the previous time' (Prokesch, 1997) and backed up this statement by continuously raising production targets or continuously cutting budgets. Teams had to search for knowledge in order to meet targets.

# The importance of making knowledge findable and accessible

Making knowledge findable means making sure it is well tagged for search and well structured for browsing. It also needs to be accessible, as there is nothing more frustrating than to see that a knowledge artefact exists, and then not to be able to open it because the folder it sits in is protected. There are a few mechanisms for supporting accessibility. Minimally, you can add a 'request access' feature to your system, which routes your request to the person responsible for the knowledge artefact. More comprehensively, your KM policy, which we cover in Chapter 23, should give guidance on how to balance information security concerns with the benefits of knowledge sharing and re-use, so that staff don't unnecessarily restrict access to content.

Your people should be aware that the knowledge resources exist for their use. At induction and orientation, they need to be provided with an orientation to the knowledge resources and an introduction to the key tools – the search engine, the community directory, the yellow pages – and told that they are expected to use these resources as well as contribute to them.

The resources themselves need to be 'ambiently findable' which means that by their very nature, they pop up when you start looking, or when you are engaged in a task that requires them (Morville, 2005). For example, in a project management portal, at the project initiation stage, as soon as the project type is selected, links could appear to the relevant synthesized knowledge on projects of that type, while a system in a law firm might automatically send relevant precedents to a lawyer opening a new piece of work with a client.

# Roles for knowledge finding and re-use

There needs to be accountability for knowledge finding, review and re-use within the line organization. The project manager or department manager is usually accountable for ensuring people seek the knowledge they need, while the individuals are responsible for performing the searches and then carefully reading the material they find. In some cases, such as legal firms and governmental organizations, researcher and analyst roles are created to provide the knowledge workers with access to documented knowledge.

Part of a **knowledge analyst**'s role will be to retrieve knowledge and information from various knowledge bases in order to prepare briefings for customer-facing staff. Typical tasks include:

- assessing the knowledge needs of these 'internal clients';
- gathering and organizing knowledge resources, compiling information and data from many sources, and preparing statistics;

- providing replies and briefings in response to queries by staff, managers and external clients.

The role of the **professional support lawyer** (PSL) in legal firms is similar to that of an analyst role. The PSL role can be any combination of (Magnusson, 2008, p 99):

- providing know-how (advising lawyers, drafting precedents, providing updates, maintaining knowledge bases);
- providing training (internal and external) and facilitating meetings; and
- business development (pitch support, client alerts and seminars).

There are also a number of key knowledge organization roles that provide the tools within the IT infrastructure to support findability.

The **enterprise taxonomist** is responsible for developing and implementing enterprise-wide taxonomies – the controlled vocabularies that connect related knowledge and information content together. These vocabularies can also be used to connect people with content – for example, if somebody is contributing a lot of knowledge on a particular topic area, then that taxonomy tag can be associated with their staff profile in the system. When somebody does a search on that topic, they can then see the knowledge as well as the people who are closely associated with that topic. When connected to an actively managed competency framework, a taxonomy can have even greater power in helping project or engagement managers find suitably qualified and experienced staff for projects (Lambe, 2007, pp 106–12). The taxonomist is responsible for mapping these connections into the taxonomy.

The **information architect** is responsible for designing the information and knowledge environment of the organization so that information resources are easily navigated and easily findable. They work very much like the architects of a physical space – ie organizing and signposting the 'information space' so that people can navigate it easily. The information architect needs to identify and analyse the information and knowledge needs of different users in the context of their work, and needs to work closely with the taxonomist. The taxonomist provides the terminology and categories, and the information architect designs the overall environment using the taxonomy to support the identified user needs.

The **enterprise search specialist** is responsible for ensuring that the search technology is deployed in a way that effectively exploits the taxonomy and supports the information architecture design.

For example, an enterprise taxonomy will usually collect all the alternative ways that a taxonomy term can be expressed, and connect those alternative terms to the controlled term in the taxonomy. Then whenever a search query uses one of those alternative terms, the search engine retrieves all the resources (and people) tagged with the taxonomy term. This is a way of overcoming 'scatter' of resources when searchers use different words to mean the same thing. The search specialist has to configure the search engine to do this.

Similarly, the search specialist will provide the taxonomist with reports of the most frequently used search queries. These are terms that should be considered for inclusion in the taxonomy or the collection of alternative terms, because they are evidence of how people are thinking about the knowledge content.

The search specialist works with the information architect to provide the targeted 'ambient findability' of knowledge resources we talked about earlier. The information architect identifies the needs for knowledge resources in a specific context. The search specialist deploys the taxonomy and the search technology to go looking for those resources and pipe them through to the relevant user interface.

# Processes for knowledge finding and re-use

The best-known process for knowledge finding and re-use is the **before-action review**. Here, finding and reviewing knowledge resources is incorporated into a discussion process. This works best as a fixed step in a project management process flow, and is held at a project initiation stage. In the British National Health Service (NHS) a before action review is part of a mandated process flow for projects, and is primarily a facilitated discussion session guided by the following four questions (Department of Health, 2010):

**1** What are we setting out to achieve?

**2** What can be learned from similar situations and past projects from elsewhere?

**3** What will help deliver success?

**4** What are the actions we need to take to avoid problems and apply good practice?

Question 2 requires some preparation by consulting prior knowledge resources and lessons, and this is where knowledge finding and re-use feeds back into the planning cycle. In the Singapore Army, the before action review is used in a similar way at the planning stage for a mission or operation (Singapore Ministry of Defence, 2014, p 208).

However, in most organizations the assumption is that individuals will search for knowledge themselves as and when they need it, with no particular process for discussing and evaluating this knowledge. This ad hoc approach can work when the other elements of the KM framework are in place, but when left as an optional exercise it is often omitted entirely.

A much more systematic process for ensuring knowledge re-use is the **KM planning** process (Milton, 2005, p 117), the outcome of which is a KM plan. This is a document for a specific project (or department, community of practice or function), which details:

● what knowledge needs to be sought, reviewed and incorporated by the project;

- known knowledge gaps, and knowledge requirements of the project;
- where the knowledge will be sought;
- how it will be acquired;
- who is responsible for its acquisition;
- when the acquisition is needed;
- what knowledge will be created by the project;
- how it will be identified and documented (which processes will be used, and when);
- who is responsible for its documentation;
- where the documented knowledge will be stored and how it will be made findable and accessible; and
- what KM framework will need to be applied within the project, including roles and accountabilities, processes and supporting technologies.

The plan is created at a KM planning workshop, held as part of the project planning and initiation activities. The workshop will include a discussion of the knowledge needed by the project, and during this discussion, actions will be assigned for knowledge seeking. The KM plan therefore drives the behaviour of knowledge finding and review, as many of the knowledge-seeking actions will involve searching for documented knowledge.

# Technologies for knowledge finding and re-use

There are four main technologies to support knowledge finding and re-use:

- tagging systems and tag clouds;
- enterprise search and search-based applications;
- autoclassification tools;
- taxonomy management systems.

**Tagging systems** are frequently used in conjunction with knowledge-sharing tools such as blogs, wikis and online discussion platforms. They allow users to define and attach keywords ('tags') to their posts. **Tag clouds** are an extension of this. Here, the most frequently used tags are presented in a cluster on the page, and the font is scaled according to the frequency with which the tag is applied. This is a good way of identifying trending topics in a rapidly flowing knowledge-sharing environment.

The disadvantage of tagging systems is the lack of control over the terms that are chosen. One person might use the term 'infectious diseases', another 'communicable diseases', another 'vector control', and another 'disease transmission', for posts that are all about the same underlying topic. Even the same user may tag the same topic differently at different times. Without some form of management or control, such as the integration of tags within an enterprise taxonomy, these related posts would not be brought together. This is where knowledge organization capabilities come into play.

**Enterprise search** refers to technologies that match queries to results. In its simplest form, a search engine takes a search query and matches it against an index of terms it has already prepared, each of which is in turn linked to knowledge and information resources. However, there is a great deal of work involved in making enterprise search results relevant to the users. This usually involves:

- Establishing rules to make sure that the terms that get into the index are highly significant to users and representative of the content. For example, a document that contains the word 'Google' is not necessarily 'about' Google, so a search engine needs to be told how to identify the 'aboutness' of a document so that it can compile a smart index.

- Establishing rules for how search results are prioritized depending on where the index words have come from – eg the taxonomy metadata, the document title, abstract or specific sections in a well-structured document.

- Establishing rules for how search results are prioritized depending on who the user is, based on what the system knows about their search, download or tagging behaviours, or their functional role in the organization.

**Search-based applications** are extremely targeted uses of a search engine, usually in conjunction with a taxonomy. For example, earlier on in this chapter, we referred to examples of 'ambient findability' where knowledge is piped through to specific situations and contexts where it will be relevant and useful. These examples are powered by the enterprise search tool, which in this case is matching resources to specific pages in a workflow. Opening the page triggers a pre-defined query, pulling all the most relevant resources connected with that activity.

**Autoclassification tools** are a means of assigning tags or taxonomy topics to documents without the need for manual tagging by users (Hedden, 2010, pp 199–229). These tools are designed to reduce the burden of manual tagging, especially where knowledge contributors are under time pressure, or where they might not be aware of the relevance of their contribution to other people, and might therefore not assign the tags that are relevant to those users. Autoclassification tools work best with named entities (places, people, organizations) or with very clearly defined technical vocabularies (such as in engineering or law), and less well with abstract topics like activities, subject areas, or concepts. This is because the tools work on term recognition – where the language is extremely variable, the tool is weaker, and where the language is reasonably tight, the tool works better.

Used in combination with taxonomy and search, they can be very powerful. For example, the BBC uses an autoclassification tool which is integrated into the story-filing interface for its journalists. As the journalist types his or her story, the system recognizes the names of people, places and organizations using a reference taxonomy, and it uses the search engine to automatically populate the right hand column with links to prior stories about those people, places or organizations. The journalists will correct the suggested terms and add their own taxonomy topics, because they immediately recognize that the tool makes their work easier (Shearer and Tarling, 2013).

**Enterprise taxonomy management systems** address the problem where large and complex organizations are using multiple knowledge sharing and storage platforms (online communities, discussion forums, knowledge bases, content libraries, portals supporting workflow, lessons databases). Without a common enterprise taxonomy, these systems become knowledge silos, each using their own sets of topics and finding aids. If related knowledge content is to be pulled together, even with an enterprise search engine to crawl across these systems, then it is important that content is tagged consistently using the same controlled vocabularies. An enterprise taxonomy management system provides a central place where all the controlled vocabularies that make up the taxonomy and the metadata can be governed, maintained and updated. The system then provides these vocabularies to the content systems that need them, and to the search engine to consult. Without such a system, the task of maintaining consistent vocabularies across multiple platforms becomes very labour intensive and error-prone (Hedden, 2010, pp 154–62).

# Governance for knowledge finding and re-use

Some of the governance elements which will support knowledge finding and review are as follows:

- a clear assignment and delegation of accountability for ensuring projects and other activities learn from the past;
- a defined expectation for searching and reviewing documented knowledge, and incorporating any relevant knowledge in future work;
- a defined expectation for the accurate tagging of documented knowledge to support findability, and for ensuring that access rights support sharing;
- a defined expectation for KM planning and the use of KM plans;
- monitoring compliance with these expectations;
- training and support in the use of taxonomy and search technology;
- collection of success stories regarding the re-use of knowledge and the value created from re-use.

**Tip**

The full technology and governance requirements for knowledge finding and re-use will not become clear until well into your trials and pilots approach. Do not commit too early to a single set of technologies or knowledge organization tools. As you run your pilots, keep a running log of the finding and re-use requirements that emerge, and regularly review them, before building an integrated set of requirements.

## Summary

Knowledge finding and re-use, the crucial step for delivering value from documented knowledge, is a step which often seems to get least attention, and is often left unsupported and ungoverned. You need to give particular attention to this element of the framework if you are to reach your goal of a complete 'knowledge supply chain' for the knowledge workers in your organization.

# Knowledge organization

## 17

**W**e have already covered several aspects of knowledge organization, such as knowledge synthesis (Chapter 15), and findability, internalization and re-use of knowledge (Chapter 16). These are all manifestations of knowledge organization.

In this chapter we focus on the need to have a systematic and evidence-based methodology for organizing explicit knowledge and supporting documents, and connecting this content with people (subject matter experts) and community discussion topics. Without this methodology, it will be difficult to guide the many technical activities involved in knowledge organization in the service of your KM framework.

In this chapter we cover:

- grounding knowledge organization in the business drivers;
- the three components of knowledge organization: taxonomy and metadata, information architecture, and search;
- taking an evidence-based approach;
- using the knowledge assets audit to focus on what counts; and
- testing and validating the knowledge organization system.

## Grounding knowledge organization in the business drivers

Knowledge organization involves designing an infrastructure to serve specific needs and purposes. These needs and purposes flow through from the business drivers, via the KM implementation objectives, as discussed in Part Two of this book.

For example, one of the objectives might be to ensure that lessons learned in one part of the organization can be re-used in other areas, so as to avoid wasted cost or to reduce risk. This has implications for the taxonomy, because it would have to provide a common way of categorizing lessons that all interested parties could make sense of, even though in their functional silos they might use different terminology. For example, in the Army, both

Military Police and Guards Formations have duties to protect strategic installations such as army bases, power stations or government offices. MPs call it 'Key Installations Protection', and Guards call it 'Protection of Installations'. The taxonomy has to broker that difference in terminology, so the related lessons can be gathered for analysis, synthesis and re-use.

Another objective might be to speed up the learning curve of new recruits, so as to maintain strategic capabilities in a period of high turnover or growth. That would have an impact on the taxonomy and information architecture design, for example in the scope of the knowledge assets being focused on (the knowledge items they need), and in the technical complexity of the terms being used (new recruits generally can't navigate technically complex language as easily as experts).

---

**Tip**

Remind yourself of the business objectives and KM implementation objectives identified in your preparation stage. Identify the priorities that impact your knowledge organization approach such as common taxonomy, information architecture and enterprise search.

---

# The three components of knowledge organization

## *Taxonomy and Metadata*

A **taxonomy** is a controlled vocabulary for a set of categories and topics, to describe what a document is about and to tag people (eg with topics of expertise), community domains, or topics of discussion in a community. This allows you to connect content with content, and content with people and communities.

'**Controlled**' means that there are defined roles, rules, and processes for approving changes to the vocabulary, to ensure that the taxonomy continues to serve its intended purpose. Without control, people will add their own terms to the vocabulary on an ad hoc basis, and the taxonomy will slowly lose its ability to bring together related resources as intended.

In many cases, a taxonomy has a hierarchical structure. Detailed topic terms are clustered together under more general category headings. This hierarchy allows us to organize a large number of topics in a user-friendly way. Other taxonomies, however, are small and simple enough that they can be presented as a flat list with no hierarchy – for example, a simple taxonomy of types of car could contain just seven terms: economy, family, saloon, luxury, sports, off-roader and commercial.

Enterprise taxonomies serve multiple user groups and multiple content collections across the whole enterprise, to enable the bringing together of content, people and communities from across functional siloes and to enable knowledge re-use and discovery of new insights. Because of the diversity of use they have to support, they should consist of multiple controlled vocabularies rather than a single, monolithic, hierarchically structured vocabulary, for the following reasons:

- Large organizations have to manage findability for many hundreds of thousands (or even millions) of knowledge and information assets – a single taxonomy hierarchy to cover all this content would be far too complex and difficult for users to navigate.

- The way a single hierarchy is organized must favour a single particular perspective. For example, if we organize lessons at the top level by project type, then by project activity, and then by customer, we are taking a 'project' view of the hierarchy, and this will be far from ideal from the customer manager's point of view. The customer manager would obviously prefer to organize the hierarchy by customer type first.

The solution for this is to build a system of controlled vocabularies called **taxonomy facets**. Each facet is a smaller vocabulary covering just one aspect of the content – in the example above, we would have three facets; a project type facet, a customer facet, and a project activity facet. A document (or conversation, or expert) would be tagged according to each facet, so that both the project manager and the customer manager can find resources equally easily, from the perspective that makes most sense to them. Faceted taxonomy structures are also much simpler and easier to navigate than large, single hierarchy structures.

The process of identifying which facets are relevant and important to the different user communities is called facet analysis, and requires a thorough understanding of the different communities of knowledge workers that need access to the same knowledge resources. Your knowledge assets audit can provide this understanding.

**Metadata** refers to structured data about a resource. For example, author, title, subject keywords, date of publication, access permissions, are all individual pieces of metadata that might be associated with a document. Metadata is also used for other resources such as people and communities. Metadata is used for three main purposes:

- Identifying content – descriptive metadata captures unique identifiers such as author and title fields and distinguishes each document from all others.

- Helping systems manage content – eg administrative and structural metadata captures things like version numbers, archiving date, security and access permissions, and file types to tell the system which applications to use to read it.

- Aiding retrieval of content – eg descriptive metadata captures things like taxonomy topics, user-defined tags, content types and document descriptions.

Taxonomy facets supply the vocabularies for the descriptive metadata components that aid retrieval. This is why enterprise taxonomists are also usually responsible for their organization's metadata schema – the framework that specifies which metadata will be gathered, how it is defined, how it will be collected, which controlled vocabularies are used and what purposes they should serve (Lambe, 2007).

## Information architecture

'Information architecture' refers to the overall design of the information environment such as websites, intranet, knowledge bases, portals and community spaces. It requires a close understanding of the different user groups and their needs, such as will be gained from the knowledge assets audit. The work product of an information architect includes:

- a high-level map of different knowledge systems and supporting tools such as search and taxonomy management systems, showing the relationships and information and content flows between the systems;
- a system-level map, or site map, showing how the system is structured for easy navigation by its users;
- a page-level map, or 'wireframe', showing the labels that act as signposts to sections, pages or information actions such as a comment, a submission, or a link to a knowledge owner's contact details. 'Pages' here refer to webpages within a KM system – whether it be an intranet page, a knowledge base page, a wiki page or page within a community collaboration space.

In order to organize an information or knowledge environment for the main user groups, information architecture design is almost always bottom up. Wireframes which meet the needs of the knowledge workers are created, tested, analysed and refined iteratively. User requirements are aggregated and analysed to provide the knowledge flow and navigation requirements for the information environment being designed. As these system-level requirements are identified, the site structure and system architecture maps are built to accommodate them in an efficient manner.

The information architecture focuses on the overall environment within which knowledge content is managed and navigated, while the taxonomy provides the core vocabularies describing individual pieces of content. Both use labels, but with different levels of granularity and different purposes. This is why information architecture labels and taxonomy labels often have overlaps but are not identical.

## Search

When people talk about **search** they often think of the technology that makes up enterprise search, while failing to appreciate the design component of search. Search technology is only as good as the rules configuring the way the tool indexes documents, the way it exploits taxonomy structures, and the way it supports navigation through the designed information environment, as we saw in the chapter on findability and re-use (Chapter 16).

Taxonomies (and other metadata), information architecture, and search are three interlocking components that make up a knowledge organization system. Very much like a KM framework, when these components don't talk to each other through an over-arching design and common implementation methodology, then their effectiveness is drastically reduced.

# Taking an evidence-based approach to knowledge organization

The facet analysis step in taxonomy design, and the iterative designs of information architecture, cannot be conducted on the basis of intuition, guesswork, or limited sets of opinions. They need to be evidence-based.

In the field of knowledge organization we talk about three types of evidence, or 'warrant':

- **Content warrant** refers to the evidence of how knowledge and information content is currently described and organized by users. This evidence can be gathered by collecting existing classification schemes and taxonomies, folder structures and site structures, labelling schemes for collections of content, content pages for synthesized knowledge products, etc. Typically this content warrant has been built up cumulatively over the years without an over-arching framework, and while it tells you what the 'ambient' vocabulary is in an organization, it does not highlight which documented knowledge is most relevant and useful at this point in time.

- **User warrant** refers to evidence about the most important and frequent work activities of the different user groups. User warrant requires building a series of use-case scenarios for the different user groups covering a range of key work activities that are dependent upon knowledge and information consumption. The user warrant provides the context and purpose of information and knowledge use, and so helps to determine which parts of the content warrant are most significant and relevant.

- **Standards warrant** refers to situations where a work group needs to exchange information and knowledge with other groups, whether internal or external, and therefore needs to use a standard shared vocabulary. For example, government funding agencies need to report upwards into their national statistical system, and so need to use standard taxonomies for industries, institutions, population segments, etc. In some cases, user warrant may conflict with standards warrant – ie the standard vocabularies do not match the way that users think about and describe their resources. In this case, you create cross-walks between the user-oriented taxonomy vocabulary and the required standard, so that the system can automatically associate the two sets of terms and connect the two sets of information content.

Taking an evidence-based approach means having a systematic method of collecting all three kinds of warrant. Start with the user warrant, which helps you understand the knowledge work which the taxonomy and information architecture will support. The content warrant then gathers all the existing vocabulary systems and organizing systems for using information and knowledge, and these either form input to the taxonomy or will need to be mapped to the taxonomy through a thesaurus, so that variant forms of terms in use are recognized by the system and associated with their respective taxonomy terms. Finally the standards warrant indicates where standard taxonomies and classification schemes need to be used.

## Using the knowledge assets audit to focus on what counts

Each of these evidence-gathering activities can be conducted separately. However, this will be labour intensive. By far the most efficient and effective way to structure the evidence collection is to use the knowledge assets audit (Chapter 11), which although principally aimed at identifying operational knowledge gaps and flows, can also be used to capture user, content and standards warrant:

- The knowledge asset descriptions represent a current overview of the key knowledge assets that support key business activities across all departments, and represent the current vocabulary of how your staff think about the knowledge they use – ie the current content warrant.

- The knowledge asset maps are organized around key work activities and provide the context in which information and knowledge are used, so they form the basis for user warrant.

- The audit can generate maps of internal and external knowledge flows that can help you identify the need for standards warrant.

In addition to the knowledge assets audit, you need additional evidence gathering for the content warrant, for example collecting existing taxonomies, classification schemes, folder structures, vocabularies, etc. You can also use reports of common search queries from your search engine, and commonly used uncontrolled tags in your tagging system, as valuable content warrant.

The challenge with content warrant is in discerning which vocabularies and organizing principles are most relevant and current now. By providing a complete overview focused on key activities, the knowledge maps give you a framework that will help you design the knowledge organization system in a way that focuses on areas of current relevance and need. All the other evidence you collect needs to be incorporated, but it is incorporated as background material, pointing to the key vocabulary that is of current concern. In Chapter 16 we saw there are several different terms to describe 'infectious diseases'. In fact, 'infectious diseases' is an historical term, and the current term is 'communicable diseases'. In this case the term 'communicable diseases' goes into the taxonomy, and 'infectious diseases' is captured into the system as an alternative term so that resources using the older term can still be retrieved using the newer term (Lambe, 2007).

### Tip

If you have completed a targeted or comprehensive knowledge assets audit, analyse your maps for key user scenarios. Pull out the knowledge asset descriptions for documents to gather the vocabulary describing document types. Pull out the activity descriptions and the knowledge asset descriptions for methods and skills to gather the vocabulary about key activities and processes. Pull out the knowledge asset descriptions about experience and natural talent to gather the vocabulary about expertise topics. You are starting to build the core of a useful enterprise taxonomy!

## Testing and validating your knowledge organization system

You design your knowledge organization system to meet the KM objectives you have defined. Once you have gathered your three forms of warrant and referred back to your business objectives and KM implementation objectives, the taxonomist can begin the facet analysis to identify the taxonomy facets that will serve key user needs, while the information architect can start identifying key use-case scenarios against which to start designing and testing the wireframes. These are both skilled technical tasks, so you will need professional help to do this, whether in house or from external specialists. Both the taxonomy and the information architecture design will need iterative testing against the use-case scenarios, to give assurance that the taxonomy and information architecture designs do actually improve findability and accessibility of knowledge resources. You will need to measure against a baseline (before and after), and typical measures would include:

- speed of completing knowledge-seeking tasks;
- quality of results in relation to the task;
- completion/non-completion rates of tasks;
- number of mistakes and dead ends in completing the task;
- confidence level in searching/browsing behaviours;
- consistency in tagging behaviours using the taxonomy (inconsistent tagging means that the same resources will be scattered);
- accuracy of user predictions in where to find specific materials.

Using metrics such as these means your design will be highly defensible. Anybody with an opinion will be able to propose 'better' designs when it comes to taxonomy and information architecture, but when you can use empirical testing to show that performance of key tasks is rendered more effective by the design, you become less reliant on opinions and can build an evidence-based culture.

Once your taxonomy and information architecture designs are complete, you can turn to the search design. The information architect sets the requirements for the role of search in delivering the information and knowledge resources to each key user interface in turn. Examples of key user interfaces might be a search page, a search results page, a topic structure page, a dashboard, and so on. These are 'interfaces' and not passive pages, as the user can take actions using the search engine to refine or sort or organize the contents on the page. The page and the interactions on the page need to be structured in a way that suits the different user groups. The taxonomy and metadata schema provide the vocabulary content for the search engine to work with.

# Summary

The role of knowledge organization during KM implementation is primarily a design task, integrating the capabilities of taxonomies (with other metadata), information architecture, and search. To be effective, it requires a systematic, evidence-based approach, grounded in a thorough understanding of the current reality in your organization. The knowledge assets audit is extremely effective at providing this understanding, as well as helping you to define the goals to be achieved by the design. The work involved in taxonomy, information architecture and search design is skilled and technical. Not all specialists combine these three sets of skills, and very often the three roles will need to work as a team to create (and subsequently maintain) your knowledge organization design.

# Influencing the stakeholders

## 18

**Y**ou can't change your organizational culture all at once; you can only change it one heart and one mind at a time. Much of KM implementation involves working with and influencing your key stakeholders on an individual basis. In this chapter we cover:

- a template for mapping stakeholder buy-in;
- the knowledge manager as salesperson;
- segmenting your audience;
- influencing tactics;
- when to use the influencing tactics;
- a case study from NASA.

## The steps of the buy-in ladder

Even when we realize that culture is changed one heart and mind at a time, we also need to realize that each individual does not change their heart and mind all at once. There are a number of steps before an attitude is changed (Figure 18.1) and it is worth understanding these steps, as you cannot move an individual more than two or three steps in any one interaction.

The steps are these:

1 **First contact** – the first time that the individual hears the term 'knowledge management'.
2 **Awareness** they become aware of KM as something that may be an issue in the organization.
3 **Understanding** – where you help them understand what KM means (in basic terms).
4 **Acceptance** – where you help them realize that KM holds value for them and for the organization.
5 **Trial** – the point at which they agree to try KM. This leads to the first commitment threshold – the commitment to act. This is your 'sell' – the point at which the individual 'buys' KM.

**FIGURE 18.1**   The stakeholder buy-in ladder

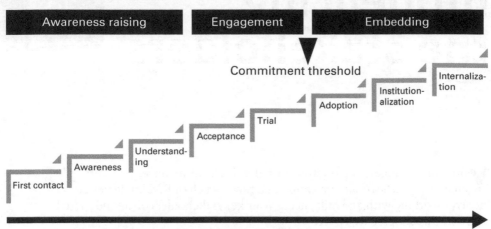

Increasing level of buy-in

6 **Adoption** – assuming the trial has gone well and delivered value, this is when the individual agrees to adopt KM in the longer term.

7 **Embedding into work process** – this is where the individual, team and eventually company embeds KM into work process, as described in Chapter 23.

8 **Embedding into culture** – this is where they internalize KM as 'something we just do'. At this stage it becomes a core value.

There are many steps, and it is easy to underestimate the importance of each one. Many key stakeholders or stakeholder groupings never go beyond the trial stage, or perhaps they adopt KM but never embed it. It is only when the majority of your key stakeholders get to Step 7 that KM is relatively safe, and even then you need to take care of the final step, the internalization step, so that the culture becomes pervasive and unconscious.

---

**Tip**

Use the 'eight steps' ladder to map the current buy-in level of each of your key stakeholders, and to plot how you want to move them up the buy-in ladder over the next few months. You can certainly raise awareness and understanding through general communications, but at some point you will need to start to involve individuals in direct conversations to get to the 'trial' stage. Use the ladder to determine the priority and timing of the conversations you need to have.

# The knowledge manager as salesperson

You can introduce the topic of KM to the organization and raise the levels of awareness and understanding among your stakeholders through general communication and education (as described in the next chapter). This can move stakeholders to the 'understanding' and hopefully 'acceptance' levels, but to take the next step, where your stakeholder commits to trying KM, you need to move from being an educator to being a salesperson.

Salespeople often have a bad reputation, based on the conventional idea of product-based selling as persuasion, regardless of the quality of the product or service. In KM, our ability to sell is as dependent on the credibility we have as it is on the 'pitch' itself. However, your effectiveness in implementing KM also depends on your influencing skills. You may have designed the best KM framework in the world, but the world will not beat a path to your door in order to use it. You have to go out and sell it, which means you need to know some of the tools and methods of selling and influencing.

## Understanding what the customer is buying

You first need to understand what the customer is buying. You may know the statement by Harvard marketing professor Theodore Levitt: 'People don't want to buy a quarter-inch drill. They want a quarter-inch hole' (Christensen *et al*, 2006) – and they want that hole to put up shelves so their house is tidy. A drill salesperson is actually selling the ability to improve your house. Similarly your stakeholders are not buying KM, they are buying something wider, which KM can deliver to them, and you need to understand what this is. Two of the more common 'wider things' that the customer wants are protection and opportunity.

KM can offer **protection** against lost knowledge, repeat mistakes, inefficiencies and risks: all of the things we mentioned as potential pain points in Chapter 4. This is the primary selling point for a knowledge retention and transfer strategy, for example. In industries and countries with ageing workforces, you can usually show worrying figures about projected knowledge loss, and you can talk about the risk that this 'corporate amnesia' poses to continued effective operation. A knowledge retention programme protects against loss of capability.

You can also sell knowledge management as an **opportunity**. Most organizations already have a lot of knowledge, held in the heads of individuals or scattered in many knowledge stores, which they are underutilizing. This opportunity to capitalize an undervalued asset is a powerful argument. Which manager would not want to gain value from an asset they already have?

---

**Tip**

Based on your knowledge of the stakeholders, what is the 'wider sell' you can make? What can KM deliver to them (eg protection or opportunity) that they may be in the market for?

---

## Segmenting your audience

Every salesperson needs to know their market and their customer base. To sell KM, you can think in terms of three market segments:

- The one in five people who instinctively 'get' KM and become immediately enthused, moving rapidly from 'first contact' to 'acceptance' and 'trial'. In our experience, about 20 per cent of staff are likely to be early supporters of the idea, and will become your allies, your supporters and the early adopters.

- The three in five people who don't care about KM one way or the other. They will engage in KM if they have to, if it's part of the job, or if everyone else is doing it. If KM is voluntary, or unusual, they won't bother. Moving them to the 'trial' phase of buy-in will require a range of influencing tactics described later in this chapter.

- The remaining one in five who really don't like KM at all. They think it is a personal threat, or a way of 'stealing their ideas'. These people will resist KM, unless it is made unavoidable and fully embedded into performance management so that their job prospects suffer if they refuse to share. These people will be very difficult to move to the 'acceptance' stage, let alone higher than that.

If you introduce KM as a voluntary activity, you only reach the 20 per cent in the first market segment. Many organizations have found this to be a typical sort of adoption rate when internal use of social media such as blogging and microblogging is introduced 'bottom up'. Adoption does not spread beyond the enthusiasts, 80 per cent of the organization remains uninvolved, and so 80 per cent of the knowledge remains untapped and unmanaged. Gartner (2013) recently showed even worse figures, and concluded that a 'Provide and Pray' bottom-up approach to KM technology has just a 10 per cent success rate.

You need to use the 20 per cent of enthusiasts to create 'social proof' (described later) which will draw in the others. Use the supporters and early adopters to conduct the pilots, deliver the benefits and write the case studies that will convince others that KM will help them in their work, and convince management to set KM as a corporate expectation.

Also you won't complete the journey until KM becomes inescapable. If the company is committed to KM, then the last 20 per cent, who really don't like it, need to know that their future is at risk if they continue to avoid or sabotage the KM efforts.

Sometimes it makes sense to directly influence these sceptics early in the implementation programme, as the case study below demonstrates.

## CASE STUDY

One very successful KM practitioner we know was working in a law firm in the 1990s. Lawyers are famously difficult to influence in favour of putting effort into KM, because their rewards are directly tied to time spent on client work, not on internal knowledge sharing. Our friend approached the most sceptical law partner and said 'We're putting a new KM framework in place. Tell me where your biggest pain points are, and we'll try to address them.' He wasn't convinced, but told her that as long as she didn't make any extra work for his lawyers, she could work on solving a few of his headaches. She chose the issues that she knew could scale beyond this partner, and got to work. Pretty soon she had other partners stopping her in the corridor, asking why this particular partner was getting so much attention, and when they could start benefiting from KM. She told them she'd bring them on to the project roadmap as soon as she could, and created a timeline for them to follow. By going for the most sceptical partner and doing a good job, she had created a 'KM pull' effect that meant she had to do very little selling anywhere else.

## Influencing tactics

The knowledge manager needs to understand the basics of influencing and persuasion in order to move the stakeholders up the buy-in ladder. The book *Mind Gym* (Bailey and Black, 2014) describes nine influencing tactics you can select from, based on the character and situation of the 'buyer'. These are described below, together with the sorts of things you might say.

**Reasoning** – using logical argument to make a case. Your argument might be something like:

> KM, if applied to the bidding process, should improve our bid conversion rate by 20 per cent, which would be worth $5 million in new business. We calculated this by looking at the bid losses over the last three years that would have been avoided through re-use of knowledge and best practices.

Reasoning will almost certainly be necessary to support your case with all stakeholders, even if other influencing techniques will create the 'sell'. You therefore need to create a compelling logical case for KM, which needs to be a case for the individual as well as a case for the company.

**Inspiring** – appealing to emotions and creating the vision. You would use this approach when you want to generate emotional commitment to the vision. The inspiring tactic demands conviction, energy, and passion, but is particularly effective with the 20 per cent of early adopters:

> Imagine what it would be like to have knowledge at our fingertips – to know, at every decision point, what we have tried in the past, what works and what doesn't work. We hold 10,000 years of experience in the heads of our staff – imagine what would be possible if that resource was available to everyone in the building.

**Asking questions** – leading the other person to make their own discovery of the value of KM:

> When do your people use knowledge? Tell me about some of the important decisions where knowledge is critical. If we had a situation where every person facing such a decision had complete access to the knowledge they needed, how much more business do you think we could win? And how certain are you that people in this situation are currently handling this vital knowledge in a rigorous, systematic, managed way?

This is one of the more difficult tactics to use because it is impossible to know how the other person will respond and you have to be able to think on your feet, but it is one of the most powerful approaches to use when talking to senior staff.

**Cosying up** – your stakeholders will almost always feel positive toward someone who makes them feel good about themselves. This is the cosying-up tactic.

> Dan, you are the smartest and most progressive leader in the whole management layer, and I know you are always looking for the next way to really improve your department. Let me tell you about this new thing called knowledge management.

Don't use this approach when talking to people who are much more senior than you, when cosying up can look like 'sucking up'. And don't use it when you don't believe what you're saying. People find it very easy to detect insincerity.

**Deal making** – when you give another person something in return for their agreement with you.

> Susie, I would like to make a deal with you. Let me set up a KM pilot in your part of the business, and I guarantee you a 10 per cent improvement in your results within three months.

Your ability to use this approach depends very much on your confidence and ability to offer something in return. Make sure you deliver on any promises.

**Favour asking** – simply asking for something because you want or need it.

> David, I really need a favour. I need an area of the business to set up a trial Lesson Learning System, and your department would be perfect. Can you help me?

This tactic works well only when the other person cares about you or their relationship with you. If used sparingly, it is hard to resist, but be aware you may have to pay back the favour at some point.

**Using silent allies (aka social proof)** – using the fact that others are getting value from KM as an argument in its favour. Social proof consists of showing stories of people, as similar to your 'buyer' as possible, who are using KM and gaining benefits as a result. This is the voice of the 'person on the street' you see in TV commercials endorsing a product. The reason the advertisers use these stories is because people are influenced by them. On a deep subconscious level, people who are uncertain about the product will use the 'person on the street' as an indication that they will get value from the product.

This technique works well with the 60 per cent audience segment who don't care about KM for its own sake but might be convinced by benefits other people got.

> Here is one of our engineers talking about how KM helped him deliver his project ahead of time by giving immediate answers that helped him solve his problems.

You can use social proof to support KM as follows:

- Begin conducting trials and 'proof of concept' studies of KM in house, with your most willing advocates (see Chapter 22).
- When the trial is a success, ask the advocate to tell their story on camera.
- Record a short YouTube-style video story, along these lines – 'this was my problem, I tried KM as a solution, this was the benefit I got'.
- Use these videos widely – embedded in PowerPoint, on the company intranet, in your KM introductions, etc, and as part of your KM communication programme (Chapter 19).

---

**Tip**

View each success in KM, no matter how small, as an opportunity to gather social proof. Keep a video camera with you (luckily most digital cameras, smartphones and tablets can record video) to record the voice of the 'person in the street' describing what KM delivered for them.

**Invoking authority** – appealing to a rule or principle.

> You have to hold your lessons learned meeting – it says so in the project procedure.

This technique is one you use late in the roll-out programme to convince the 20 per cent of laggards; once you have the support of senior management, when the KM policy is in place (see Chapter 23), and when KM has become a clear expectation. You can make excellent use of a statement or short video from your chief executive as a way of invoking authority. BP, for example, used a quote from the chief executive, John Browne, to support the expectation for KM.

**Forcing** – 'Do it or else'. The best example of the use of this tactic in KM comes from Bob Buckman, CEO of Buckman Labs, with his statement that 'the people who engage in active and effective knowledge sharing across the organization should be the only ones considered for promotion' (Buckman, 2004, p 145). This is a technique that senior management can use on your behalf, and which may be needed to remove the last few vestiges of KM non-adoption late in the roll-out phase. Obviously this tactic cannot be used until KM has become fully adopted and fully embedded, and until managers and knowledge workers alike are completely convinced of the value of KM.

**Tip**

Before trying these techniques on your stakeholders, practise on the KM team and KM champions until you (and they) have a repertoire of influencing tactics that can be used with different people.

# When to use the influencing techniques

Figure 18.2 shows when to use the various influencing techniques. Reasoning, inspiring and question asking are useful at any stage, but they are your primary influencing strategies in the early stages of implementation, and when working with senior management. Deal making, favour asking and cosying up come into their own when trying to influence middle managers to host a KM pilot. The use of social proof/silent allies is particularly important during the roll-out phase. Invoking authority and forcing can only be used later on, during or after roll-out, once KM has become a clear corporate expectation.

**FIGURE 18.2** When to use the different influencing techniques

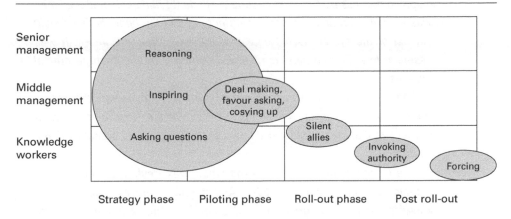

Conduct an after action review after each 'sales' conversation. What worked? Why was it successful? What did not work? Why not? What will you do differently (or repeat and reinforce) in the next conversation?

## CASE STUDY

The story below is told by Michael Lipka, the KM specialist at the NASA safety centre, and it underscores the message that stakeholder engagement is as important as KM framework design (Lipka, 2015). Lipka had previously worked for the US Air Force and had launched a platform for online communities on the assumption that in a military organization people would participate if told to do so. They didn't. Lipka learnt a hard lesson:

*Just giving people a system and expecting them to use it is wishful thinking. The hard work of engaging and winning over potential users is at least as important and demanding as designing and building a system for them.*

*So I worked to develop an implementation plan for that Air Force initiative. I held two-day workshops to discuss knowledge gaps the system could help*

*fill, to define community roles and responsibilities, and to explain knowledge-mapping processes. The most important element I had neglected until then was the value proposition: convincing people that the benefits they would get out of the system would outweigh the effort they put into it. It was essential to keep that message simple, limiting it to two or three critical benefits.*

*The implementation plan and workshop made an immediate difference. During my time with the Air Force, the 'Knowledge Now' community of practice tool gained over 100,000 users globally across all branches of the military.*

*The lesson of that Air Force experience was fresh in my mind when I came to work at NASA in 2011. And it guided me as I developed a knowledge-sharing programme for Office of Safety and Mission Assurance (OSMA)... Rather than simply scheduling events and expecting people to show up and participate, I spent a lot of time speaking to SMA leadership and personnel from other agencies, such as the Department of Defense, to ensure I was providing useful and informative sessions. Those early efforts have paid off. The events typically attract about 80 participants, who rate them highly. The rocky start to my Air Force initiative was painful, but it was a valuable lesson that helped spur my current knowledge-sharing effort and will continue to influence me throughout my career.*

## Summary

Implementing KM involves working with the stakeholders, systematically taking them up the buy-in ladder one step at a time, using sales techniques and influencing tactics. Make sure you are fully aware of these techniques and tactics, make sure you have practised them and rehearsed your arguments. This is the hard work of KM implementation: changing the hearts and minds of the key stakeholders one by one and step by step.

# Culture, communications and change

## 19

Any KM implementation must understand and engage with the underlying organizational culture (or in a large organization, subcultures). By culture, we mean common and widespread patterns of values, attitudes and habits of behaviours and thinking. Because these are habits they are largely automatic, and are reinforced by the frequency with which they are seen in other people. This makes cultural traits self-reinforcing and hard to change. For effective communications and change, it is essential to have a very clear view of the traits and behaviours that both support or oppose your KM implementation goals. Once you have this view, you can target the specific cultural traits that you want to leverage or address, in both your communications and your change management efforts.

In this chapter we cover:

- KM as an agent of culture change;
- mapping the current culture – using a dimensions approach and an archetypes approach;
- cultural drivers;
- communication and change;
- the communication plan.

## KM as an agent of culture change

KM requires a supportive culture, yet how do you develop the culture without doing KM? Should you wait for the culture to change, and then start your KM initiative, or should you start your KM initiative knowing you have to reshape the culture? Our advice is to do the latter. KM is itself such a powerful agent of behaviour and culture change that there is no point in waiting for a favourable culture.

Use the introduction of KM as a programme of culture change through the following steps:

- First map the culture, so you understand the barriers you need to address and the cultural habits you can work with.
- Then look for small areas of the business where the cultural barriers are weakest and/or the need for knowledge and KM is strongest, and make these your pilot areas (see Chapter 22).
- Deliver success in the pilot areas, then use these success stories in your communication programme as 'social proof' (Chapter 18).
- Repeat the last step as many times as it takes for the new cultural habits to catch hold.
- At the same time, lobby your sponsor and steering team to start removing the institutional barriers to the new culture that you have identified.

# Mapping the current culture

Your first step is to understand the current culture, and identify those attitudes that are likely to create barriers to KM behaviour as well as those attitudes and behaviours that may support it. There are two main ways of mapping organizational culture:

- the cultural dimensions approach; and
- the cultural archetypes approach.

## The cultural dimensions approach

In this approach, distinct cultural traits are identified as separate dimensions, and each dimension is presented as a scale with opposing traits at each end (see below). A representative sample of the target audience are surveyed, usually through a questionnaire, to find out where they score on each cultural dimension, and the results are aggregated to form a cultural profile for the target group. As with any framework, the dimensions you select depend on what aspects of culture you are interested in exploring. In our case, we are interested in cultural traits that affect learning and knowledge use in organizations. We have identified 10 potential dimensions to an organizational learning/KM culture, listed below.

Open vs defensive. The extent to which people feel comfortable having their performance (including mistakes) analysed for learning purposes. The negative aspect of this is defensiveness – the sort of behaviours you see developed in a 'blame culture'.

Honest vs dishonest. The extent to which people will filter knowledge and information when communicating with peers or seniors. This is sometimes known as 'transparency'. There is some overlap between openness and honesty, but dishonesty and defensiveness are recognizably different.

**Empowered vs disempowered.** The extent to which people feel able to act on knowledge, independent of approval from their leaders. A disempowered culture is where you have to ask your manager's permission to re-use the knowledge, or a culture of micro-management.

**Learner vs knower.** The extent to which people put a value on acquiring new knowledge as opposed to the knowledge they already hold in their heads. This distinction is explained well by Maddock and Viton (2010) who describe a 'knower' culture as one where new ideas are shut down, and a 'learner' culture as one which is not only open to new ideas but goes out of its way to find concepts contrary to its own.

**Need to share vs need to know.** The extent to which people offer their knowledge to others rather than keeping it secret. This refers to the level of risk that people perceive is related to sharing knowledge with others. 'Need to know', 'for your eyes only', 'top secret' are all part of the need to know culture.

**Challenge vs acceptance.** The extent to which people seek to understand why things are the way they are. It is more about intellectual curiosity than just learning and it encompasses a willingness to embrace innovation and to challenge the status quo.

**Collaborative vs competitive.** The extent to which people identify with and share in the success of others, rather than feeling they are in competition with them.

**Remembering vs forgetting.** This is the extent to which people acknowledge and incorporate the past when making plans for the future and the extent to which they consciously record decisions, judgments, knowledge, etc for future reference.

**Strategic patience vs short-termism.** This is the extent to which people consider the 'bigger picture' and try to understand how their actions fit into the broader, longer-term vision for their organization.

**Relentless pursuit of excellence vs complacency.** This is the extent to which organizations acknowledge there is always room for improvement. Organizations most deserving to be called 'learning' ones are those that admit how far they have yet to go.

## CASE STUDY

A common cultural trait is the 'not invented here' syndrome. This is classic 'knower' behaviour, indicating that people do not trust knowledge that comes from others, and if they haven't invented it themselves, they won't accept it. One team leader countered this by what he called 'no single source solutions'. He set the rule that he would not accept any solution invented only by the team. He wanted every solution to come from multiple sources, which meant that the team had to learn what others had done. This was a simple rule, but he was able to use it to drive 'learner' behaviour and eliminate 'knower' behaviour.

## The cultural archetypes approach

The archetypes approach, pioneered in KM by David Snowden (Snowden, 2005), involves gathering stories about both positive and negative experiences around knowledge and learning behaviours from groups of around 8–12 people. To get a representative collection of experiences, you will need to run 6–8 workshop sessions with different groups, involving staff of different profiles and length of service.

After the stories have been gathered, each group reviews its transcribed stories and tags them for values, attitudes and behaviours, using Post-it notes.

- Values describe implicit beliefs in the culture, and may be expressions of the cultural traits described above.
- Attitudes describe the way that people respond automatically to each other – for example, confrontational attitudes when challenged.
- Behaviours describe typical responses to situations and people, and they themselves reveal the underlying values and attitudes.

Collectively, these Post-it notes give a revealing picture of the underlying culture. After the tagging exercise, the stories are removed, and the participants cluster their Post-it tags by affinity, then take a cluster of attributes and create a fictional character embodying those attributes.

Any single session can create 5–15 archetypal characters that are fictional representations abstracted from the behaviours and traits that occurred in their stories. This abstraction process is important, because it allows the group to generalize from specific experiences, and not to point the finger at individuals. Over the series of focus group sessions, you will find that similar archetypes emerge, which are clustered and given to an artist for representation, and the descriptions of the archetypes are consolidated and tidied up (Lambe, 2007).

Typically this exercise will identify 10–15 archetypes that collectively represent the dominant cultural behaviours of the organization. These archetypes are very context rich – behind them are numerous example stories of how this pattern of behaviour plays out in practice.

For example, a common archetypal behaviour we have encountered is called 'the squirrel', which represents the behaviour of building a private hoard of all the information and knowledge assets that one needs to do their work. The squirrel is hesitant to share this because, while it works for their job duties, they are not sure whether it is appropriate for other colleagues, fearing it might create problems that bounce back on them.

Over several years, we have identified archetypal behaviours that occur across many different organization types, and we have created a set of cultural archetypes cards (available at **http://www.straitsknowledge.com/ store_new/organization culture cards/**). With these, a less time-intensive approach can be adopted, where a sample of the different staff groups selects cards for patterns of behaviour they recognize. The results are aggregated, and the 10–12 most frequently selected cards are taken to represent the cultural profile of the organization. However, while very rapid, this method lacks the contextual richness of the background stories that give specific examples of how these behaviour patterns work in practice in that organization. To mitigate this, you can run short focus groups just sharing stories on the most frequently recognized archetypes.

### Which method should you use?

Both approaches have different strengths and weaknesses. The dimensions approach is highly structured and focuses on known factors that affect knowledge use, knowledge sharing and learning in organizations. It is also fairly easy to run, analyse and draw high-level conclusions from, and it provides a baseline to measure cultural behaviour changes in future surveys. However, it may not capture unusual cultural traits that are not represented in the framework, but that have an impact on knowledge use in that organization.

The archetypes approach is more labour intensive, but can capture cultural traits that fall outside standard frameworks. The stories that are collected provide rich contextual background to the frequently recognized behaviours, and this often helps in analysing the drivers and constraints that shape the culture, but is less appropriate for creating a baseline. If you have the time and the resources, then a combination of both methods is ideal and will give you a more holistic picture.

# Understanding the cultural drivers

Once you understand the culture, the next step is to understand what drives, shapes, or reinforces the culture. There are often factors such as leadership behaviours, infrastructure issues, and incentive systems that reinforce the current culture. For example, the 'squirrel' behaviour is often reinforced by a poor quality of the common information platform, and a lack of information governance and quality control.

The dimensions approach also helps to identify potential drivers of change.

- Defensiveness is driven by the way the organization responds to failure. Where failure is punished, either formally or informally, people will be defensive.

- Dishonest behaviour is often influenced by leadership behaviours. Where leaders model an honest and transparent leadership style, employees often follow.

- Disempowerment is driven by many factors, such as the number of layers of approval required for new work, or the details of the objective-setting system, or micro-management of employees.

- Knower behaviours are driven by the ways in which people are recognized and rewarded, particularly the recognition of 'lone heroes' and knowledge hoarders.

- Need-to-know behaviours are driven by a concern for information security, and by relying on the individual to be secure rather than the IT system.

- Acceptance and complacent behaviours come directly from leadership. If leaders do not challenge the status quo, neither will their staff.

- Competitive behaviours are driven by competitive incentives such as 'forced ranking' of individual staff appraisals, or by requiring operational units to compete for bonuses, budgets or prizes.

- Forgetting behaviours are also driven by leaders, and reinforced by the lack of a KM framework which makes remembering easier.

- Short termism is often driven by the incentive system, the prime example being the hourly billing system employed by many consultancies and legal firms. Here the pressure to deliver work in the short term acts against the need to reflect and capture knowledge that can be used in the long term.

Understanding the cultural drivers helps us to identify the levers of change that can be built into the change management plan, and this helps in shaping the messages in the communications plan.

## CASE STUDY

One of the authors worked with a company trying to introduce best practice sharing between a number of factories who competed for an annual 'factory of the year' award. The company decided to make 'best practice sharing' part of the award criteria, with each factory required to submit a quota of best practices. The wily factory staff waited until just before the award deadline, then issued all their best practices in one submission; early enough that they counted towards the award, but so late that none of their rival factories could benefit from re-using the knowledge. Competition therefore trumped knowledge sharing.

# Communication and change

Communication is a big part of your change management strategy. It is through communication that you move the bulk of your organization up the first three buy-in steps described in the last chapter: first contact, awareness, and understanding. In a 2009 blog post, Seth Kahan described his lessons from leading KM at the World Bank, and contrasted his first KM initiative (which failed) with his second (which succeeded, thanks in part to increased communication).

The first initiative was 'comprised of a few select, world-class thought leaders who drew on a dedicated budget to design and implement a powerful new tool they hoped would revolutionize the way business was done. We met in closed meetings, witnessed remarkable demonstrations, and marvelled at the power of the Internet to spread knowledge.' In other words, KM was being pushed by a closed group, who were interacting only with other enthusiasts. Unsurprisingly, nothing came of it.

The second initiative, with no budget and no resources, 'told everybody what we were up to. In fact, we spent a good deal of time in the beginning figuring out how to tell as many people as we could, as fast as possible. We even met regularly with our detractors, as their input was sometimes needed the most'. The second initiative was being run as a change programme, with communication extending beyond the closed group of supporters, and engaging with everyone. Within two years, it had changed the organization. Seth identifies seven lessons for KM change based on his experience:

- Communicate so people get it and spread it. As he says though, this is not one-way communication, but a conversation that spreads.
- Identify and energize your most valuable players. These are your supporters and KM champions who can help to drive KM forward.
- Understand the territory of change. Seth had a method for mapping stakeholder support, similar to the method we describe in Chapter 18.
- Accelerate evolution through communities – at least in large dispersed organizations. Smaller co-located organizations may find other ways to introduce and implement KM.
- Blow through bottlenecks and logjams. Seth suggests a 'SWAT Team' mentality. But please don't bulldoze people!
- Create dramatic surges in progress. Seth suggests special events to drive progress. Another way is to create energy around early successes, and to build on social proof.
- Keep your focus when change comes fast. When KM is successful, it can accelerate alarmingly. (Kahan, 2009)

> ### Tip
>
> Ensure your communications are not written in KM jargon, but use the language of the business. Terms such as innovation, collaboration, providing know-how to the front-line workers, finding best practices, learning from experience and speeding up the learning curve are easier to understand than terms such as knowledge creation, knowledge synthesis, tacit knowledge sharing and so on.

# The communication plan

Communication is key to a change campaign, and we believe that communication planning needs to be one core component of KM implementation. Your communication plan should be based on the following principles:

- Start the communication plan from day one – the same time as you start the KM strategy.
- Make a member of the team accountable for the KM communication plan.
- Ensure 'communication' is a line item in your KM budget.
- Identify your main stakeholder groupings and the main communications channels and messages that are appropriate for each one.
- Draft a 'simple message' which provides the logical case for KM and also paints the vision (thus covering the reasoning and inspiring tactics described in Chapter 18).
- Address the cultural drivers directly in your communications, using plain language.
- Create a standard communication pack, for example a standard set of PowerPoint slides and videos, which all members of the KM team and all KM champions can use.
- Brand your communications with a logo and strapline. Consider the use of collaterals such as mugs, corporate calendars, mousepads.
- Ensure communication to 'all staff' happens at least quarterly.
- Build an internal mailing list or social media channel.
- Ensure communication to the most important stakeholders is face to face, using the influencing techniques described in Chapter 18.
- Communicate your plans, even if the details are not yet clear.
- Until any early wins are demonstrated, all widespread communications should be internal within the organization, and

should focus on the first buy-in steps of first contact, awareness and understanding.

- As soon as you have some successful proof of concept exercises, the communication campaign should use these to deliver social proof, and you should begin communicating outside the organization so that external perspectives can trickle back in.

---

**Tip**

You need to balance the expectation of the senior business managers with the expectations of the knowledge workers. These two customer groups may have different expectations and requirements from KM that need to be taken into consideration, and they certainly have two value propositions. Your communication channels therefore need to communicate 'what's in it for the business' for the senior managers, and 'what's in it for me' for the knowledge workers.

---

## Summary

Shortly after Michael McCurry, Clinton administration press secretary, left the White House, a writer for the *Harvard Business Review* asked him what he says when people ask him how to become better communicators. 'Know what you're trying to say and say it precisely and simply', McCurry answered. 'And be committed to telling the story over and over again. You have to persevere' (Coleman and Barquin, 2010). Perseverance and repetition are especially important when trying to influence cultural change, because cultural habits are deeply engrained.

Plan your KM communication, make someone accountable, decide your audiences and key messages, and persevere! Be reassured – you can never over-communicate.

# Preparing the KM implementation plan

## 20

When you prepared your first KM plan and budget, as described in Chapter 8, you had not yet conducted many of the defining activities such as the knowledge assets audit, the stakeholder analysis, the culture survey and the outline KM framework. By the time you reach the end of the planning stage, however, you will have far greater clarity on the challenges you face, the missing gaps in the framework that need to be filled, the people you will need to engage, the potential business pilot areas, and the communication programme you will need to run. Now is the time for detailed planning. In this chapter we cover:

- how to create the plan;
- possible components of the implementation plan.

## How to create the implementation plan

In the Mars case study (Chapter 27) Linda Davies describes how she developed an implementation plan for her KM programme following standard business planning practice, detailing costs, resources and proposed activity, with a broad three-year time horizon and a detailed one-year plan, submitted annually as part of the regular business planning cycle. This is a good approach to take, creating a one-year detailed plan as part of a longer outline plan.

Prepare the detailed plan in an interactive workshop, involving the whole KM team and as many KM champions as you feel appropriate. A workshop format utilizes the collective knowledge and organizational experience of the whole team. Book a meeting room with a long blank wall, and line this with a long roll of paper. Bring a large supply of Post-it notes. Mark the months for the first year along the top of the paper, followed by the quarters for the two subsequent years. Use one colour of Post-it note to mark the main milestones for KM implementation. These might be, for example:

- strategy approved (if this has not yet happened);
- implementation plan approved – start of piloting;
- end of piloting – approval for roll-out;
- end of roll-out.

Then begin to identify, through discussion or brainstorming, the main tasks you will need to perform to reach each of these milestones. A list of possible tasks is provided later in this chapter. For each task, mark down on a separate Post-it note (one per task):

- the duration of the task;
- the number of working days it will take to do the task (effort is not the same as duration – a task might take a month, but only require a few days' work during that month);
- the resource you will use to do this task – for example a KM team resource, an external resource like a consultant or contractor, or a KM champion.

Put these tasks on the papered wall in rough order. Ask the attendees at the meeting to review the set of tasks and, wherever necessary:

- Move tasks so that they follow other tasks on which they depend (for example, the task of delivering the first internal KM training course needs to come after the tasks of creating the training material and publicizing the course). Draw lines between dependent tasks.
- Add new tasks which should be on the wall and aren't (for example presenting the first KM engagement workshop can't be done until the communication plan is completed, and the engagement slide set created).

Once you have all the tasks on the wall and agreed, photograph the wall to create a record, collect the Post-its and close the meeting. The tasks then need to be moved to a spreadsheet or a project management tool. You may have your own standard project planning template, but we present one here that works well.

Create a spreadsheet with rows for tasks, and columns for weeks of the year, as illustrated in Figure 20.1. Mark in the main holidays such as Christmas, New Year or Eid. Place the tasks on the rows, clustering them into major groups. Where you have two types of resources assigned to a task, for example a KM training course delivered by an external consultant and attended by the internal KM team, enter this as two rows, one for each resource. Then place the number of days this resource will be working on this task into the relevant week. For example, Figure 20.1 shows that an

**FIGURE 20.1**    A portion of an example KM planning spreadsheet

| | Task | Resource | Total days | Piloting phase | | | | | | | | |
| | | | | Jan | | | | | Feb | | | |
| | | | | W1 | W2 | W3 | W4 | W5 | W6 | W7 | W8 | W9 |
|---|---|---|---|---|---|---|---|---|---|---|---|---|
| KM team | Appoint internal Chief Knowledge Officer and Knowledge Management team | Int | 6 | | 1 | 1 | | | | | | |
| | Train CKO and KM team in knowledge management tools and techniques | Ext | 10 | | | | 5 | | | | | |
| | Attend above training | Int | 20 | | | | 20 | 1 | 1 | 1 | 1 | 1 |
| | Ongoing coaching for CKO and KM team | Ext | 19 | | | | | | | | | |
| | Attend coaching above | Int | 27 | | | | | 1 | 4 | 1 | 1 | 4 |
| | High level briefing, in the absence of a CKO | Ext | 4 | | | | | | | | | |

external resource (Ext) will spend 5 of 10 allocated days in week four providing KM training, which will be attended by the KM team.

A sum of the horizontal rows determines the total of working days spent on each task (which should agree with the working days estimate on the Post-it notes), while a sum of the vertical columns gives the total working days for each week.

Plot the working days per week onto a chart, to visualize the resource requirements, and identify tasks that need to be reassigned or rescheduled in order to smooth out the resource. An example of this is shown in Figure 20.2, where the required days per week are plotted for three resources; the CKO, an external consultant, and the internal KM team. You can see periods (for example in week five) where the CKO will be overloaded, working more than five days per week, so some of the CKO tasks need to be assigned to the KM team members or to the consultant. The resource requirements from the KM team are up to 15 days per month and will rise higher once the CKO tasks are reassigned, implying a three-person KM team is needed. This particular plan is based on a Middle Eastern example, and the long gap in between weeks 24 and 34 represents Ramadan and the hot summer months.

Once the KM implementation plan is complete, and you have a good view of the resource requirements, then the next step is to present this to your steering committee for their review and endorsement.

**FIGURE 20.2**  A resource plot created from a KM plan spreadsheet

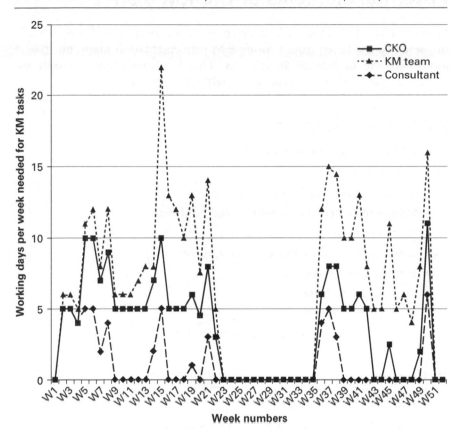

> **Tip**
>
> Beware of 'Planner's Droop'. This is the phenomenon where the first few
> months, where you have a good idea of what will happen, are filled with
> tasks, but the later months are almost empty because you do not yet know
> what you will be doing. This can be seen to an extent in Figure 20.2 where
> weeks 43 through 49 look suspiciously quiet. Revisit the tasks, brainstorm
> what else may be needed at this future date, increase the resource
> requirements, and if necessary add 20 per cent contingency for the things
> you don't yet know you will need to do.

# Potential elements of the KM plan

Below is a list of potential tasks which may appear in the detailed plan. Each of these tasks is taken from real-life KM implementation plans, but few if any plans will include all these tasks. This list simply suggests options, intended to remind you of tasks you might otherwise overlook.

## KM team development

- select and appoint team members;
- train team;
- schedule team meetings and study time;
- team attendance at conventions and conferences;
- representation on seminars, courses, etc;
- team learning and knowledge-sharing activities;
- manage team knowledge;
- create team website;
- manage team website;
- provision orientation pack for new team members.

## Culture analysis

- conduct culture survey;
- conduct culture workshops and focus groups;
- identify culture drivers, enablers and blockers;
- review these with steering team and develop action plan for removal of blockers;
- repeat culture survey.

## Stakeholder engagement and communications

- create communications and stakeholder management strategy;
- conduct stakeholder mapping;
- create the communication plan;
- decide logo and branding;
- define the high-level message;
- define other messages;
- ongoing regular communications (eg quarterly);
- identify and design promotional collateral;
- seek and gather success stories;

- publicize success stories internally and externally;
- create engagement material for KM champions;
- plan and deliver internal KM conference;
- one-on-one stakeholder engagement;
- prepare for, and speak at, external conferences;
- prepare and implement awards and recognition scheme.

## Training and coaching the knowledge workers

- finalize training content:
  - for each new role;
  - for the KM champions; and
  - for general awareness training.
- plan and advertise the training;
- deliver KM training;
- set up KM community of practice;
- facilitate knowledge sharing in KM community of practice;
- coach and support the KM champions and KM team members.

## Framework definition

- develop audit tools;
- conduct audit of current state (eg knowledge assets audit);
- analyse business process and knowledge flows;
- identify best in class approaches;
- identify gaps, opportunities and options to fill the gaps and meet opportunities;
- define potential roles;
- define potential processes;
- define potential governance;
- review these with steering committee;
- finalize first-pass framework.

## Technology definition

- conduct user survey;
- define use cases;
- analyse business process and knowledge flows;
- conduct technology requirement analysis;

- compare requirement against a range of options including 'do nothing';
- select technology.

## Knowledge organization system definition

- translate KM implementation objectives into requirements for taxonomy, metadata and information architecture;
- conduct user warrant, content warrant and standards warrant analysis;
- conduct facet analysis for taxonomy and metadata;
- create use-case scenarios to test the taxonomy and information architecture design;
- design and test taxonomy;
- design and test information architecture;
- integrate search engine with taxonomy and information architecture design;
- define governance and maintenance framework and processes for the taxonomy, information architecture, and content/document management lifecycle.

## Proof of concept work (examples)

Lessons learned:

- select opportunity for lessons learned;
- meet the project managers to agree the approach;
- conduct and document the lessons learned session;
- train internal staff in lessons facilitation;
- trial of lessons management and lessons re-use;
- continued lessons learned support;
- capture learning and stories.

Knowledge retention:

- select opportunity for knowledge retention;
- meet with HR to agree the approach;
- identify priority individuals for knowledge retention and engage with their line managers;
- conduct workshop to create knowledge transfer plan;
- facilitate knowledge capture;
- facilitate knowledge transfer;
- create and review knowledge asset;
- capture learning and stories.

Knowledge transfer:

- select opportunity for knowledge transfer;
- meet the stakeholders to agree the approach;
- facilitate the knowledge transfer session;
- train internal staff in knowledge transfer facilitation;
- continued knowledge transfer support;
- capture learning and stories.

Technology test:

- select opportunity for technology test;
- meet the stakeholders and test user population to agree the approach;
- work with IT on procuring evaluation copy of technology;
- coach users in use of technology;
- facilitate application of technology;
- review and monitor usage;
- make decision on permanent implementation and integration;
- capture learning and stories.

Community of practice (CoP):

- find opportunity for community of practice launch;
- identify domain, sponsor and potential members;
- launch CoP;
- develop CoP charter and business case;
- coach and support CoP leader in roll-out and growth of community;
- work with CoP facilitator on capture of good practices from community experts;
- work with CoP facilitator to define community activities;
- work with IT on appropriate tools and collaboration spaces;
- ongoing review of CoP activity;
- regular CoP maturity assessment;
- capture CoP learning and success stories.

## *KM pilot projects*

- select high-grade pilots using experience from proof of concept stage;
- engage pilot business area;
- appoint and train business pilot lead;
- scope pilot;
- conduct audit and map knowledge of pilot area;
- define pilot terms of reference;

- define pilot area KM framework working with pilot business area;
- finalize roles and responsibilities and governance process;
- develop detailed pilot plan;
- deliver pilot KM activities;
- identify, share and/or and capture knowledge in pilot area;
- coach business pilot lead;
- coach pilot team members;
- create pilot knowledge asset or knowledge base where needed;
- monitor and report pilot metrics;
- capture learning/success stories/case studies.

## Finalizing the framework

- review and update organizational KM framework based on pilot experience;
- collate benefits and develop business case for roll-out;
- review roles and accountability statements with steering committee and HR;
- draft templates for KM job descriptions and performance contracts for KM roles;
- review technology plan with steering committee and IT;
- review processes with steering committee and relevant business units;
- finalize standard templates;
- review governance with steering committee and relevant senior managers;
- finalize leadership KM accountabilities;
- finalize role descriptions, accountabilities and performance contract for the operational KM team;
- define KM interfaces with other organizational units;
- gain approval for roll-out.

## Running roll-out workshops

- create manuals and reference material;
- create schedule of workshops;
- trial roll-out workshop;
- improve workshop material;
- invite participants;
- arrange logistics for workshops;

- deliver workshops;
- follow-up workshops.

## KM embedding

- draft and agree the KM policy;
- draft and agree the KM metrics to be used;
- define and agree the KM reporting structure;
- define and agree the KM recognition and reward mechanism;
- create list of required roles;
- update project management guidelines to include new KM processes;
- update operational guidelines to include new KM processes;
- update reporting guidelines to include new KM governance;
- change performance management or rewards and recognition system to support KM activities.

## Reporting and planning

- apply KM metrics;
- define reporting structure;
- monitor and measure KM activity, outputs and outcomes;
- annual reporting and planning;
- steering team meetings – preparation and reporting.

# Summary

The detailed planning described in this chapter will be needed to secure your budget for the next stage of KM implementation, and to coordinate your activities once the plan and budget are approved. In the following chapters we will look at some of these implementation activities in more detail.

# PART FOUR
# The implementation activity

## Executive summary

Part Four covers the core of your KM implementation activity. Chapter 21 outlines how to set up a KM champions network, to help you in your implementation. Chapter 22 describes how to select and run proofs of concept and pilot projects, which will help you test and refine your KM framework in the business. Chapter 23 covers the steps involved in transitioning to a full KM roll-out, and Chapter 24 gives you a framework for establishing KM metrics for the business. Chapter 25 provides advice and guidance for those occasions when your implementation hits obstacles or barriers, and Chapter 26 covers how to make the transition from an implementation programme to fully embedded KM.

# Building the KM champion network

## 21

In this chapter we cover one of the most powerful ways of scaling up KM activities, and embedding KM awareness and practices throughout the organization: building and empowering the network of KM champions. The topics we'll cover are:

- what a KM champion is, and is not;
- what KM champions are expected to do;
- how to identify potential KM champions;
- keeping KM champions motivated; and
- supporting KM champions in their role.

## What is a KM champion?

If KM is to be sustainable, KM roles will need to be embedded into the normal working practices of your organization. The KM team remains to manage KM (Chapter 26), while accountability for managing knowledge itself will become embedded within business roles such as CoP leaders and facilitators, knowledge managers and practice owners (described in Chapters 13–16).

There is also a third type of KM role, which is a vital part of the culture change programme, even before these business accountabilities are assigned. This is the role of the KM champion – a temporary change management role required to broaden the reach of the company's KM activities.

In the early KM literature, KM champions are mostly described as senior level activists promoting and advocating KM at a strategic level (Duffy, 1998; Santosus, 2002; Jones *et al*, 2003). However, within KM implementation there is also a strong need for operational level KM activists, and this is the type of KM champion we describe in this chapter (Abell and Oxbrow, 2001; Bishop, 2002). The content of this chapter is based on our work in helping clients build KM champion networks, with input from a 2006 research project conducted with the actKM community (Lambe and Tan, 2006).

KM champions play an important change management role for KM, but they differ from KM roles such as knowledge managers and community leaders, in that KM advocacy is often not a part of their job description. They have operational, full-time work obligations and performance requirements while acting as unpaid advocates for KM. For this reason it is important not merely to select the right kind of people with the right kind of attributes, but also to make sure that your performance management policy and framework does not penalize them or impose undue pressure on them.

## What KM champions do

KM champions have three main roles in support of KM at an operational level. Depending on the stage you are at and the projects you are rolling out, their responsibilities can be any mix of these three:

- **advocacy** – spreading the KM message;
- **support** – acting as local department level representatives for KM implementation activities, providing coaching and advice on KM issues;
- **knowledge brokering** – linking their department colleagues to knowledge and information resources outside their immediate context.

Typical activities under each of these three roles might be:

- Advocacy:
  - communicating KM messages to their department from the KM team;
  - helping to influence stakeholders on behalf of the KM team;
  - encouraging knowledge sharing and learning behaviours;
  - leading or facilitating KM awareness sessions;
  - being a reference point for clarification and explanation of KM activities;
  - gathering and communicating feedback from colleagues to the central KM team; and
  - collecting stories about KM impact from within their department.
- Support:
  - acting as KM liaisons between the central KM team and their department manager and colleagues;
  - playing a role in KM projects at department level;
  - coaching colleagues in KM-related duties;

- facilitating KM activities such as after action reviews or peer assists;
- providing feedback on the usefulness/impact of KM initiatives at department level;
- proactively providing ideas and suggestions for new initiatives or improvements to KM processes and tools;
- identifying potential proof of concept exercises or KM pilots;
- mentoring and supporting new KM champions; and
- representing their department in KM initiatives planning, review and needs analysis.
- Knowledge brokering:
  - networking with other KM champions;
  - identifying major knowledge and information needs in their own department and seeking out resources that will address those needs;
  - responding promptly to requests for help from colleagues or other departments; and
  - pointing colleagues towards relevant resources or colleagues when they mention an information or knowledge need.

# How to identify potential KM champions

The attributes of KM champions have a big impact on their effectiveness. For this reason, it is always better to let KM champions 'emerge' than to select and nominate people for the role based on their job function or technical skills. Because their role can at different times span 'lighter' advocacy work and 'heavier' implementation work, and because they have a strong peer-influencing role, KM champions need to have the trust and confidence of their peers as well as their managers.

Successful KM champions will have the following qualities:

- well established in their work group, knowledgeable about the group's activities, and respected by their colleagues;
- helpful and approachable to their colleagues; and
- able to communicate effectively with peers, superiors and subordinates.

A more detailed set of attributes to support each of the three dimensions of their work is given in Figure 21.1.

KM champions are often identified and nominated by their department managers, because they will need the support of these managers in the definition, discharge and recognition of their KM-related duties. Before they make their nominations, managers need to be briefed on the roles the KM champions will play, the attributes required to be successful in those roles, and how to properly support their KM champions.

**FIGURE 21.1**    Attributes of successful KM champions

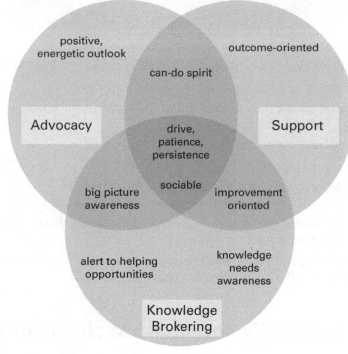

KM champions will be most effective when their KM role is:

- formally and explicitly integrated with their main job role;
- a recognized part of the department's work priorities;
- embedded in the job-related processes of the organization (such as job descriptions, performance management, job reviews, and rewards and recognition mechanisms).

There are two common mistakes in appointing KM champions: appointing the 'new kid on the block', and relying on the 'overloaded hero'.

## The new kid on the block

While newer, younger recruits may have more energy and ideas than long-time staff, they find it harder to operate effectively as KM champions. Because they may not be familiar with all aspects of the department's work, they are usually not well networked and they may not be able to positively influence their more experienced colleagues.

### The overloaded hero

Many departments will have staff members who have all the right qualities and attributes to be a KM champion, but these staff members are the usual targets for all new change initiatives. As they take on more and more, they become over-stretched and sometimes burned out. While it might make sense to group related change initiatives (such as innovation, KM and quality) under one person, the risk of overloading is a serious one.

# Maintaining the motivation of the KM champions

Even positive, informed KM enthusiasts can become intimidated by the seemingly broad and open-ended duties of being a KM champion. They can worry about what is expected of them, how this role will affect their 'normal' work, and whether they will get the support they need from their managers, and recognition from their organization.

Here are some of the questions that new KM champions commonly worry about (these questions are taken from KM champion orientation sessions):

- How important is this role to the organization at large?
- Will my manager support me?
- Will the central KM team support me?
- What specifically do you want me to do?
- Will I be equipped with the relevant knowledge and skills to be effective in this role?
- How much empowerment do I really have to influence processes, roles and behaviours in my department?
- What is the timeframe of this responsibility?
- Do I have a choice? Can I opt out?
- Is this over and above my normal job responsibilities? How do I manage both?
- How will I know if I'm doing a good job in this role?
- Will I be rewarded or recognized for taking on this additional responsibility?

Underlying most of these questions is a desire for clarity and detail. Even if the role appears challenging, you will improve the motivation of the nominees significantly if you can reduce the uncertainty surrounding it. Provide a clear, specific set of terms of reference, and ideally an appointment letter from your senior KM sponsor.

Here are some other ways you can help keep the KM champions motivated, brainstormed by KM champions themselves at their orientation sessions. We find this list works well as a checklist to prepare for building a KM champions network.

1  **Reduce uncertainty by being specific,** for example about criteria for appointment, timeframe of appointment, amount of time to be allocated per week, known duties, key performance indicators, recognition mechanisms, and available support.

2  **Provide immediate, regular, visible support,** for example regular face-to-face sharing opportunities between KM champions, and between KM champions and the central KM team. Provide training on a regular basis.

3  **Give them a sense of ownership,** for example by allowing them to have an influence in how their role is defined, to negotiate priorities and balance of duties with their managers, to discuss their role with other KM champions and with the KM team.

4  **Give them a sense of identity and recognize their efforts,** through a formal appointment, by organizing a kickoff and orientation session, by communicating regularly with their managers and the senior management team about the importance of their role, and by collecting and publicizing stories of their impact and effort.

5  **Recognize them for their achievements.** If possible ensure the champions are recognized through traditional methods in their performance management process. If the KM champion role can be made part of their job description, then provide feedback to their manager about how well they have played this role. For the best performers, recommend to their line manager that they receive a bonus, remembering to cite examples of where they performed particularly well. If the KM champion role is not a formal part of their job description, then find a way to recognize them through your centrally coordinated KM activities, for example through a central awards scheme (Chapter 23).

---

**Tip**

Draft a set of terms of reference for the KM champions in your organization, bearing in mind the implementation stage you are at, and the pilots you may want to implement. Remember to cover the following questions:

- Why this role?
- Why have we nominated you?
- How long is this appointment for?

- What are your duties in the next three to six months?
- How many hours per week are you expected to devote to this role?
- How often will the KM champions meet?
- What support will the KM team provide?
- What are your key performance indicators?
- How will your performance in this role be reviewed?
- How should you hand over to your successor?

# Supporting the KM champions

There are a number of ways in which the KM team can provide support to KM champions. We describe five of these ways below.

## Train the champions

The KM champions will need to be trained in the skills they need to perform their role. Certainly you should offer them training in the KM skills and generic skills such as facilitation, but you may also offer them training in change management and influencing skills.

## Provide them with resources to do their job

Much of the KM champion role is communication and advocacy, so they need access to the communication resources of the KM team. We described the communication plan and strategy in Chapter 19, and the KM champions will play a key role in this strategy. Give them access to the slidesets, videos, posters and other communication mechanisms, so they can spread the word in their own part of the organization. Better still, create a communications pack specifically for the KM champions, to ensure a consistent message is spread throughout the organization.

## Build a KM community of practice

Once KM implementation is over, KM will be an established discipline and like all disciplines will need its own community of practice (CoP) so the practitioners can support each other in their KM roles. Kick off this CoP early in the KM programme and use it as a way to connect and support the KM champions to become independent champions for KM within the organization, by giving them access to knowledgeable peers, and helping them feel that they are 'not alone'.

## CASE STUDY

One of the authors was the moderator for an organizational KM community of practice, known as the KMUnity. About 180 KM champions and advocates shared their knowledge in a virtual workspace, with an e-mail discussion forum, a facilitator, and a website for storing collective knowledge. The conversation within the community ebbed and flowed but proved to be an invaluable way to keep alive a sense of purpose around the topic of KM, and to answer the questions of the KM champions. Some examples: a knowledge manager in Australia wrote saying he was finalizing his performance contract and objectives and could anybody assist by describing KM performance indicators. A supporter in internal audit raised a question about virtual meetings: did anybody have any experience or guidance to offer? A community facilitator asked for help in sharing large documents across the world. Many other similar queries were raised and were quickly answered by others in the community.

## *Make the KM champion role a recognized role in the organization*

Work with the champions' line managers to ensure their KM duties are embedded in job duties and subject to performance review and recognition. Work with HR to ensure that their role as KM champions is taken into account in considering promotion possibilities. Recommend key performance indicators for the role. Gather and publicize stories of KM champion contributions, so that the organization recognizes this as an important role for business success.

## *Hold KM events*

Provide a regular rhythm of face-to-face events for the champions, as a way for them to provide support to each other. At these events the KM champions identify and share common issues, give feedback and ideas, undertake training in KM-related skills, and consolidate their sense of collective identity and confidence in their role. This might be a monthly, quarterly or annual rhythm depending on the size and geographic dispersal of the KM CoP.

The central KM team will play an important part in organizing these sessions, and should be present to share updates and progress with the KM champions, and to listen to and record their input. While initially the agenda for such meetings may be quite highly structured by the central KM team, it is desirable that ownership of the content and structure of the meetings gradually transfers to the KM champions themselves. This strategy will more likely produce a vibrant and resourceful CoP, with a longevity that will outlive the central KM team.

## CASE STUDY

Gorelick *et al* (2004) tell this story about a regular face-to-face meeting of local KM champions in BP, told from the point of view of the KM team representative at the meeting.

*It was a mixed group sitting around the small meeting table in Brussels; mixed not only in terms of nationality but also in terms of understanding of, and commitment to, KM. Some were enthusiastic converts, already driving forward their own initiatives in the business. Some were new to the topic, but had heard enough to know there was some potential. These were the members of the KM pool for BP Oil, Europe – the major part of BP's fuels and lubricants marketing business – and this was one of the monthly pool meetings.*

*We were going around the table reviewing what we were doing in our parts of the business to deliver value through management of knowledge. Clyde had been sitting quietly in the corner looking rather puzzled. When we got to him he spoke up. 'Look, I'm still not really sure what value there is in this KM stuff. I mean, if my manager asks me to justify to him the time I spend here with you, what can I reply? Where is the real business benefit here?'*

*I took a deep breath, ready to trot out the examples and success stories that I'd used so many times to justify expense on KM, but before I could start to speak the others had already begun to reply. Richard explained the value that had been generated by reducing the cost of service station construction in Europe. Sath talked about how much value could be generated if the different call centres that we were implementing around Europe could learn from each other. Someone else mentioned the peer assist on leaky storage tanks. Clyde nodded thoughtfully; yes, he could see the value. He would try a peer assist for himself. I thought to myself, 'these people do not need the KM team any more, they have each other for support.'*

## Summary

In this chapter we have covered the important role of the KM champions in helping to advocate, promote and support KM in every part of your organization. It's important to recognize that this is probably a non-specialist part-time role, and that the KM champions, particularly at the beginning, will need a lot of support. However, the skills and attributes you need in your KM champions network are common to many of the skills and attributes you will need in your core KM team. Together with the KM champions network the KM core team can form a KM community of practice, to develop skills, heighten KM awareness, stimulate KM activity, and provide feedback and ideas on KM implementation.

# Trials and pilots 22

The 'trials and pilots' stage is where you begin to test KM in the business. In this chapter we distinguish between two types of test:

- The 'proof of concept' trials where you apply a single KM process or technology to a single business issue, in order to demonstrate that it can be applied in your organization, and sometimes to deliver a quick win. A proof of concept trial usually lasts a few days, or weeks at the most.
- A KM pilot where you apply a complete (but often simplified) KM framework to a business problem, in order to gain knowledge and create success stories. A KM pilot can last several months, or even a year.

This chapter covers the following topics:

- proof of concept trials;
- where to look for quick wins;
- selecting KM pilot projects;
- the 'minimum viable KM framework';
- delivering KM pilots;
- reaching the organizational decision point.

## Proof of concept trials

In the early stages of KM – potentially even when you are still drafting the strategy – you may need to deliver a number of 'proof of concept' trials, to show short-term progress and provide immediate tangible results, so people can see KM in action and understand the value it brings (this was described in Chapter 2 as the 'opportunity-led programme' that should run in parallel with your strategic programme). These trials are small interventions with a KM tool or process, so people can see it in action, and realize that 'KM is not all smoke and mirrors – it can work here'.

As you talk with your stakeholders, you and they may be able to identify many opportunities to test KM processes and technologies. Suitable opportunities might include the following:

- A lessons-capture meeting such as a retrospect for a tricky (or successful) project. For one of the companies we have worked with this was a project that had gone disastrously wrong, and they effectively said to us: 'if you can get learning from this project, then we will believe what you say about KM'. We did gather learning – some very powerful learning – and this opened the door to management support.

- A peer assist for a high-profile project. This has been the proof of concept for many companies – a straightforward demonstration that valuable knowledge can be shared between project teams, and can make a positive impact to project plans. In Chapter 29 Tan Xinde describes an early trial of peer assist in a product development unit.

- A facilitated exchange of knowledge on a key topic. In another organization we worked with, the proof of concept was getting experts together from all over the world to build a company best practice on bidding and winning large government contracts.

- Creating a knowledge asset on a key topic. Another client we worked with was going through a series of mergers, and compiled knowledge in the form of a set of guidance summarizing 'what we have learned about delivering effective mergers'.

- A launch event to kick off a community of practice. One of our clients was seeking to develop knowledge-sharing behaviours, and a successful community launch gave them the evidence they needed to convince them this was worth supporting.

- A retention interview from a departing expert. This has been the proof of concept for many retention-based KM strategies. Management want to see what is possible, and they want to be convinced that KM can generate valuable output.

In each case, you should seek to create two things from the proof of concept. The first is some valuable knowledge, either exchanged between people, or captured as lessons or guidance. The second is stories, reaction or feedback from the people involved, saying 'Hey, we tried KM, it was great, it was not difficult, and it created real value'.

## CASE STUDY

This story, adapted from Gorelick *et al* (2004) describes an early proof of concept exercise at the charity Tearfund, conducted by their knowledge manager, Paul Whiffen. Tearfund had a tradition of careful planning and consultation and was unfamiliar with a trials and pilots approach, but Paul was keen to start with some small-scale demonstrations of KM processes.

One of the key activities of Tearfund – critical to its success and to delivery of its vision and mission – is providing aid in response to disasters. Learning was not being transferred automatically from one disaster response project to another, as disasters in different parts of the world are often attended by different staff, and may have very different characteristics. However, there was huge potential benefit for increasing the effectiveness of response and therefore saving human lives, if knowledge could be captured, saved and re-used. Paul chose disaster response as an opportunity to test knowledge capture and re-use. Paul reports as follows:

> There is no doubt that demonstrating the Bangladesh retrospect in the summer of 1999 was a great thing. It was much better to just do something and demonstrate to people how simple and yet how powerful these processes are.

The Bangladesh retrospect was well received by people who attended, and several lessons were identified and recorded which could be used in future flood response programmes. However, this turned out not to be just an academic exercise, because shortly after the retrospect had been completed, the Orissa cyclone hit India, and flooding started there.

Although the Orissa cyclone was a sudden-onset disaster, unlike the floods in Bangladesh that had developed over a period of weeks, Tearfund found that many of the lessons from Bangladesh were immediately applicable to Orissa. The first thing that the Asia team leader did was to look for the Bangladesh lessons, because they were fresh and applicable. He was impressed by the process, and became an effective advocate for KM at management level

# Where to look for quick wins

Delivering business value through a proof of concept trial will be easiest when the trial is based on knowledge pull rather than knowledge push, ie driven by a specific business need for knowledge. Many companies seem to start instinctively with knowledge push, and with sharing and replicating best practices. Seductive though this idea is, it doesn't deliver the quick wins to the business. You might capture best practices on mergers, for example, but it may be a long time before another merger, and there may be no short-term opportunity for knowledge re-use. And even if there is an opportunity, there may be a 'not invented here' barrier to deal with.

Instead find part of the business that has a problem, and help them use KM processes to acquire knowledge in order to solve the problem. This acquired knowledge will find an instant application and a willing audience, and there should be little or no 'not invented here' to contest against.

# Selecting KM pilot projects

Pilots are intended to test and refine the KM framework. The purpose of piloting the KM framework is to:

- understand what works (and what doesn't work) in terms of KM within your organization;
- test the framework and look for ways to improve it;
- deliver success stories for future influencing; and
- gather enough evidence of value that senior management will then commit to the roll-out of KM.

An effective pilot will address a knowledge domain or practice area – one that could cover many business teams and divisions – rather than covering a single business project or team. It will therefore test the validity and value of the KM framework in a cross-organizational setting. Suitable business problems for KM pilots, where better access to knowledge can significantly help performance, are listed below. Some of these may have been identified during your strategy stage when identifying the key business drivers (see Chapter 4). All of these are 'areas of business improvement' which KM can address, rather than an opportunity to apply a single KM tool in a specific situation.

- A business-critical activity which is new to the organization, where rapid learning will deliver business benefits. If the activity is new to only one part of the organization, then transferring learning from where it has been done before may give huge benefits.

- Repetitive business activity where continuous improvement is needed, and where KM can help accelerate the learning curve.

- Activity which is carried out in several locations, and where performance level varies, in which case KM can help exchange knowledge from the good performers to improve the poor performers.

- A business area which is subject to rapid change, where innovation and rapid learning are critical to survival, in which case KM can help by providing team sharing and learning processes, as well as access to relevant knowledge bases.

- An area of rapid business growth where deep experience and skills need to be scaled up to deliver on projects and services.

When you start looking around, you will find very many business opportunities for KM piloting. Your 'opportunity jar' will soon be full to overflowing, and you will need to find a way to compare and rank these piloting opportunities to find the most promising. We have a set of ranking criteria we have been using for about 15 years, which includes looking at the following questions:

- If the project is successful, can we measure the value, and so demonstrate that the pilot has 'worked'?

- Is there strong management support for the pilot, and for KM, within the potential pilot area?
- If we create, capture or share knowledge, is it purely for the pilot team or can others use it across the business, allowing us to leverage the results and spread the benefits?
- Will what we learn in the pilot allow us to scale KM across the organization?
- Finally, is there a high probability of successfully completing the pilot in the required timeframe and with the resources available (money, staff, KM support, etc)?

Any pilot where you can answer a strong YES to all of these questions will be a top-ranking pilot, suitable for selection as part of your KM programme.

---

**Tip**

Make sure you don't miss the high-level pilots. Lots of managers assume that KM is 'something my staff need' and that pilot projects will address routine tasks at low levels in the organization. However KM is of value at all levels, and managers are knowledge workers too. When you are proposing KM pilots, look also for pilots at senior level – pilots that look at divestments and acquisitions, for example, or business restructuring. Delivering a high-level KM pilot on areas such as these can deliver massive value, and also get senior managers on your side by solving their problems for them.

---

# The 'minimum viable KM framework'

There is a concept in lean manufacturing and in start-up companies known as the 'minimum viable product', which is the simplest and easiest version of the product you can build that delivers customer value. The manufacturer builds and releases (often to a customer subset such as the early adopters) a simple bare-bones version of a product in order to get customer feedback, learn about the product in use, get some revenue, and gain experience that will inform the next version of the product.

In many ways, these are the objectives of the first few KM pilots. The first KM pilot can be seen as an early version prototype of the full KM framework, released to gain learning and user feedback as well as to create business value. There is real benefit in releasing a 'minimum viable KM framework' as early as possible in the piloting stage. 'Viable' means the framework should be complete, rather than one or two elements. 'Minimum' means it should be as simple as possible while still adding value. You don't need to wait for the full technology or the fully documented process – start with something simple and gain learning and feedback.

For example, if you want to pilot KM in an area of the business where knowledge needs to be shared between multiple business units you could take one of two approaches. The all-too-common approach is to introduce a technology (Yammer, for example, or Jive) and anticipate that people will start to use it. However, this is neither minimum (both of these technologies are well developed, with many features), nor is it viable (technology alone is not a full framework). Better to introduce a simple framework such as a community coordinator (role) who sets up monthly discussions (process) using dial-in conference calls (technology) to discuss an identified agenda of critical knowledge issues (governance). Once the community realizes this minimum system adds value, then they can start to build upon this system, adding complexity and sophistication until they have a KM framework that fully meets their needs. This is exactly the approach taken in the case study below.

## CASE STUDY

One of our former colleagues was a KM champion in an organization that was just starting KM. Enthused by the first company KM workshops, he decided to conduct his own KM pilot. He set up a simple framework with a group of colleagues who, every 10 or 11 weeks, would hold a telephone conference call about key operational problems and how to solve them. They called themselves the Operations Forum. The knowledge sharing which took place attracted more people to the call from different countries, some of them staying up into the night to join in. One night the head of operations sat in on one of the calls, and was excited by the knowledge sharing that he was hearing. He gave his endorsement to setting up an operations excellence community of practice, supported by a portal website as a common area to gather knowledge and ask questions. The community then started to grow, driven by the success stories that were being delivered, and its successor communities are still working nearly 20 years later.

That first conference call involving 10 people on telephones was the 'minimum viable framework' from which a sophisticated community of practice grew. It proved a much more robust starting point than beginning with a portal might have.

# Delivering KM pilots

## *The three key roles*

There will be three major roles in the pilot project.

The first is that of the **business sponsor,** who acts as the customer within the business. They play an active role in setting the direction for the pilot, providing resources, and agreeing objectives and deliverables. The business sponsor is likely to be the manager of the business unit hosting the pilot, and it is crucial that they are committed to the success of the project.

The second is that of the **local pilot project manager.** This person will be accountable for delivering the results of the project. It is important that this role is owned by somebody within the business, so that the project is seen as internal to the business, rather than something 'which is being done to us by outside specialists'.

The third role is that of the **KM team member** who works closely with the local project manager in implementing the project and provides the KM processes, tools and technologies. The KM team member can carry learning from the pilot project back to the KM team, and may work full time on the pilot project, depending on its complexity and scope.

## *Sequence of activities*

The following section describes a generic set of activities within a KM pilot project.

**Scope the pilot** to determine the constraints and context. The scoping phase may take a week or more, as you get to know the nature of the business in detail. Find out:

- the key stakeholders in the pilot part of the organization;
- the main business issues which KM needs to address;
- the current flow of knowledge within the working practices, its bottlenecks and hold-ups;
- the leverage points for KM;
- the business metrics KM will address (you may even conduct a benefits mapping for the pilot, using the process from Chapter 9);
- the current (baseline) level of those metrics;
- how well those metrics could be improved with good access to knowledge; and
- whether there are other initiatives going on which could conflict with KM.

After the scoping phase, the three roles described earlier work together to **develop a terms of reference document** for the pilot programme, containing the following sections:

- **context** – background and a brief introduction to the groups or practice area conducting the pilot;
- **stakeholders** – list of key stakeholders and their requirements;
- **key knowledge topics to be addressed** – including a glossary, if required;
- **KPIs to be impacted, and conditions for success** – including an analysis of baseline metrics, so you know what the 'pre-KM' metrics were;
- **pilot project approach and scope** – the approach to be used, the (minimum viable) KM framework to be applied, and the in-scope and out-of-scope elements;
- **deliverables from the pilot** – including dates and accountabilities;
- **implementation plan** – tasks, durations and resources;
- **risks and obstacles to be addressed** – including mitigating actions; and
- **resources** – funding and manpower.

**Introduce the concept of KM.** Work with people in the business area to explore what the value of KM might be to them. Run some proof of concept exercises. Discuss the proposed KM framework, and be prepared to adapt this if necessary based on feedback. Select suitable and simple KM technologies, considering local culture, local practices and local work habits. Identify and engage, or launch, any communities of practice that will support the pilot. Use activities such as peer assists to engage people in the community of practice. Use technology to support community discussion and question-and-answer dialogue. Identify appropriate needs for confidentiality.

**Train and coach the team members to do it for themselves.** Initially the KM team member will need to facilitate the KM processes. Eventually this activity can be transferred to the people in the business; the KM champions perhaps, or the supervisors or project leaders. Tailor the training to the experience of the audience and choose a training style that they are familiar with. Try to gain access to people at all relevant levels in the organization; not just the managers, but the factory floor workers, the sales staff, the craftsmen, etc.

Knowledge leadership can occur at any level. Make sure the KM team provides regular and on-call support until the framework is fully embedded, but limit your role to support – the people in the business have to 'do' the KM. In particular you need to continue to support and coach the local pilot project manager.

**Build the knowledge bank in cooperation with the local business.** You will need some sort of store of explicit knowledge as part of the KM framework. You may pre-populate the knowledge bank to be able to demonstrate the value, but afterwards hand over construction and maintenance of the knowledge bank as soon as possible to someone within the business. The more you do for the business, the harder it will be to get them to take over.

**Review the project against its deliverables.** If all goes well, which it certainly should, then your pilot project should be on track to deliver its objectives of significant measurable business value through the management of knowledge. If you conducted a benefits mapping exercise during the scoping phase of the project, then this will help you track how things are going and adjust your focus accordingly. Help the local project manager to deliver the project on time, on budget, and on specification. Hold periodic reviews, just as you would with any other sort of business project. Look for evidence that the project is on track against timeline and budget, that the objectives will be met, and that the benefits will be delivered.

**Monitor and report the delivery of value.** If you selected business metrics you hoped to impact (lower delivery time, higher delivery quality, greater sales volume and so on) and determined the baseline for these, then you need to monitor when the business metrics start to improve on the baseline. This improvement may not be solely due to KM, so you also need to find stories that connect specific KM interventions with specific business outcomes.

**Look for ways in which the project can be used as a 'showcase' for other projects.** If the project has gone well and delivered value, you want to be able to use it as marketing material, or as an example that other projects will want to follow. Collect as much material as you can that can be used as 'social proof', while still giving the business the credit for delivery. This material might include:

- a measurement of the value delivered, in hard business metrics (money saved, cycle time shortened, business created, etc);
- a written or recorded statement from the business sponsor that 'KM has generated real business value, demonstrated by the following business metrics';
- anecdotes and stories of the value created by the exchange of knowledge, from people at all levels in the organization. Record these on video as social proof for your communication and influencing (Chapter 18);
- the history of the pilot project, told if possible by the local project manager or business sponsor.

**Learn from the pilot project.** Hold your own AAR at the end of each stage, and hold a retrospect at the end of the pilot to capture what you have learned. Feed this knowledge into the company knowledge asset on 'implementing KM'.

# Reaching the organizational decision point

If you selected your pilot projects wisely, organized them well and supported them in delivery, you should now have some good case studies of real business value delivered through the use of KM. Your KM implementation programme has reached the crucial decision point – the decision whether or not to fully adopt KM as a required discipline for the whole organization.

This decision is the point of no return for KM, and needs to be taken at the highest levels in the organization. Firstly, your steering committee needs to be convinced that you have enough evidence from the pilots to support this decision, then they need to support you in taking this decision to senior management.

Put together a business case which will be convincing to top management, based on your pilot evidence. Use the value delivered through the pilots to estimate the total value of KM to the organization. For example if you were able to use KM during the pilot phase to reduce the cost of a project by 12 per cent, then make an estimate of how much you could reduce the cost of all projects. Maybe it would be a bit much to attempt to reduce them all by 12 per cent – the pilot project was after all chosen because it was a particularly attractive case for KM application – but what if you would reduce the project bill by 6 per cent? Or 4 per cent?

Then estimate the costs to the organization in making this reduction. The costs will include any further spend on new technology, the cost of the roll-out effort, and the annual cost of a KM operational team. You do not need to include the costs of the people playing a KM role in the business, unless you are arguing for the creation of new roles where they did not exist before, such as a full-time community of practice leaders or a full-time lessons management team. You also need to list on the debit side of the equation any changes that will have to be made to embed KM, as discussed in the next chapter. These changes may not cost money, but they may cause disruption, and they will need senior management support.

Hopefully this business case will provide the basis for a firm commitment to KM. If not, then ask the senior management what evidence would convince them that KM was valuable enough to adopt, and then continue piloting until you have gathered that evidence.

## Summary

In the trials and piloting phase, KM comes out into the open. The proof of concept trials and the full business-led pilots are where the knowledge workers at all levels begin to see KM at work in their own context. The proof of concept trials provide the continual feed of quick wins and demonstrations of progress, while the bigger pilots not only provide the testing ground for the KM framework (remember to start piloting with the minimum viable framework), they also deliver the success stories and social proof that will convince the managers and workers alike that an investment in KM is a wise investment.

# Roll-out, embedding and governance

We suggested in Chapter 3 that the goal of your implementation programme should be to embed a robust approach to KM in all elements of the business, adding demonstrable value to the business and supported by a sustainable KM culture. This chapter describes what embedding means, and how it is done.

In this chapter we cover the following elements:

- what embedding means;
- some examples of KM embedding;
- finalizing the KM framework;
- governance;
- the KM policy and expectations;
- rolling out KM; and
- tracking and reporting progress.

## What does embedding mean?

Embedding KM means making it part of normal work, rather than an add-on. You do this through embedding each of the four KM framework elements: roles, processes, technology and governance, in support of the main knowledge transactions (both push and pull).

Firstly, KM roles and accountabilities must be integrated into the organization chart. You will need to introduce new full-time roles or additional responsibilities where needed (for example, lesson management teams, leaders and coordinators for large communities of practice, practice owners, information architects and so on). You will need to change some of the accountabilities of existing roles such as the senior experts, so that they are held accountable for stewardship of your organization's knowledge. You will ensure that these new accountabilities are written into their job descriptions, so they are measured and rewarded for the KM component of their job, as they would be for any other component.

Secondly, you should write KM processes into the work cycles and work processes. For example, you might change the project management requirements to include mandatory processes for capture of knowledge at the end of the project or after key milestones, and mandatory processes for reviewing past knowledge at the start of the project. You might change the rules for project support, so a project gets no money if it hasn't done any pre-learning or knowledge seeking. You might change the product delivery process, so that product development includes a stage for identifying knowledge gaps, and so that the product work stream is supported by a knowledge work stream working in parallel with it (see the case study later in this chapter).

Thirdly, you will need to change the technology suite so that KM tools are available and used as part of the working toolkit, and integrated into the existing working tools. As we suggested in Chapter 3, if e-mail remains the number one work tool for your organization, then link your KM tools into e-mail rather than requiring people to acquire new working habits. Build technology additions outwards from existing habits.

Finally, you will need to change elements of your organization's governance. Make KM part of the company values. Write it into the company policies. Write a KM policy to be signed off by the senior management team. KM governance elements are discussed in greater detail later in this chapter.

Do all of these things, and KM will be fully embedded as part of 'the way you work'. However, to make all these changes you will need the support of senior managers as described at the end of Chapter 22.

# Examples of embedded KM

Two illustrative examples are described here, showing how two of the six components of KM described in Chapter 1 – communities of practice and lesson learning – have been embedded in organizations.

## Communities of practice

- The organization's critical knowledge areas have been identified, and are each owned by senior staff (eg the head of engineering, the head of sales and so on) who have targets and deliverables relating to the company's knowledge capability.
- The leaders of the communities of practice report to these senior staff, and have a performance contract with the senior staff, stating how they will develop the communities.
- The community leaders take accountability for the development of the communities and of their knowledge base.
- They may have a budget which they can spend on community development and development of the knowledge base.
- The communities work through defined processes such as Q&A and face-to-face knowledge sharing, and are supported by a suite of collaboration tools such as discussion forums, expertise finders or wikis.

In such a system the communities of practice perform a key role in developing the organization's competence through enabling knowledge sharing and knowledge building; the network leader can track activity and value through community metrics, success stories and performance metrics, and they can report this to the senior staff who have oversight and exercise accountability to the business.

## Indicators that lesson learning and learning from experience are fully embedded

- The organization has targets for project delivery (cost, time or quality targets).
- These targets are owned by the head of projects.
- A lessons management team reports to the head of projects, and takes accountability for the delivery of effective lesson learning.
- The project leaders are accountable for making sure the project teams learn before, during and after project activities, re-use previous lessons, and document and publish new lessons.
- Delivery against these accountabilities is measured using standard project management methods such as stage-gate reviews.

If this accountability chain works well, the lessons management team can track the development of effective learning through metrics, and through improved project delivery (including shortened learning curves for repeat projects). They report this to the head of projects, who reports against their own targets and deliverables.

In both of these illustrative examples, KM is given a clear and specific job to do ('improve or protect strategic organizational capabilities through CoPs', 'improve company performance through project learning'), there are individuals who are accountable for that job, and the reporting chain supports oversight, accountability and performance management. The job is clear, accountabilities are clear, the KM framework is defined, performance is tracked, and KM is embedded.

## CASE STUDY

The pioneer in KM for product development is Toyota. Based on their KM successes in manufacturing, they developed the Toyota product development system, which is an efficient and effective combination of lean manufacturing and KM (Morgan and Liker, 2006). More recently this has evolved into the concept of 'knowledge-based product development' (Kennedy *et al*, 2008; Melvin, 2013).

KM expectations, processes and roles are embedded into knowledge-based product development as follows:

- the product development process includes a knowledge gap analysis step, a knowledge-gathering stage, and a stage-gate meeting to ensure all knowledge gaps are closed;
- a defined set of knowledge products are created throughout the process, in the form of 'knowledge briefs';
- accountability for the knowledge briefs is clear and is monitored by the chief engineer; and
- the knowledge briefs and a knowledge-based product description called a check sheet collectively form the knowledge products that accompany the physical product.

# Finalizing the KM framework

Embedding KM roles, accountabilities, processes and technologies assumes that you know what these elements should be, and that you modify the company structures to include these elements. However, before you can modify anything, you need sign-off from the senior managers of the organization that your KM framework is acceptable and will become adopted. Here your steering committee becomes crucial. If it contains the right people, such as the head of HR, the head of IT and the head of projects, then you are in a good position. They will have been involved in your steering committee throughout your journey, and so will have a good understanding of what is needed to bring KM to the next level. However you and they still have some work to do, namely, working with:

- HR to develop the new job descriptions;
- HR to define any changes to the rewards and recognition scheme needed to remove disincentives for KM such as internal competition or forced ranking of staff;
- the head of projects and the head of operations to finalize new requirements to be incorporated into the project management process and the operations management process;
- the head of IT to add the necessary capabilities to the technology suite;
- the functional heads, or 'heads of discipline' to develop the ownership structure for knowledge domains, and to identify the communities of practice and practice owners; and
- your sponsor to determine the changes in long-term roles and responsibilities for the KM team itself.

If these core people were not in your steering team, this engagement will take a lot longer and be a lot more challenging, as you may need to talk each person through the whole history of KM in order to win them over.

Once all these agreements have been made, then they should be enshrined in a KM policy.

# The governance elements of the KM framework

In Chapter 1 we introduced the idea that governance is one of the four enablers of KM, and in Chapter 12 we stated that governance is one of the core dimensions of the KM framework. Chapters 13–16 worked through examples of how governance gets translated into KM activities. Once your KM framework has been finalized and agreed with the steering committee and senior management, then you can look at KM governance in a broader sense. This higher-level governance contains three aspects:

- The first aspect is the rules, guidelines and expectations for KM within the organization, which will be rolled out together with the definition of roles, processes and technologies, and which may be laid out in a KM policy document.
- The second aspect is performance management for KM, which includes monitoring and measuring KM activity, and linking it to recognition and reward (discussed in Chapter 24).
- The third aspect is providing continuing support for the business, including KM training, coaching, and the provision of specialist services. The permanent KM support organization is covered in more detail in Chapter 25.

# The KM policy

There are three main reasons why people don't do KM – they don't want to do it, they don't know what to do, or they don't know how to do it. The first is solved through performance management, the last through training. To address the second reason – not knowing what to do – you need a KM policy. The policy defines, at a high level, what the organization expects from its staff in the area of KM. The policy clarifies areas such as:

- the importance of KM;
- the KM approach to use;
- the expected level of KM activity;
- the size of project where lesson learning becomes mandatory;
- whether community membership is encouraged/expected;

- the rules for document classification and storage; and
- how the competing requirements of information security should be balanced with knowledge sharing.

As well as clarifying expectations, the KM policy also acts as a visible public management commitment to KM.

There is no 'one size fits all' approach to KM policy writing. Focus on the areas where you expect there may be doubts, uncertainty or competing priorities.

Typical elements in a KM policy would be:

- purpose and desired outcomes from the policy;
- scope of the policy;
- concise and clear statement of the policy in one or two sentences;
- guiding principles behind the policy;
- roles and responsibilities under the policy;
- guidelines and examples for implementing the policy;
- glossary of key terms and definitions; and
- how the KM policy connects to other corporate policies.

**Tip**

When you create the first draft of your KM policy, share it with your KM champions. Tell them that they will be the first line of support for explaining the policy to their colleagues, and ask them to brainstorm all the questions they might be asked. Use the most frequently asked questions as input to refining and sharpening your draft policy, so that it focuses on issues of concern to staff.

## CASE STUDY

One of the more complete KM policies you can find on the internet is the NASA KM policy (NASA, 2013). Knowledge is very important for the success and safety of NASA missions, and they have a strong corporate commitment to KM, laid out in the policy, which contains the following elements:

- a strong first sentence – 'Compliance is Mandatory' – which makes the intent of the policy very clear;

- an owner for the policy, namely the Office of the Chief Engineer;

- a description of the intent of KM to 'cultivate, identify, retain, and share knowledge in order to continuously improve the performance of NASA';

- the responsibility of all NASA staff for 'retaining, appropriately sharing or protecting, and utilizing knowledge';

- an identification of critical KM activities to be applied, including learning from experience and knowledge retention; and

- the requirement that each NASA organization 'shall implement continuous improvement of knowledge management processes'.

Model your KM policy on the style of other internal policies already in existence in your organization, such as the HR policy or the IT security policy. Make sure that your internal policies reference each other where appropriate, and make sure that there are no inconsistencies or conflicts with existing policies.

Use the policy to define the minimum acceptable level of KM activity that is expected of an employee. Do not set the expectation too high – a policy should be something that people can easily exceed but are required to comply with. Find a high-level champion who will own the policy; in the NASA case above this is the chief engineer.

# KM roll-out

Once the final KM framework has been defined and the roles, processes, technologies and governance are clear, KM roll-out becomes largely a process of education through communicating, training, coaching, and developing performance support tools and reference materials.

## Communicating

The communication programnme described in Chapter 19 changes gear as you enter the roll-out phase. Continue to publish success stories as fast as you can collect them, but you will also need to:

- publicize the new KM expectations and policy;
- introduce the new roles (for example by publishing an interview with a community leader);

- explain the new processes and technologies;
- give use-case examples of how the policy requirements should be acted upon;
- advertise the training events; and
- try to get some articles from senior managers to endorse the message that 'the organization has now committed to knowledge management'.

## Training

You will need to provide training at three levels.

- General awareness training for the knowledge workers in the organization, introducing the elements of the KM framework, explaining the new KM expectations, and demonstrating the value that KM can bring to the knowledge worker. Make the training interactive; one organization we worked with created a 'knowledge treasure hunt' which challenged people to find five key nuggets of knowledge using the new tools, thus giving people hands-on experience of the tools while showcasing some of the knowledge content.
- Specific training for the people with KM roles – the community leaders, the practice owners, the process facilitators and knowledge engineers – in order to give them the skills they need to do their jobs. The different roles may need separate training; for example a course on community building, a course on lesson capture, and so on.
- Awareness training for the managers to explain the expectation they need to set for KM within their teams, and their own roles in modelling and supporting the KM culture.

## Coaching

People with specialist KM roles will need ongoing support. You can provide coaching and regular check-ins from the KM team, and should also invite the people with KM roles to join the KM community of practice. As this community grows in size and activity it should become self-supporting while also allowing the KM team to monitor the development of KM practice within the organization.

## Developing reference resources

Every new role needs a role description, every new process needs a process description and facilitator guide, and every new technology needs a manual that can be easily understood by the users. You need to write these and put them on a wiki (so they can be continually improved), and potentially also develop e-learning content for the people who can't attend face-to-face training.

# Celebrating the successes

Roll-out is the time to begin the regular celebrations of KM within the organization. These could take any of the following forms:

- An annual internal KM conference, to bring together the KM champions and the KM professionals to exchange knowledge, experience and stories. This can be a powerful event to strengthen the KM CoP, and a good way to gather success stories and present awards.

- For large organizations, an annual knowledge fair to show off the benefits of KM to the organization at large. This is an opportunity for CoPs, networks, and innovation and learning teams to share what they have achieved through the year, and for knowledge-intensive parts of the business to show off their wares and contributions. Knowledge fairs can also be combined with 'knowledge markets' where participants are encouraged to register knowledge gaps and needs, and also areas of knowledge that they are prepared to share. During the event, 'askers' and 'offerors' can be matched up by topic through the clever use of noticeboards, nametags, or even software apps.

- Some organizations have implemented annual 'fail fairs', inspired by the 'annual failure reports' first issued by Canadian development organization Engineers Without Borders in 2011. Major failures that were learning opportunities for the organization throughout the year are presented, diagnosed, and the key learnings and follow through actions are described and celebrated. While this is not something that all organizational cultures would embrace, it sends a very strong signal about the organization's commitment to learning processes.

- An annual collection of success stories, as in the case study that follows.

## CASE STUDY

The US construction company Fluor started their 'Knowvember' campaign in 2001 to collect KM success stories. As Will (2008) explains:

*In addition to recognizing outstanding knowledge-sharing behaviours, one of the primary functions of the campaign is to gather and share 'Success Stories' of the specific ways employees have benefited from using Knowledge OnLine [the Fluor KM framework]. These are intended to emphasize the ease and benefits achieved from using Knowledge OnLine. For example, one award-winning story was from a member of the engineering community in South Africa. He was commissioning a plant and found that a* *transfer line from a fired heater was leaking. The cost of having to flare natural gas is approximately US $120,000 per day; therefore, time was of the essence to obtain a solution. Not having the expertise available locally, he posted a discussion forum topic to the piping community with an urgent response time requirement of three days. Within two days, he received responses from Houston, Haarlem and New Delhi providing the answers needed to fix the plan.*

Stories such as this, shared during Knowvember, act to celebrate success, and spread the message that knowledge management is both important and valuable.

## Tracking the roll-out phase

During the roll-out phase, the purpose of KM implementation is to spread the KM transformation across the entire organization, while continuing to add business value. You need to track this roll-out, in order to identify areas still to engage, and to report progress. This tracking is not to be confused with the permanent measurement and evaluation system you will put in place once KM is fully embedded and operational (Chapter 24). There are three main ways to track roll-out.

The first way is to track the percentage of the organization which has reached a defined KM level. The levels might be the same eight levels we discussed in Chapter 18 for measuring stakeholder buy-in, and the aim for the roll-out phase is to get every part of the business to the 'Adoption' level. You could also track roll-out metrics such as the number of training courses run in each region, the number of people trained, the number of communities launched, the number of KM champions and so on.

The second is to collect activity metrics for those elements that cross-cut the organizational divisions, such as the communities of practice and the lessons learned system. Such metric schemes will be discussed in more detail in the next chapter.

The third is to track the value added by KM to the business. Although the crucial moment for demonstrating value was when you made the business case for KM adoption at the end of the piloting stage (Chapter 22), you need to continue to reinforce the message that KM adds value. The success stories you collect at the KM conference and via awards programmes will provide plenty of material for your communication campaign, and you should also keep a running tally of the total value. Someone at some time is sure to ask you 'just how much value has KM delivered so far?' It would be good to have an answer ready to hand!

> **Tip**
>
> Be prepared to let go of the 'KM' term as KM becomes embedded. In an organization with fully embedded KM, you don't hear a lot of mention of 'knowledge management'. However, you hear a lot about the tools and processes. Instead of people saying 'we must do KM', you hear 'we should hold an AAR', 'we should ask the community', 'why don't we put this on the wiki'. The conversation is now about the activities and the tools and not about the system itself, and the term 'knowledge management' takes a back seat.

## Summary

The roll-out stage of KM implementation involves finalizing the framework, deciding the governance elements such as the KM policy, determining how KM will be embedded in the organization, and then running a large-scale campaign of communicating, engaging, training and coaching. This stage of the implementation may take several years for a large organization, but once this roll-out and embedding campaign is complete, KM has truly become part of the way the organization works on a day-by-day basis.

# Setting up the KM metrics and reporting system

A robust measurement and reporting regime is an essential component of sustainable, embedded KM within an organization, because it supports the continuing oversight and administration for KM activities, and allows the future KM operational support team to:

1 know where to support and intervene;
2 report the status of KM to senior management on a regular basis;
3 evaluate the continuing benefits and impact of KM to the business; and
4 identify any changes to the framework that might be needed as the business changes.

In this chapter we cover:

- the different kinds of metrics and their purposes;
- examples of KM metrics;
- KM performance management;
- KM metrics reporting; and
- KM metrics as a learning opportunity.

## The different kinds of metrics and their purposes

There are four main types of KM metrics, and each has a specific purpose. It is important not to confuse them, for reasons we explain below. Together they form an integrated system of measurement for ongoing administration, learning and governance. The four types are:

- activity metrics;
- performance (or compliance) metrics;

- impact metrics;
- maturity metrics.

## Activity metrics

The purpose of activity metrics is to monitor KM activity and trends and so track the level of application of KM processes and use of KM technologies. Activities might be contributions to an online knowledge base, lessons learned activities in projects, frequency of community of practice meetings, peer assists, question asking and answering, and so on. Specific examples of these metrics are given later on in this chapter.

Activity metrics will generally be collected by people with KM roles in the business such as the community leaders and knowledge base administrators, who may create a dashboard that shows key activity metrics on a month-to-month basis. The KM team (initially the KM implementation team, but handing over to the KM operational support team) should review these dashboards to identify trends that may need attention – either downward activity trends that may need further enquiry and support, or upward trends that may need some reallocation of resources or indicate opportunities for further value creation.

---

**Tip**

It is natural that specific KM activities will ebb and flow in regular cycles, so do not be alarmed immediately if some activities seem to trend downwards. These downticks are simply signals for you to monitor more closely and check in with the relevant people in the business, but you should not panic at the first sign. As time goes on, you will start to see how a natural cycle develops in the metrics, and will become better at spotting significant shifts that may warrant further investigation and intervention.

---

## Performance metrics

The purpose of performance metrics is to ensure you have compliance to your KM policy, identify areas where staff may need support or guidance, and spotlight exceptional performance. Performance metrics should relate to critical non-negotiable compliance essential for the value-add of KM to the business, and should enable line managers to recognize and reward exceptional contributions. Instances of non-compliance to the KM policy need to be picked up and addressed quickly, so habits of non-compliance do not build up. Hence the metrics need to be built into the business process monitoring dashboards.

Do not confuse activity metrics with performance metrics. It is a common mistake to turn non-critical activity metrics (such as number of contributions to the knowledge base, or attendance at community of practice meetings) into key performance indicators or targets for employees and teams. When this happens, staff will go through the motions of completing the activities but the quality of the contributions will likely suffer, and your activity metrics will no longer represent genuine trends in the underlying KM activity.

---

**Tip**

Handle the instances of non-compliance with your KM policy quickly and sensitively, and investigate with the relevant line manager what the probable cause of the non-compliance is. Don't jump to the conclusion that it is an attitude problem. It may be an awareness problem, in which case the staff will need guidance and support, or a skills problem, in which case they will need training or skilled assistance, or a prioritization problem, in which case they may need some additional resourcing. Deliberate recurring non-compliance, however, may need firmer treatment.

---

## Impact metrics

The purpose of impact metrics is to enable senior management to assess the continuing contribution of KM to the business, and should link back to the intended benefits and outcomes of KM outlined in your KM policy. Right from the very beginning of your KM implementation you will have been projecting the intended benefits of KM to the business. It is essential that you do not lose track of this once KM has become embedded.

Impact metrics can be 'hard' in terms of quantifiable benefits to the business (eg reduced costs, improved sales, improved quality), in which case they will be derived from specific examples continuously gathered from your KM activity streams. Impact metrics may also be 'soft' in the form of evaluations from managers in the different lines of business as to the added value that KM brings to the way that work is conducted. 'Soft' evaluation metrics like this can be gathered through surveys, interviews or focus groups. These mechanisms, if conducted periodically, are also useful ways to identify opportunities to streamline, enhance or fine-tune the KM processes or the support that is offered by the KM operational team.

## Maturity metrics

The purpose of maturity metrics is to trace the progress in KM maturity of the organization over time. This can be done for your organizational culture for example, or it can be done for an aspect of KM such as communities of practice.

You can monitor the maturity of your culture by conducting regular culture reviews as described in Chapter 19. Here you will not have prescribed targets but you will be looking for positive trends in the culture. If you see the emergence of worrying trends this is a signal that you should investigate further, for example through focus groups. Organizational cultures generally evolve slowly, so biennial or triennial reviews are probably going to pick up more changes than annual reviews.

Some KM activity streams such as communities of practice also have maturity levels. Wenger *et al* (2002) identified five typical stages in the lifecycle of a community of practice (potential, coalescing, maturing, stewardship, transformation) and Gongla and Rizzuto (2001) developed a detailed maturity model based on these lifecycle stages, both of which provide good options for measuring CoP maturity.

The purpose of a maturity model is to be able to track longer-term 'big picture' trends over time. Similarly to activity metrics, it is important that you do not turn your maturity metrics into targets – as soon as they become known as targets, then the respondents who are giving you the feedback for the components of your model will be incentivized to give you indicators that are positive rather than negative.

# Examples of KM metrics

Metrics related to KM can be collected through a variety of mechanisms, and depending on the elements in your KM framework, you will need to decide on a core set of metrics and introduce them as part of the roll-out. Here are some examples of metrics grouped by KM activity streams.

## Project KM metrics

These may be collected by the project knowledge manager, by a lessons management team, or by the project management office, and reported to the head of projects. The key metrics will be as follows:

- Compliance with the project-based expectations of the KM framework, such as the creation of a project KM plan, conducting peer assists, or holding lessons-capture meetings. The target should be 100 per cent compliance (performance metric).

- Completion of all actions within the project KM plan, again with a target of 100 per cent compliance (performance metric).

- Number of lessons learned activities, lessons added to the lessons database, and instances of lessons re-use (activity metrics).

- Evidence of value added through KM activities in projects, and presented as success stories (impact metric).

## Community of practice metrics

These will be collected by the CoP leader or facilitator and reported to their sponsor. Key metrics are as follows:

- Community maturity level, reported on an annual basis (maturity metric).
- Evidence of community value, delivered through solutions to members' problems, and presented as success stories (impact metric).
- Examples of exceptional contributions to the community, collected for example through nominations of members or through evaluation of community activity metrics (performance metric).

In addition, the community leader may collect community activity metrics such as:

- number of community members;
- number of active community members;
- number of community activities and levels of participation in those activities;
- number of questions asked per month;
- number of answers per question;
- individuals who make most contributions;
- time between question and first answer;
- number of forum posts per month;
- number of readers of the community blog;
- frequency of articles on the community blog.

## Knowledge library / knowledge base metrics

Knowledge base metrics may be automatically generated by your knowledge base software, or may need to be created manually. They will be collected by the relevant practice owners or the knowledge base administrator, and may include the following:

- user feedback and satisfaction ratings, collected through a user rating system (performance metric);
- evidence of value, gathered through user feedback, and presented as success stories (impact metric).

In addition, the practice owner or the knowledge base administrator may collect activity metrics such as:

- number of reads per knowledge asset or knowledge item;
- number of comments;
- frequency of edits and update;
- number of new items;
- most regular users;
- individuals who make most contributions to the knowledge base;
- re-use rate of knowledge assets;
- frequency of searches of the knowledge base;
- search success rate.

## Metrics associated with the lessons learned cycle

Lesson-learning metrics are often automatically created by the lessons management software, should be collected by the lessons management team, and should be reported to the head of projects. Metrics may include:

- lessons submitted per month (by project, product line, and/or region) (activity metric);
- number of lessons embedded into procedure vs number waiting to be embedded (activity metric);
- time taken to close lessons (activity metric);
- individuals who make most contribution to lesson learning, tracked through a combination of numbers and evidence of value and re-use (performance metric);
- lesson re-use rate (activity metric);
- evidence of value delivered through the lessons learned system, and presented as success stories (impact metric).

## KM metrics collected through staff survey

Metrics can also be collected through regular staff surveys. Surveys can be a good way to assess the maturity level of the organization culture, for example by a re-run of the culture survey described in Chapter 19, or by including a couple of questions on KM culture in annual staff questionnaires. Surveys of managers in the different lines of business can be used to gather evaluations of the impact of KM upon the business, to complement the specific examples of impact gathered through other means.

# KM performance management

If KM is to become truly embedded into behaviours and culture, it needs to be linked to rewards and recognition. People who perform well at the KM aspects of their job should feel that this is recognized, and people who perform poorly should feel that this impacts their rewards. The metrics described above should allow good performers and poor performers to be identified. KM activity can then be linked to recognition and reward in the following ways:

- All individuals with an accountable KM role (knowledge managers, knowledge engineers, CoP leaders, process owners, lessons management team members, knowledge base administrators and so on) should have this role explicitly documented in their personal objectives, to be reviewed during annual appraisal and rewarded through the normal means of salary increments, bonuses and promotion.

- KM activity in projects such as lessons review and lessons capture should be reviewed at project stage gates and reported in project dashboards, and thus linked to the project manager's performance. It is worth recalling the quote from Bob Buckman, CEO of Buckman Labs, which we mentioned in Chapter 18: 'the people who engage in active and effective knowledge sharing across the organization should be the only ones considered for promotion' (Buckman, 2004, p 145). Poor KM performance should therefore be challenged, as well as good performance rewarded.

- It may also be possible to reward KM activity directly. Dora *et al* (2002) describe how employees of Siemens Information and Communication Networks were incentivized to submit tips and hints to the online knowledge base through the award of 'premium points' which could be redeemed for prizes within a bonus catalogue. However, care must be taken that such submissions are of high quality, and in Siemens each tip was validated against a set of agreed criteria.

- A KM award scheme can be created and run on a regular basis, to recognize good KM performance. Non-monetary KM awards should be given to people who have delivered real value through KM, as in the case study example that follows.

## CASE STUDY

An excellent example of a KM awards scheme is the Conoco Archimedes awards (Conoco, 2012). This contains the following awards categories:

- the Grab award for the person or team who generated the most value through re-using knowledge from elsewhere;

- the Give award for the person or team who shared the knowledge of greatest value to others;

- the Integration award for the community of practice that has generated the most value through knowledge sharing;

- the Guts award for the person or team that has shown the most courage in sharing lessons from failure.

# KM metrics reporting

In addition to defining the metrics, you need to define who will collect the metrics, and how, when and to whom they will be reported. A typical reporting structure is shown in Figure 24.1.

In this structure the KM operational support team collates metrics supplied by the knowledge base administrator, the CoP leaders, the lessons management team, the projects and staff surveys, and provides a collated report to the KM steering committee. This report could take the form of a master KM dashboard or KM balanced scorecard.

Some metrics work on longer reporting cycles than others. Activity metrics should be collected continuously, but generally reported on and acted on periodically (eg quarterly). Compliance-related performance

**FIGURE 24.1**   Typical KM metrics reporting structure

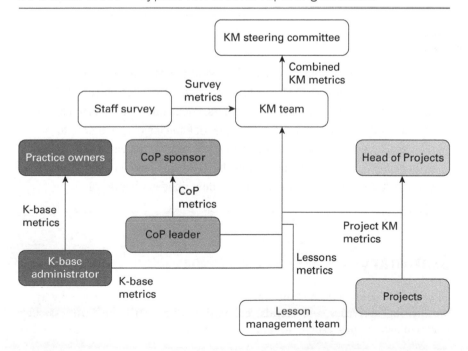

metrics need to be picked up immediately at the point where completion is due, so that instances of non-compliance can be identified and acted upon quickly. Reward and recognition performance reporting should be synchronized with the (normally annual) performance management cycle. Impact reporting should be done regularly as part of the KM communications programme, and again annually in consolidated form as part of the business review cycle. Maturity reporting may be done at longer intervals (eg biennially or triennially) since organizational maturity levels generally take longer periods of time to make significant shifts.

## KM metrics as a learning opportunity

Each of the metrics we have described has a different primary purpose: monitoring activities and trends, identifying performance lapses and excellence, evaluating impact and benefits, and tracking progress in maturity levels.

However, they also have a secondary purpose, which is to provide opportunities for feedback and learning to the operational KM support team. Karl-Erik Sveiby, who developed detailed systems for measuring intangible assets, believed that metrics provided the opportunity to open up 'learning dialogues' around trends and changes in the indicators captured by the metrics. He believed that this was an even more powerful benefit than the opportunities that metrics provide for control or influencing (Sveiby and Armstrong, 2004).

---

**Tip**

At least once a year, use the highlights of your activity, impact and performance metrics as the focus for a learning retrospect with the KM operational team and any key stakeholders. Focus on the lessons to be gathered from these highlights and trends. Use the insights gathered to plan adjustments and refinements to your KM support activities and arrangements. These retrospects can also feed useful data to your periodic KM framework refresh, which is described in Chapter 26.

---

## Summary

Your KM metrics system should provide a systematic and integrated way of monitoring activities and trends, evaluating impact to the business, key performance issues and examples of performance excellence, and, on a longer-term basis, shifts in the maturity of KM (or aspects of KM) in your organization.

At an administrative level, activity metrics and the trends they show help the operational KM team identify areas for additional support or need for further investigation. Impact metrics ensure that the KM activities continue to support the business, and retain the support of business leaders. Performance metrics help your KM governance and support the rewards and recognition processes you have set up. Maturity metrics help you trace improvements in KM capabilities over longer periods of time. All of your metrics also provide an opportunity for continuous learning and adaptation in your KM activities.

# Dealing with bumps in the road

## 25

No matter how well framed and implemented your KM implementation is, it is likely you will run into challenges that are unpredictable or beyond your control. As we pointed out in Chapter 3, KM implementation is a long and complex process, and it is vulnerable to misunderstanding, shifts in leadership priorities, resourcing issues, and continuity in both your stakeholders and the core KM team. In this chapter we cover:

- dealing with common objections to knowledge management; and
- four major challenges to KM implementation:
  - Scenario 1: over-enthusiastic support;
  - Scenario 2: death of a thousand cuts;
  - Scenario 3: perpetual reset mode;
  - Scenario 4: the show stopper.

## Dealing with common objections

There are a number of common objections to KM that you will hear as you deliver your implementation programme. It is worth anticipating these and preparing your reply in advance. Here are the five most common, and how you might address them.

### Objection 1. 'We do this already'

'We already have a training programme', 'all of this is covered by staff induction', 'we have a library that takes care of this', or 'we have SharePoint'. These are the objections of someone who wasn't listening when you explained that KM is not a single tool. You need to explain again how KM is a framework of people, processes, technology and governance. It's not training (because KM deals with organizational learning, not individual learning), it's not staff induction (because learning is for all staff, not just new staff), it's not just a library (because KM is as much about conversation as content, and as much about tacit knowledge as it is about explicit knowledge), and it certainly isn't just SharePoint.

## Objection 2. 'We tried knowledge management. It didn't work'

This is a common objection in a company that has already unsuccessfully attempted KM, and it's a valid objection. Why try again? What's different this time? You need to firstly understand why it failed last time (usually this will be due to one of the KM pitfalls listed in Chapter 3), and then you need to explain how you have learned from the failure, as well as from successful implementations in other companies, and demonstrate how your approach will be different this time.

## Objection 3. 'It won't work here; we are different'

'It may work in western engineering companies, but we are different. We are lawyers/non-profit/Venezuelan, etc.' Firstly, it is very useful if you have a few case studies of KM working in a similar context, so you can say, 'it works at organization X, and they are lawyers/Venezuelans/not-for-profit'. However, at its heart, KM is about how people work effectively while interacting with and learning from other people, and all organizations are made up of people who are supposed to be working effectively. Unless they can argue that their people are really not like other people, their argument doesn't really stand.

## Objection 4. 'Our people are too busy for this. It will take too much time'

Too busy to learn, but not too busy to reinvent wheels, rework solutions, and revisit old problems? Going back to your business case and ROI analysis for KM, you need to explain that KM is a time saver that can cut project times by up to X per cent, and that it's the efficient person's way to work. As one of my colleagues said, 'You work surrounded by the knowledge of others, why on earth would you not use it? It will save money and time, it will make your life easier, and you will do a better job'. Basically, if people are too busy, there is a strong signal that KM is needed.

## Objection 5. 'It's simple – let's just do it'

This isn't really an objection; it's more of a misunderstanding, but it can short circuit the careful preparation, planning and resourcing required for effective implementation. Certainly KM is simple, but it's not easy. Getting people to change the way they prioritize things, and to move from seeing knowledge as a personal property to seeing it as collective property requires a significant culture shift, and culture change is never easy. So you need to recognize the enthusiasm of this person, and then explain why you can't just 'tell people' to do KM – it requires a hearts-and-minds change.

> **Tip**
>
> Get together with your KM champions, and while working on some of your practice sales and influencing conversations, build a knowledge base of 'Objections to KM and how to answer them'.

# Challenge scenario 1: over-enthusiastic support

One of us worked with a client where there was a clear business focus, a well-articulated strategy, and where some early proof of concept projects had been very successful. These successes were used to build enthusiasm and support at senior leadership level. Soon they had the strong endorsement of the Chief Executive who would, at every meeting where an organizational challenge presented itself, translate it into a 'knowledge-related' challenge, and call on the KM team to pick it up. The team struggled to integrate these requests into their KM roadmap, which became progressively more complex and unwieldy.

The core elements they were working on stalled, and the calls for support to the middle management layer became increasingly tiresome and were ultimately ignored. Two years later the team found themselves being heavily criticized by the same Chief Executive for slipping behind on their roadmap, and failing to deliver what had been promised. As quickly as he had given support he withdrew it, the senior KM sponsor was moved to another position, and the team gradually fell apart.

> **Reflection**
>
> What would you do differently from this team? How would you deal with the increasing demands that come as a signal of senior level support for KM?

What this example shows is that while gathering support and buy-in is critical, especially at senior levels, there can be such a thing as 'too much' support, as well as 'too many' stakeholders. In another case, an attempt to involve too many stakeholders with conflicting agendas also resulted in a disastrous loss of focus (Lambe and Tan, 2003). So while an opportunistic approach can be a powerful one, it must always be connected back to the business focus. Saying 'yes' to every request that comes along is a recipe for over-extension of resources, becoming stretched on too many fronts, failure to show results where it counts, and ultimately rapid burnout of the team.

Choose your opportunities carefully, and do not be afraid to say 'no' or 'not yet'. Maintain a portfolio of your implementation activities currently under way and currently under plan, as part of your live KM implementation plan (Chapter 20). This should include proofs of concept and pilot projects, where they are, and how they are resourced. Every new request should then be carefully evaluated against three criteria:

- Is the request aligned with the objectives set out in the KM strategy and the aims and objectives of the KM implementation plan (Chapter 4 and Chapter 9)?
- Does the request meet the criteria for a proof of concept or pilot project as outlined in Chapter 22?
- Does your current level of resourcing permit you to take on this work, or will you need to ask your KM sponsor and steering committee to re-evaluate priorities and resources?

Work through these questions with the person making the request. It will help to communicate the framework within which you are working. If you say 'no' but they insist that the request be considered, then take it up with your KM sponsor and steering committee.

# Challenge scenario 2: death of a thousand cuts

One of us was working with a client (a regulatory agency) to develop a KM strategy, framework and implementation plan. Much of the most important work in this agency was case-based, and decisions on cases became precedents for how the regulatory framework would be interpreted in future. However, cases might take some years to resolve, and there was frequent turnover of the officers assigned to the case.

Technology was clearly an issue, with personal computers and e-mails being the preferred modes of working. Coordination and collaboration were critical but difficult in such an environment, so technology enhancements became a priority. However, there were also issues around poor technology literacy (which was why the previous technology platform had not been fully exploited), lack of consistency around case processes and workflows, and lack of clear policy and being held to account by leadership for following the processes that did exist.

The leadership team recognized technology enhancement as a risk factor, and so an integrated plan was approved combining minor technology enhancements, development of policies, a performance management framework, and training in business process alignment. Soon afterward, the KM team began running into a series of roadblocks.

The HR group, responsible for the performance management framework, said it was too stretched to take on the performance management review. The IT team started building out and extending the technology requirements because they saw the end of life of the current platform coming along in the next 18 months. The requirements for the IT platform were dramatically expanded and the budget became very large. The CEO left, and in the subsequent reshuffle, the leadership team got distracted from the policy development work. The KM team watched as the different elements of their KM framework were cut out one by one.

### Reflection

How would you deal with this issue? What do you do when some stakeholders in the components of the KM framework (in this case technology) want to expand their scope and pace, and others (eg people, process and governance) claim that they are not ready and want to move slower?

In the absence of progress on the people, process and governance fronts, the KM team quite rightly decided not to attempt the business process alignment exercise, because this depended on policy and accountability, and on an enhanced technology platform. Trying to move on just one of the fronts would have been fruitless, and would have called the credibility of the KM team into question. The IT team went ahead with their very large budget request for a more complex platform, but it was refused.

A year later, with no progress made, the issue of the renewal of the IT platform came up again. The KM team went back to senior management and reminded them of the interlocking components of people, process, governance and technology. The senior management finally decided to act on all four components.

Sometimes, you have to stand firm and keep pointing to the interdependencies between the elements of the KM framework. Having a visualization of a framework that shows this clearly in the context of your organization will help to demonstrate how the combined elements of the framework help the organization achieve its desired business outcomes – in this case, successfully prosecuted cases, more accurate management oversight of case progress, and much more effective use of their professional staff's time.

# Challenge scenario 3: perpetual reset mode

One of us worked with a client over a period of about three years, supporting them through the diagnostics and strategy-building phase of their KM implementation. In that time, the KM leader left and was replaced by somebody with little experience in the company, the whole KM team was gradually replaced, and the CEO of the company also changed. The second KM leader left to pursue further studies, and a third person was transferred in from another part of the organization. We discovered that we were effectively the organization's own outsourced memory of the KM implementation project, and had to keep briefing the new incumbents and stakeholders on what had been done before.

Every time there was a major change in personnel, the KM activities and projects were set back by about six months, despite the best efforts of the hard-working KM leaders and staff. As change agents, they needed to spend significant time rebuilding familiarity, trust, and effective relationships with their various stakeholders and customer groups. This is the kind of work that cannot easily be transferred from person to person. Rapid turnover in the KM team therefore significantly slowed KM implementation, as stakeholder relationships needed to be built from scratch again and again.

---

### Reflection

How can you work to protect continuity in the core KM team? How would you mitigate the impact of losing key people in mid-implementation?

---

The importance of continuity in the KM team and their stakeholders is an often-neglected feature in KM implementations. In fact, in a global survey of knowledge managers conducted by Knoco, internal reorganization was the most cited reason for the abandonment of KM. This is something you should communicate early to your KM leader and steering committee in the preparation stage when first introducing them to their roles (Chapters 5–7). In the case of our client organization, they were expecting significant organizational change, and should have incorporated succession planning into their KM resourcing plan, with job shadowing for key people.

In the event that you unexpectedly lose key people, look to your designated KM appointment holders (Chapters 13–16) and KM champion network (Chapter 21) as potential replacement resources. They are familiar with the way your organization works, they have seen and understand how KM is applied in the business, and they will have been building networks and relationships at least within their own spheres of influence.

To avoid the withdrawal of support for KM because of leadership changes, you need to use the advice in this book to make your KM implementation robust. Each of your proof of concept and pilot exercises should be gathering both evidence and allies in support of the value of KM. When your evidence base and credibility are pervasive across the organization, it will be difficult to pull the plug even if leadership changes.

# Challenge scenario 4: the show stopper

One of us worked with a large funding agency. In the assessment and planning stage, the team identified a major issue with the way that funding policy knowledge was communicated across the organization. Policies were kept in large, complex Word documents in a folder in the finance division's shared drive, with frequent policy updates sent out as circulars by e-mail to all staff. The policy documents themselves were infrequently updated, so staff were expected not only to be familiar with the contents of the policy documents, but also to keep track of which circulars superseded which sections of which policies. This had a big impact on work effectiveness, with mistakes, re-work, and time spent on making verbal checks with finance staff. In addition, high staff turnover meant that new staff were taking up to six months to get up to speed on funding policy and approvals.

The KM team decided that this would make an excellent pilot project to demonstrate the value of KM. They mapped out the steps in a single funding process flow and linked each step to the relevant policy sections, along with FAQs, guidelines, templates, and spreadsheets for making calculations. They identified a wiki tool for hosting and updating the policy directly in easily navigated sections, while e-mail notifications just pointed back to the relevant updated policy section. The wiki also maintained the 'history' of each section, so past policy positions could be checked. The team then tested the new system on new and recent recruits, and demonstrated clear improvements in helping new staff to get up to speed.

Then they hit a brick wall. The finance department refused point blank to adopt the new tool and process. Some of their influential people were deeply attached to the current method of maintaining policy knowledge, and they told the KM team to go try the new approach on another area of the business.

## Reflection

What would you have done differently to avoid this situation? How would you deal with apparently irrational behaviours among critical stakeholders that are detrimental to the business lines?

The KM team had clearly failed to get a critical stakeholder on board before they started the pilot. They had approached the finance department at the pilot planning stage, and were told to go ahead 'without disturbing the funding policy people'. They took that as a green light, where it was really passive resistance. The KM team then assumed that demonstration of 'obvious business value' would convince the finance department to make the necessary changes.

Sometimes you will meet behaviours that are apparently irrational when considered in the context of the business as a whole. People will protect well-established ways of doing things, even if it compromises effectiveness for themselves or others. There are two ways of mitigating this:

1 Send the decision up the leadership chain. Outline the business benefits and seek endorsement and direction from above. Unfortunately this can normally only be done quite late in the implementation process when you have a solid evidence base to draw on, and wide and deep support at senior levels.

2 If this pilot area is crucial to your implementation, then commit to spending a lot of time with the resisting party. Sit with them, identify the specific barriers to change, acculturate them to the new tools, hand hold them through each single change they need to make, and focus on this single issue with persistence, patience and sheer hard work. Apply some of the influencing techniques listed in Chapter 18.

To avoid getting into such a situation, take a good hard look at all of your stakeholders when evaluating your different pilot options, as outlined in Chapter 22. Use the buy-in ladder in Figure 18.1 (Chapter 18) to understand the current level of each stakeholder. Try to anticipate objections and barriers that may emerge from unexpected quarters.

## Summary

In this chapter we have looked at how to prepare for the inevitable objections that will come your way, and considered four types of challenge that can emerge in a KM implementation. Driving organizational change is difficult, and not everything that should go according to plan, will do so. The approach and framework we have given you in this book should help you to prepare for these challenges, avoid them, or mitigate them when they happen. Remain calm, stay focused on your course of action, and use your preparation and planning to steady you when needed.

# When implementation is over

## 26

Throughout this book we have stressed that KM is a programme of change. It requires cultural change alongside the development and implementation of an organizational framework. The focus on culture change is absolutely vital if KM implementation is going to succeed. Sometimes that leads people to think that once the change programme is over, the job is done, and that KM becomes something that 'just happens'. They think that everyone will then be naturally sharing and reusing knowledge, and that the need for KM professionals, a KM department, or a KM organizational framework will then disappear.

This is not true. The change programme will deliver an embedded KM framework, and like any management framework such as quality management, safety management or information management, it needs a small group to monitor and maintain it on an ongoing basis, as well as to respond to changes and new challenges in the organization and environment.

The change programme can only be considered complete when the framework is in place and under the care of an operational support team for KM. Without this operational support team, and an embedded framework, an organization can all too easily tip back into a pre-KM state or the KM framework can drift away from changing organizational needs. If either of these things happen, then the risk is that KM will be declared as another 'failed initiative'.

In this chapter we discuss:

- the decision to close the implementation programme;
- the role of the KM team after implementation; and
- knowledge management refresh and update programmes.

# The decision to close the implementation programme

We were recently having a discussion on KM implementation with an experienced knowledge manager, and he made the point that when organizations view KM as a project, they can often view it prematurely as a failure if it doesn't deliver all of the designated deliverables at the predetermined end date. This 'start and stop' mentality is a risk with KM, because so much of KM implementation is indeed structured as projects and programmes with defined phases, budgets and timelines. However, KM implementation activity should not stop until KM has been fully embedded, even if this means extending the project.

Making the decision to close the KM implementation programme is the last in the series of decisions we first introduced in Chapter 2. You should not stop the implementation project until you have good evidence to support making this final decision, and until you have fully completed the handover to the KM operational support team.

Here are some examples of the evidence you should look for:

- KM roles are in place for all major divisions and projects (and, if necessary, for all support functions);
- practice owners are in place for all major areas of business-critical knowledge, and are already performing their jobs well;
- communities of practice are in place and active for all major areas of business-critical knowledge;
- all the main KM processes are in use and delivering value, and training and reference material is available;
- lessons are being captured, documented and re-used, for business gain;
- all the main classes of KM technology are in regular use;
- the principles and rules of information architecture, taxonomy and metadata are being regularly applied to a high standard;
- the company expectations for KM are well defined, for example in a KM policy;
- there are many great examples of KM success stories;
- a re-run of the culture audit (described in Chapter 19) shows a marked shift towards organizational learning and knowledge-sharing culture and behaviours;
- you have a robust measurement and reporting process in place.

Take this evidence to your steering committee, and make the case to them either that KM is not yet sufficiently well embedded to transition from roll-out to operational state, or that it is sufficiently well embedded, and that KM implementation can make the transition.

## CASE STUDY

One of the authors has personal experience of a KM programme that was ended too soon. In 1999 the KM implementation at BP was just starting its third year when it was prematurely terminated as a result of massive cost cutting associated with the aftermath of the BP–Amoco merger (the biggest merger in history at the time). Many supporting programmes within the business were wound down, and KM was one of them. The first two years of KM implementation had been devoted to assessment, proof of concept and business pilots, as described in Gorelick *et al* (2004), and the third year was to have been the start of roll-out.

The team had the vision of '99 in '99' – 99 business unit knowledge managers by the end of 1999 – and were in the process of drafting a KM policy known as the Knowledge Management Assurance Standard (KMAS). Terminating the KM programme at the end of the piloting stage meant that success was not complete, with KM only partially embedded. The existing communities of practice continued, as did KM within the drilling function, while in other areas KM died away. KM was re-introduced several years later in the major capital projects area (Gibby *et al*, 2006) and KM is at last finally embedded in BP's Exploration and Production segment (Valot, 2010).

# The role of the KM team after implementation

The KM team's role as described in this book thus far has been to design, test, roll out and embed a robust and sustainable KM framework, accompanied by the required changes in behaviour and culture. Once that job is done, the role of the KM team changes to become one of ongoing operational support. Roles and responsibilities will change, but the need for KM support professionals will not disappear.

Here are some of the key elements of that continuing role.

1 They need to support usage of the KM framework. This includes training people in its use, coaching the KM professionals, running the KM CoP, launching other CoPs, and maintaining the knowledge asset about KM.

2 They need to monitor and report on the application of the KM framework, collecting and reporting the metrics described in

Chapter 24, including compliance checks on the KM policy, monitoring activity trends for any evidence of need for intervention or support, measuring the maturity of key CoPs, and collecting evidence of value.

3 They need to coordinate any KM performance management, as described in Chapter 24. This includes running annual awards schemes and events, for example, or finding other ways to recognize the star performers.

4 They need to continuously improve the KM framework. This may include improving the KM policy, it may include bringing in new technology, or improving the existing technology, and it may include adapting the processes and roles as the organization adapts to changes in its environment. We cover this 'refresh and update' activity in more detail later in this chapter.

5 They may take on specialist roles themselves, such as lessons management roles, facilitating major lessons capture events, or helping develop KM plans. If your KM strategy is a retention strategy, the KM team may run the retention process (planning, prioritizing, interviewing, etc).

6 The KM team will manage any outsourced KM services. If you need to bring in specialist providers for lessons capture, for example, or for information architecture services, then the KM team act as the in-house buyers. This ensures coordination and consistency across the consuming business groups.

# Knowledge management refresh and update

As part of their monitoring and reporting role, the KM operational support team need to monitor the application of the KM framework, and look for ways in which the framework can be improved. Generally the improvements will come through the addition of new processes or the acquisition of newer and better technology. Occasionally they come from an extension of the KM expectations. For example an organization that initially applied KM expectations only to large-scale capital projects may decide, after a year or two of successful operation, to extend it to medium-scale capital projects as well. Improvements and adaptations may be required as a result of corporate restructuring or changes in the business strategy.

All updates to the KM framework should be treated as new projects, with a definition phase, a piloting phase and a roll-out phase. Rather than running the risk of 'continually tinkering' with small elements of the KM framework and losing the overall shape and focus on supporting the business, upgrades and changes should be bundled together into a new version of the framework to be released as a new project. In Chapter 3 we stressed the importance of keeping all four elements of the KM framework in balance. Tinkering at the edges with parts of the framework requires regular sense checks to ensure that the overall balance is being maintained. New versions of the framework can be released every few years, separated by periods of stability, consolidation and usage.

## CASE STUDY

One of us worked with a client (a large government organization) that had successfully rolled out a KM framework including all four elements in balance with each other. After some time, the IT infrastructure underwent a major overhaul, and the KM team was given the responsibility to project manage first an intranet revamp, and then the implementation of an enterprise content management system. Other teams were working on a business process redesign supported by a business process management system across the entire organization. As each responsibility was added, there was a rationale as to why this responsibility should be managed as a part of KM. The organization became so preoccupied with the IT-led and explicit knowledge-led activities that the balance of activities started to suffer badly. Components and responsibilities were being added to the KM portfolio without clear consideration of the impact on the shape of the overall KM portfolio and maintaining the balance and complementarity between the elements of the KM framework.

### Tip

At least once per year (half-yearly if the intensity of change in the organization is high), undertake with your team a review of KM activity trends, any significant changes in KM activities in the business, new requests for support, and responsibilities allocated to the KM team. Map these to the KM framework and determine whether a formal review and rebalancing is likely to be needed in the foreseeable future.

# Summary

The end of KM implementation should not be the end of KM, nor should it be the end of a KM team, although their roles and responsibilities will change. The distribution of competences required within the KM team will shift, from being project oriented with heavy emphasis on influencing and change management skills, to more operational competences and technical and functional specialities, with an emphasis on tracking and reporting. For these reasons there should be a clear decision to hand over KM to an operational support team, with a transition management plan and a new team profile for the KM team, until it is time for the next update and release of the KM framework.

# PART FIVE
# Case histories

## Executive summary

This section contains five detailed case studies written by KM practitioners about KM implementations in a variety of different organizations and geographies. They demonstrate that KM implementation is not a one-size-fits-all, linear methodology. It is an adaptive, iterative, learning process, focused on delivering business value. Chapter 27 provides a textbook illustration of gaining senior support for KM, based on consistent focus on business value. Chapter 28 describes how knowledge networks were used as part of a comprehensive KM framework in a global oil and gas company. Chapter 29 describes an iterative piloting approach in a fast-moving, rapidly growing technology business. Chapter 30 provides an unusual case of a 'green-field' KM effort for the Singapore Youth Olympic Games, using very simple technology and a grounded focus on consistency, learning and knowledge transfer. Chapter 31 illustrates the power of piloting when introducing a new training approach in a legal firm.

# Implementing KM at Mars

## 27

By **LINDA DAVIES**
former Knowledge Management Director, Mars, Incorporated

---

**Context**

Mars, Incorporated (Mars) is an American global manufacturer of confectionery, pet food, and other food products. The company is privately owned and employs more than 75,000 'Associates' in more than 74 countries. This chapter details the main implementation phases of knowledge management at Mars, which took place from 2003 to 2011.

---

Knowledge management (KM) and networking have a long history in Mars. The company is typified by very informal means of communication, and networking is a key element in the way things are done. In earlier days, when the company was smaller, much of the connectivity and knowledge sharing was achieved by Mars family members travelling to business units, spotting connections and prompting people to get in touch and work together. As Mars grew this was no longer an efficient method of connecting associates and the journey to an embedded KM organization began. This journey has provided a number of key learning points.

## Know why you're doing what you're doing

KM in Mars started formally in 2003 with a KM conference attracting around 100 associates from around the business. Initial KM work streams in that first year led to a second conference one year later that came to the attention of the Mars CEO. The great excitement at such senior support was rapidly muted by his strong guidance that whilst he 'instinctively believed that KM would benefit the business', until he could understand specifically how it would help, the conference could not go ahead.

I now look back on that series of events and see it as the key that unlocked KM at Mars. It taught me the utmost necessity of knowing why we were doing what we were doing, of focusing on the business need, and determining the size of the benefit KM could bring. It made me realize that we must be able to articulate the business gains we were aiming to achieve with the KM initiatives and how we would deliver these gains. And it highlighted that unless we ourselves could clearly explain the importance of our activities and how they would help the business, we could not expect anyone else to understand KM and what it could offer.

In March 2004 we went back to the CEO with a plan that focused on how KM could help deliver on the Mars strategy. This revolved around the four techniques that we believed offered most benefit within the Mars culture – communities of purpose, communities of practice, peer assists and knowledge capture. For each of these we detailed how it would be of benefit and when it would be of benefit, accompanied by examples from other companies of the benefits achieved. The plan was approved and we were given 18 months to 'prove the concept' of KM.

# Focus on critical activities that help deliver strategy

The first few KM initiatives chosen were critical. The initial plan notes that 'There is neither the time nor the money to capture all information and simply hope that this helps us do everything better. KM effort must be focused on key performance drivers where it will have maximum impact.' With limited timescale, resource (a KM team of three) and budget, the pilot applications had to be chosen carefully, to avoid spreading the resource too thinly. Only those activities that promised an obvious and demonstrable effect on the achievement of a key strategic objective were undertaken. We developed a flow chart to assess each potential project to ensure the team stayed focused and did not get distracted by less impactful initiatives. We developed a habit of focusing on how to use knowledge to solve the business problem, rather than on how to use a particular KM approach more widely.

Initially the whole KM team was focused on a few key areas to demonstrate the gains that could be achieved. Communities of purpose were believed to offer the biggest potential, and senior associates were invited to nominate key strategic challenges that were proving difficult to crack using standard approaches. Four were chosen for further review, one of which was subsequently dropped as the challenge was too broad. This delivered a valuable lesson about bounding problems and dividing them into manageable pieces. The remaining three challenges provided a framework for the following year's activities, with a community of purpose formed for each.

Each KM team member was responsible for one community of purpose. When required, other resources were either borrowed from the business units or contracted in from outside. In general there was one KM team member and around half a contractor per challenge. The communities of purpose were set a clear business objective and specific targets that could not be achieved by each unit/region working alone. We set impact metrics and measured them regularly. Each had a senior associate as champion and a community leader who was visibly responsible for global progress, resource and funding. These communities provided a forum that focused expertise on the specific challenge, provided a route for knowledge to flow around the business, and created a targeted network of associates who could call on each other for advice and support.

Within each community of purpose, the principle of focus on business impact continued. Each community focused on two or three work streams at a time, mainly using peer assists or knowledge capture and dissemination. The work streams were reviewed every six months and, as soon as they were substantially completed, were replaced by new activities. The impact of the communities of purpose was measured several times per year and reported at a senior level, keeping visibility high and ensuring motivation/commitment to the activities. The communities rapidly delivered significant benefits to the business, providing buy-in to KM activities at the very top of the business.

The power of focusing on two or three challenges in any one year became apparent, resulting in rapid progress and big wins and proving the concept of the value that KM can bring to the business. This led to a regular increase in KM budget and resource which enabled subsequent initiatives. The principle of focus became core to the KM team, with a structured plan submitted each year containing initiatives clearly focused on a maximum of two to three key business objectives.

# Plan the roll-out to build the KM story

From the beginning, KM was run as a separate division with its own business plan, detailing how and why KM was to be implemented. The initial plan in 2003 noted:

> Knowledge is an asset and must be treated as such. Working our knowledge assets requires as much effort and attention to detail as any other asset.
> The acquisition of knowledge is not accidental. It has to be actively planned and the implementation of this plan must be resourced.

The business plan followed standard business planning practice, with a broad three-year time horizon and a detailed one-year plan submitted annually as part of the regular business planning cycle. This detailed the overall objectives for the following year, the timescale for the planned activities plus the costs and resource requirements. In this way, KM became part of the standard operating timetable, which ensured budgets were agreed and incorporated in the right timeframes and provided another route to communicate KM activities and performance to a wide audience.

With Phase 1 (communities of purpose) delivering significant benefits, the next phase was designed to investigate the benefits achieved when KM was applied widely within one functional area. All the KM resource (outside of the communities) was focused on activities within Sales – a function which offered big potential benefits from KM activities and where there was 'pull' for KM. The functional leader was passionate about connecting people and developing/sharing best practice and clearly saw the potential to be gained from widespread KM. A number of networks of senior associates were created around the key Sales challenges, which drove the development and dissemination of best practice and training in key areas. Sales directors from all segments and regions were connected through a managed network, and a website was created and actively managed to link all sales associates globally. These combined to deliver significant benefits, both in terms of sales growth and cost savings.

# Go where there is 'pull' and keep all activities relevant to the business and to associates

Communities of practice (CoPs) have been widely used in Mars, and have been most successful when focused on a specific challenge that is part of associates' daily activities. They have had greatest success when headed by an associate with an individual passion for the challenge, and where the line management chain understands and supports the purpose and benefits of the community. However, some communities failed to thrive, often due to the lack of a core purpose linked to the day-to-day job of associates. If the activities of the community did not directly deliver against business objectives, the community ultimately ground to a halt. The solution was for the senior network formed around each challenge to identify the business areas where knowledge sharing could help, so that CoPs could be formed around each of these.

Likewise, knowledge sharing and best practice development has thrived where it has been related to day-to-day activities, linked to key business challenges. The communities of purpose identified the key practice areas and serve as senior champions for the development of best practice. Additionally, community leaders were charged with ensuring that each community member both gives and receives knowledge and expertise, to ensure benefit to all.

The key learning was to 'go where there is pull for KM'. There have been areas that offered potential for KM but where the appetite for KM initiatives was lacking – these areas never succeeded. When there was a clear need allied to a keen interest in KM, the potential for success was much higher.

# Measure the business impact of KM activities

The need to demonstrate the impact of KM initiatives means that you must measure impact. It quickly became obvious that it was the impact metrics in relation to the business challenges that demonstrated the power of KM to the business and generated acceptance, rather than the KM activity metrics (we did use activity measures to help trace the link from KM activities to results). For example, the number of hits to a website or people involved in a knowledge capture is only a diagnostic aid; the real measure is the impact on the bottom line, whether a cost saving, increased sales or other performance improvement.

The need to measure the impact meant that each KM initiative had a clearly articulated business performance objective, and each work stream had a cost and a value (defining these often took a significant chunk of time!). The means by which performance would be measured was agreed at the beginning of each initiative, wherever possible using existing business measures. Performance was reported to the sponsor and project champions at regular intervals, never more than six months apart.

In addition, the KM team's performance was formally reviewed on an annual basis. Progress against the objectives was reviewed and the plans and budget for the following year agreed. This review provided a showcase for KM, demonstrating how it had helped strategy. It also generated senior-level understanding and acceptance of KM activities. Once KM had achieved a high level of acceptance, the formal review was no longer necessary and KM is now reported as part of the standard business review.

# Be consistent

Once the KM concept had been proven in the Mars culture, we needed to develop a position and presence within the business. Consistency was key to this, including the consistent focus on a few key activities, regular reporting of the team's activities in a standard format, and inclusion in the normal business planning cycle. Branding of the team and marketing of the activities was also necessary. A team logo and team colours were developed along with a suite of marketing brochures outlining the key KM techniques, where they could be used, how they deliver value and examples of where they had been used in the business. These were made available in hard copy and online. Standard formats for reports and presentations ensured the work of the KM team was recognized. A regular rhythm of communications, in a consistent format, to key stakeholders helped to keep KM initiatives 'top of mind' as a valuable business tool to solve critical issues.

# Select the team members carefully

The central KM team began as a small team focused on large-scale projects that spanned product categories and/or regions and that targeted specific global business challenges. Its areas of responsibility included:

- full support for selected communities of purpose;
- global knowledge capture around key strategic challenges;

- communication of the benefits of communities of practice and training associates in their use; and
- identifying and developing the KM techniques and approaches most suited to the Mars culture, and training associates in these.

As belief in the approach grew, the team increased in number, gaining an additional team member every one to two years. As each additional team member joined, KM activities for an additional function or business area were added. Each team member therefore had overall responsibility for a specific business area, which provided continuity and built the experience base.

Choosing the right type of person to join the team was paramount. Team members were selected on the basis of business acumen and experience, interpersonal skills, especially listening skills, and 'political' agility. There was no requirement for KM qualifications or experience – these can be taught. The team members came from a wide variety of disciplines and backgrounds, which builds strength and experience into the team. The one thing they have in common is a strong ability to interact and build relationships with people. KM at Mars is about building strong and vibrant networks and those facilitating this have to possess very strong people skills.

# Build top-down support

Top-down support has been critical throughout our KM journey. From day one the understanding and sign-on from senior leaders has enabled KM to deliver its potential. Each project had a senior-level sponsor whose role was to identify the focus areas, ensure the initiative remained relevant to the business, and communicate with their peers. They also set the expectation that associates within their division should share and use knowledge. The role of the KM director was to 'sell' KM throughout the business. Using a clear understanding of the key challenges of the business and the needs of senior leaders, the leadership communicated the potential benefits and directed the team to the areas of greatest need.

Ensuring the senior leaders understand and appreciate the value of KM has been a constant requirement, as the various leadership teams change and evolve over time. There has been a constant communication programme amongst senior leaders to ensure their understanding of KM and its impact in their area – this has been rolled out as the initiatives reach each function. This is particularly important when associates change, especially those leading or championing an initiative. It is at this time that some initiatives have stalled – 'a new broom sweeps clean'. Support from the most senior leaders has helped ensure the new incumbent knows the expectation on them to continue key KM activities.

# Embed critical knowledge via existing business processes

A number of activities have been identified through KM initiatives that are deemed to be critical to future Mars strategy. Chosen by the business leaders in each function, these have been incorporated into Mars standard approaches that are documented and mandated throughout the corporation. This route is only taken for the very few actions that are deemed to be critical. These are chosen by the business leaders within each function.

Other knowledge areas have been embedded through training. Mars University offers a comprehensive training programme for associates; key elements from knowledge capture have been developed into training courses, workshops and booklets. Other activities have been launched at workshops or conferences and are positioned as 'concentrated experience' for use by others in a similar situation. These are adopted by associates because they deliver a real benefit – the initial work to identify critical areas and understand how KM would deliver benefit helps ensure the output is relevant to associates' daily work lives.

# When is it over?

What happens when implementation is over? In my experience it is never over! There is a continual need to keep the focus on key strategic issues and to ensure the team is not distracted by other activities. The constant rotation of senior leaders, community leaders and sponsors requires a continual communication of the role and benefit of KM. However, as KM spreads more widely throughout the business and the number of associates directly impacted by KM increases, the role changes. Associates new to roles are increasingly arriving aware of the benefit of KM and/or arriving to find teams regularly sharing and using knowledge and demanding to do so. Our role then becomes more about communication around specific applications and a continual communication of the benefits achieved from KM.

## Summary

The implementation of KM at Mars is almost a textbook illustration of many of the principles in this book. The constant focus on business drivers, the selection of key knowledge areas, the communication programmes, the step-by-step approach to delivering business value at each stage – all of these are real-life applications of the recommendations from previous chapters. The result for Mars has been an ongoing journey of embedding KM as a crucial element of business performance.

# KM implementation in a global oil and gas company

## 28

By **DAN RANTA**

## Context

The company described in this chapter as Oilco is an independent and international oil and gas exploration and production company, with offices all over the world. The story starts in the early 2000s – a time of consolidation, mergers and acquisitions in the oil sector, when many organizational leaders found themselves in charge of a decentralized collection of autonomous business units. Each unit had their own practices and knowledge, with multiple barriers to knowledge sharing including time zones, language, rewards, recognition, and most importantly a dearth of trusted relationships, based mainly on the fact that many people did not know each other. This story explains how these barriers were gradually dismantled within Oilco as part of their KM implementation programme.

The genesis of KM within Oilco came when the leaders who had orchestrated many of the strategic transactions saw first-hand that workers in different parts of the world were effective, but not connected. This led to a massive amount of 'reinventing the wheel' – solutions to a problem that had been solved in one location were not being shared with other locations. The leadership recognized the potential value of enterprise-wide knowledge sharing as a way to meet the company's safety, environmental and operational challenges. They felt that global collaboration within and across job functions and business units could deliver significant cost savings and productivity benefits, especially if operations were made more consistent. Moreover the leadership knew that collaboration represented the 'horizontal' movement of knowledge across business units and that this was their desired knowledge-sharing culture.

# Connecting sharing to the business – a bold approach

Oilco recognized that it needed an initial catalyst to show how collaborative behaviour could benefit employees around the world. The first attempt was an effort to collect success stories of where employees had shared knowledge leading to business success. After more than six months, the success story collection results were abysmal. Employees did not see why they should take time to fill in a form documenting successful examples of knowledge sharing, and very few submissions were made. The problem was that there was no clear connection between the desired behaviour and the bigger prize – global knowledge sharing coupled with business value.

To overcome this, the company leadership made an astoundingly bold decision. They told their regional leadership that participation in knowledge sharing would be part of Oilco's annual bonus programme. This was astounding since very few other companies would ever, even to this day, consider being this overt about the connection between collaboration and business value.

The result of linking knowledge sharing and the bonus programme immediately got the attention of business unit leadership and employees. The number of knowledge sharing success stories increased dramatically, to an almost overwhelming degree for the small central KM team. There was another problem: what kind of rewards could match the energy and the emerging importance of knowledge sharing?

The central team quickly put a programme in place for global awards, with award categories named in conjunction with the desired collaborative behaviour. In retrospect, the awards were a masterful stroke that went on to become highly coveted and represented the fact that the most significant reason employees shared knowledge was professional pride and the fact that they wanted to help others.

The KM team recognized that this initial success would be fleeting at best if there was no sustainable framework put in to place to ensure that knowledge sharing was both effective and yet simple enough that employees did not see it as a burdensome part of their daily jobs. The answer to this was the disciplined and formal creation of knowledge networks (a term Oilco preferred to the 'more fluffy' term 'communities of practice').

# The link between knowledge networks and business results

From the beginning, Oilco's knowledge-sharing programme was linked to the business drivers, so that collaboration between people in different regions or units would directly impact the business results. To make this linkage, the knowledge networks had to demonstrate a clear business case with support from leadership before they could be approved, and then had to create a set of deliverables in the service of the business at a global or regional level.

These two principles had a profound effect on the nature and character of knowledge sharing at Oilco. The business alignment provided clear justification for why network members should invest their time in a knowledge network, and ultimately led to more focused 'purposeful collaboration'. They also supported connectivity and horizontal integration across disparate and siloed business units and disciplines.

Oilco's approach to building and sustaining effective networks focused less on finding the right technology and more on guiding people to change the way they related to one another and their work tasks, and to adopt new behaviours such as:

- proactively seeking answers or solutions from experts or peers;
- getting rid of the 'not invented here' mindset;
- actively sharing know-how; and
- seeing knowledge sharing as the way to do business.

The network portal site template was then adapted to reflect or enable these behaviours.

# Connecting people and governance

Systematically connecting people through business-focused networks became the primary driver for Oilco's knowledge-sharing strategy. These were networks of practitioners in specific knowledge domains, such as engineers, geologists, and drillers. The networks were supported by social technology such as discussion forums and wikis, and were headed by a network leader, reporting to a network sponsor. The networks enabled employees to break down artificial barriers, build up reservoirs of trust, and engage in dialogue and other collaborative activities to improve work performance. Network members could exhibit professional pride by sharing their experiences to help others mitigate risk, influence decisions and increase safety as well as improve overall operational efficiency.

The knowledge networks were strengthened and stabilized by a set of specific rules for every aspect of the networks. The creation of this governance framework was an ongoing journey that required regular interactions with employees and leadership across Oilco to ensure that the governance was both adopted, and provided clarity on (for example):

- the approach to measure business value, through measuring the impact of problem solving;
- the approach to network creation, with a business case followed by appointment of the network leader, followed by network launch;
- the approach to continued development of the network through a series of maturity stages; and
- protocols on how knowledge would be managed in the network, including guidance on discussions, content, expertise, workgroups, and wiki articles.

One of the factors identified by Jim Collins in his book *Good to Great* is what he calls the contribution of 'relentless discipline' in achieving breakthrough results (Collins, 2001). This was the effect of the governance created by Oilco's central KM team in charge of knowledge sharing. The disciplined and systematic approach to governance led to consistent results and an overall system that supported collaboration and made sense to global users.

# Visible leadership led to knowledge network growth

Oilco began its most significant knowledge network push in late 2004. The company's KM team of experienced consulting advisors worked directly with senior leadership to create and implement the ambitious governance-based knowledge-sharing model and strategy. The executive leadership support enabled the launch of the first few knowledge networks in early 2005, representing the beginning of collaborative bridges between siloed business units and disciplines scattered around the globe.

By year two, the number of networks had grown to nearly 60; by year three about 80 networks were operating. The governance in place allowed for the efficient and consistent creation and launching of the knowledge networks. All the networks were global in order to create the biggest reach and greatest value. Eight years into the programme, the number of networks had grown to about 150, with membership representing the vast majority of all knowledge workers. Employees often belonged to multiple networks, averaging about three to four networks per member, thanks in large part to the consistency of each network's look-and-feel functionality. The systematic sharing and capture that this consistency enabled, formed the cornerstone of the company's strategy to retain critical knowledge from the most knowledgeable people and to make it accessible to everybody, with finding and re-using knowledge becoming a major focus. This provided a major boost to employee productivity.

By this time knowledge sharing at Oilco was widely driven from the top, with executives at all levels supporting and promoting the knowledge networks and elevating the importance of knowledge sharing as it became embedded in the culture and the company's DNA. In an Oilco employee opinion survey, for example, knowledge sharing received the second-highest increase in employee satisfaction results, even though, when the strategy was formulated and the programme began, most employees would likely not have recognized terms such as 'knowledge sharing' and 'knowledge networks'.

# Building sustainability

Once each network was launched, the centralized support team provided guidance and support through coaching, technical solutions and best practice sharing across the networks. Guided by this team, Oilco developed a process for networks to evaluate themselves against pre-determined success factors. Knowledge network leaders met with network specialists on a regular basis for a detailed assessment of the network's health and business impact. These were mandated sessions, with every network requiring at least one per year, where solutions were discussed to increase the network's business performance across the standard success factors. Competition through internal benchmarking with other networks became a key success factor over time, and this evaluation process, along with audits of network portal site effectiveness and analysis of the network business cases and KPIs, clearly increased the likelihood of continued network success.

# Discussions and lesson learning

A core component of Oilco's KM approach was connecting people through collaborative portals so they could discuss and share best practices and lessons learned. Since about 50 per cent of the global workforce spoke English as a second or third language, the portal sites (all in English) became the 'great equalizer' and employees were often more comfortable communicating in writing on the portal sites than discussing on the phone. Collaborative portals helped technical professionals who were faced with similar problems around the world to seek knowledge and expertise from their peers and so make quicker, better informed decisions.

The network portal sites, managed and monitored by the central team, also enabled newer and less experienced employees to tap the deep well of expertise from global subject matter experts. They could seek clarifications, input, ideas and validation of approaches to problems, acting and operating as part of a global company. It actually became frowned upon for an employee to act independently on a complicated work task before conferring with the appropriate knowledge network.

The cumulative number of discussion threads surpassed thousands annually across all knowledge networks, and the number of hits across all portals soared to more than 2 million per month as more and more network members realized the positive results of global collaboration.

# Promoting re-use

As the discussions evolved, so too did Oilco's sophistication at expanding the impact gained from lessons learned. The central team developed a unique technology that enabled network leaders to share with other networks a single discussion thread from their portal, without duplicating the thread and while keeping the integrity and flow of the replies in a single thread. Discussion threads were usually initiated by a network member asking for help and advice on an operational problem, and this feature dramatically expanded the number and global reach of potential solutions. On average, discussions shared with related networks received twice as many responses as those that took place within a single network.

The discussion-sharing tool was widely used and greatly enhanced the value from lessons learned, as decisions were influenced across functions and streams of the business. Network members could use the portal for peer-to-peer problem solving, or broad-based learning through discussions guided by senior practitioners and subject matter experts, or could search or browse through organized stores of existing knowledge and lessons. This not only reduced the degrees of separation between the knowledge workers, but also increased cross-organizational trust through the demonstration of 'human vulnerability' that asking questions in public networks demands.

# Synthesis: closed discussions and an enterprise wiki

As discussion within the networks flourished, a natural second order question arose – 'What should we do with all the unstructured knowledge collected in the discussion threads?' The two-pronged solution consisted of closing discussions, and creating an enterprise-wide wiki – both enabled by unique technology and processes.

The central team recognized that the knowledge within online discussions should not be left to age on network portals. Many discussions contained detailed analysis and background information that represented an extensive body of knowledge from experienced network members. The KM team researched those discussions that were deemed to have successfully reached their conclusion, and created a process and policy to encourage network leaders to officially 'close' those discussions. These closed discussions were turned into searchable documents and added to a knowledge network's content library for members to re-use. This resulted in the formation of a valuable, vast and searchable repository of knowledge assets, and the next step was to begin linking them through the development of an enterprise-wide wiki.

The wiki concept was familiar to Oilco staff, and this proved to be a natural place to capture the insights and wisdom that had originated from the knowledge networks, and to keep it up to date. Internally branding the wiki sent an important message that this was the one and only place for contextual, encyclopaedic knowledge for Oilco. To introduce the wiki to the enterprise, the central team created a set of high-end, computer-based training modules. The team also met regularly with individuals from the business who were deemed 'wiki moderators' to ensure they were aware of the newly created and emerging wiki governance standards.

# Measuring knowledge network activity

Oilco believes that 'you manage what you measure'. Keeping detailed records of the business impact delivered by the networks served to galvanize sponsorship and attract and sustain new members. Success stories provided a measure of the overall benefit of knowledge sharing, while knowledge networks also provided more specific measures of delivered value based on their business case objectives. Some networks used non-monetary measures for success, such as health, safety and environmental improvements, or mitigation of risk. The central team learned to be flexible with measurements to ensure that measures could be made, so long as those measures were aligned with the high-level business objectives of Oilco.

The overall business impact directly related to knowledge sharing measured in the hundreds of millions of dollars over a period of several years. This was calculated by adding the business benefits from operational problems solved through the re-use of knowledge, or best practices re-used for business gain.

## Summary

Oilco worked for more than a decade with unwavering commitment towards its vision of creating a workplace where employees continually delivered additional value through global collaboration and knowledge sharing. At Oilco, support for knowledge sharing and collaboration came from the executive level and cascaded downward and outward throughout the company, supported by a robust framework of knowledge networks, and supporting roles, technologies and governance. Oilco learned that creating a collaborative culture is a never-ending journey with two elements at its core – shaping behaviours, and business value.

# KM implementation at Huawei

## 29

By **TAN XINDE**
leader of the Huawei KM programme

## Context

Huawei Technologies Co. Ltd is one of the world's fastest-growing global brands, and one of the few giant Chinese multinational companies. In 2015 the company was the world's largest manufacturer of telecoms equipment, and among the largest smart phone manufacturers. One of Huawei's divisions designs and manufactures telecoms equipment and smart phones (referred to in this chapter as the R&D domain), and another builds and operates telecommunications networks (the delivery domain).

KM addresses three business issues for Huawei: the need to cope with rapid staff growth (in the early 2010s the company was growing by 10,000 staff per year), the need to learn rapidly from expansion into new markets and offers, and the need to transfer knowledge from headquarters in Shenzhen, China, to staff in projects and service teams worldwide (referred to in this chapter as 'front line staff').

As a company with more than 150,000 employees, you can't do anything at Huawei without someone asking you 'what's the value in this?' Only after you've created value in Huawei's business and earned your own credentials, will others accept you. The path we've taken in the past several years is like the north route to the peak of Mount Everest; which is to say, it has been extremely challenging.

# The value of KM to Huawei

When I first took this position, I was thinking hard about how to do KM. In the first few months, I was very unsure about the approaches that I should take according to the KM standard at Huawei, and I struggled constantly to find the uplifting words I needed to convince myself. Then I read a statement quoted by one of my colleagues: 'The value of knowledge management depends not on knowledge or on IT, but on the use of knowledge by an organization's members.' These words left a lasting impression on me. Our corporate CEO also says often that, 'everything we do, we do to live', and these words touched me. I put them on the front page of my 2012 report to the corporate executives and elaborated on them in a few minutes. Later the executives told me they thought this statement was very appropriate.

Everything that KM at Huawei has advocated in these last few years, in every domain, boils down to the question: 'does what you do help those on the front line improve their use of knowledge?' Of course, one's use of knowledge must in turn help improve the quality and efficiency of one's work.

Jack Welch said, 'An organization's ability to learn, and translate that learning into action rapidly, is the ultimate competitive advantage.' I've always supported this idea, but never quite found the best place to reference it, until last year when I visited our Nanjing research centre to discuss KM with some team leaders, and one of them shared their experience from new employee training, touching on this point exactly. The vast majority of new employees are straight out of university, and they all have something in common, which is that they need a long period of time before they can work independently. New employees have one week of orientation training, and then another round of training with their departments. This training is not particularly helpful in translating learning into action rapidly. In R&D, generally it takes about six months before new graduate employees are ready to do their own work independently, but this team managed to do it in less than two months. How?

Simple: after entrance training, new employees were split into teams of five, each team assigned to one module in a previous version of a product. These modules already had their source code altered, bugs added, and the goal was to have it debugged in less than 20 days. Teams were under intense pressure during these 20 days because this time was a critical part of the review process for graduating from training. During these 20 days there was an expert on hand, but he/she wouldn't actively help you, of course, only answer questions, and even then would only provide basic guidance; the rest was up to the employees. After these 20 days of training, new employees would essentially no longer produce the kind of basic bugs that novices generally produce. As long as they were able to completely debug their modules in the first 20 days, they would be able to start working on the next version without too much worry, and they would have a thorough under-standing of the system and Huawei's coding standards. This colleague's story made me understand completely that our relationship with HR's learning and development department is interdependent, and that ultimately our goal is to accelerate the rate at which employees translate knowledge into action. The faster this rate is, the greater our competitive advantage will be. This is something that we can accomplish step by step.

# The start of Huawei's KM journey

Prior to the year 2000, Huawei had had an internal Bulletin Board System (BBS). In common with many Chinese workers, Huawei employees have the custom of taking naps during lunch breaks, but I can remember vividly, around that time, that there were a lot of people who gave up napping and instead spent the lunch period in forums online. For example, one morning I'd be doing some software development, and I'd run into something I didn't know how to deal with – so what would I do? I would ask the forum and instantly had a flood of peers responding to share their experience. But in 2003 and 2004 the company became especially serious about information security and, unfortunately, closed the forum. I know there are still many in R&D nostalgic for that forum.

Prior to 2008, each business unit had already started building their own domain-specific knowledge portals, and at Huawei these kinds of spontaneous, diverse, standalone knowledge repositories were extremely common. In 2008, however, although information security was still a top priority, the practical demands of research and development (R&D) on knowledge sharing were too great to ignore.

Why was R&D able to bring about KM? Simple: because those in R&D naturally require knowledge to help them, equip them, and allow them to deliver their products better and more efficiently. Soon, other departments like marketing and Global Technical Service (GTS) followed the footsteps of R&D, using Web 2.0 tools to break down walls between departments and build two knowledge-sharing platforms, one for R&D and one for non-R&D employees.

In 2010, our software company faced a huge challenge: seeing as we offer tailored solutions for our many telecom operators, how can we take the knowledge and experience from our corporate HQ and deliver it quickly to our teams at the front line? As we were in this type of situation, we sought consultation from Ernst & Young on KM. Knowledge management at Huawei distinguishes between two types of knowledge: one is explicit knowledge, the kind that can be written down and seen with the eyes. The other is tacit knowledge, the kind that exists only in the brain. The knowledge that exists in the brain is certainly greater and more valuable than the kind that can be written down. Looking back, Ernst & Young's plan focused more on the management of explicit knowledge. Our software company went to corporate management and asked for some policy support, hoping to set a precedent in KM. Corporate management told them to go ahead and decided to set up a corporate-level project team for KM.

In 2011, corporate management's directive on the KM project was to focus on finding its value. We experimented with a few development teams, introduced consultants, made some progressive trials, and found a bit of footing. Those in R&D at the time found these 'project learning' piloting methods eye-opening; they didn't realize that knowledge could be 'managed' like this, and the results were very effective.

Then we asked the consultants to offer a report to corporate management. There was a story in this report that management found very inspiring: a case study on BP near the end of 2001. BP has oil wells all over the world. The cost of drilling wells in one oil field was close to $600 million, but through KM they succeeded in reducing that cost to $540 million on the next field. For BP it meant additional pre-tax profits of $60 million. Combined with our own R&D's initial successes, this case study convinced corporate management of the tremendous value of KM. They charged me with organizing a full-time, corporate-level KM team, and with gradually establishing a full-time or part-time knowledge manager (we call them KMers) in each business department.

In 2012, we did two things. The first was to integrate our knowledge platforms. At the time we had two separate technology platforms hosting discussion forums for knowledge sharing: one for R&D employees, which was built in Huawei's R&D zone and later transferred to a common zone, and the other for non-R&D employees, also in the common zone. There was still concern over information security, so we asked the leadership for an executive decision to unite the two platforms and integrate knowledge from both R&D and non-R&D. We took a lot of criticism, and there were some in R&D who objected, but looking back it's now accepted as a move in the right general direction.

The second thing was to implement the KM methodology. In 2012, our KM implementation team in the R&D domain focused on one development team and delivered two pilots in the span of about a year. In the first pilot, we tested several methods, and the business departments felt it was interesting and indeed beneficial to the quality and efficiency of their work. So when it was time for the second pilot, the head of the relevant product develop-ment unit (PDU) decided on a complete trial and appointed a key business employee to be a dedicated knowledge manager. This knowledge manager led the PDU in focusing on the key problems and knowledge gaps most likely to crop up in this version. After some analysis, we found some teams with relevant experience and did some interviews and exchanges with them which allowed our development team to better understand their experience and do some focused optimization. This pilot delivered so much quality it earned the development team's first ever five-star rating. This case study shows how KM can directly improve the quality of our products and the efficiency with which we deliver them.

Going back to the BP case study mentioned earlier, according to the way we distinguish different domains at our company, it is our delivery domain rather than the R&D domain that has most in common with the BP case. For example, we once had an overseas project budgeted at $1 billion. Where did all that cost come from? There were a few key elements. We would install our base stations in buildings or on utility poles, each of which we would call a 'site'. At the time we had a project in a certain country where it would take our engineers 20 trips or more to finish a site; it was extremely expensive.

In fact, we already had mature, integrated solutions from our successful experience in other countries, but the local teams didn't understand them and never used them. We changed to a project manager who pushed hard for an integrated solution, and eventually got the number of trips needed to finish a site down to eight. You might ask how much that really changes things, 8 trips vs 22 trips. Well, every time our engineers visit a site, we take our partner's engineers with us, and with every visit we pay them a certain amount of money, so essentially by cutting the number of trips to eight we cut costs by almost two-thirds. This is just another reminder of how sharing knowledge has a direct benefit on production and efficiency.

In 2013, we in R&D piloted KM with 10 or more product teams. At the time there were five or six teams performing better than ever. Later we did an analysis and discovered that fully implementing KM was a very difficult undertaking, the most difficult part being a true understanding and adoption of the theory and methods behind KM by our business teams. As I just mentioned, the path we chose is a very difficult one, and at its core this is because we chose the most realistic path, dealing directly with value creation.

According to plan, by the end of 2014 our KM implementation project was approaching completion, and from then on KM would be carried out by the business departments. From the first pilot project in R&D to various domains in the whole company, our corporate-level KM department still only has three or four people, but with the improvement that each domain now has its own dedicated KMers; 30 or so people in total. In our business departments KM is gradually taking root in R&D, sales, delivery, and even in the operations of several overseas countries.

# Going from the HQ to the frontline

Our KM is now going farther than R&D in HQ. We defined our KM goals as 'three ones': it should take one minute to be able to find basic work knowledge, one day to get questions answered in a community forum, and one month to capture the experience of a frontline project after it completes. In the middle of 2014, I went to one particular country, where our software company's first 'full IT' delivery project was deployed. The project was successful and our clients were satisfied.

The competence centre at Huawei HQ invited a knowledge management expert to the country to lead a 'knowledge retrospect', spending three days to figure out how Huawei successfully delivered the project. At 4pm on the third day, just as the retrospect meeting was drawing to a close, the consultant asked if anyone had anything to say, and everyone said, 'Everything I've learned was spoken out!'

This is exactly what KM does for us in the real world: when a project is completed well, we must use KM methods to gather up all the lessons we've learned. When a project begins, we must use KM methods to identify what difficulties and challenges the project faces, where the knowledge gaps are, and which company resources we can call on to help you make it happen.

In the area of explicit knowledge management, we're not quite as advanced as a lot of other companies. From what I've seen in many companies' presentations, they've all done some excellent work in managing explicit knowledge, especially knowledge base building. At Huawei many departments are already building their own knowledge bases, so our first step wasn't to start from here, because it would likely encounter serious resistance. The path we're on requires that we first prove our own worth before we prove that we can do a little more. This is what we have to share from our experience.

All in all, the past few years of KM have been difficult, because the departments we're in are so far from the business departments, who don't always understand KM right away. The previous success of R&D was due to colleagues in R&D who had an interest in KM. We seized the opportunity and leveraged the influence of consultants and gradually pushed for implementation.

## Explicit vs tacit knowledge management

Our consultant once gave us some empirical data, telling us, 'Out of 100 per cent of the captured explicit knowledge, often only 5 per cent will make it into real-world application.' This was a great inspiration for me. If you only do explicit knowledge management, this means that 95 per cent of your work is wasted. The transfer of explicit knowledge comes through collection; the transfer of tacit knowledge comes through conversation. There is an ancient Chinese saying: 'You can learn more in one sitting of listening to a wise man than from ten years of reading books.' These are wise words indeed. Therefore we should focus on learning during projects, doing what we call 'learning before, during, and after implementation'. This kind of learning has been project-tested, and is very effective. Of course, the process is very difficult, because you have to convince people to do it, and that doing it will be effective, which is hard. That's why it has been so difficult to go down this path.

# The current state of KM in Huawei

This is a panoramic view of what we promoted last year. We do KM in R&D, and in each business group we have test cases, all basically in operation at this point. With Huawei's current agile development process, we have a focused KM plan for each project. For each iteration in a product version we do an after-iteration review, and at the final stage of a version we do a full retrospect. This is a plan we are currently testing, and within R&D we have pushed it through universally.

The platform is something we haven't emphasized much. Our platform still isn't as 'internet-enabled' as others, but we do focus on a few points. First, we focus on solving real-world problems. We have a test user who raised a question in our community, a question that had troubled him for two months, but after just five hours in the community his question received a complete answer. Success stories such as this are the only way users will come to trust and rely on our community. Our community generates an average of 16 million page views per month, of which 88 per cent are related to team activity: essentially every user will at some point join several small teams. We're currently focused on developing these teams into true communities of practice. We have a standard when it comes to the CoP, which is that more than 70 per cent of content should answer questions about basic-level operations. A lot of people thought this standard was too strict, but from Huawei's perspective, we start from the ground up, and a central tenet of the community is to help users solve business problems, or help business teams solve problems about business innovation. Huawei currently has 3,500 active teams on our knowledge-sharing platform, but at present we've identified only one team who actually meets the CoP standard, and that's our KMer community (the community of practice of KM professionals). In the KMer community forum, anyone who asks a question will receive an answer within an hour.

Second, we focus on people. We've done micro-interviews, honorary titles, medals, and special headlines, to honour our users and to self-actualize ourselves. Every year we invite users from all over the world to discuss their needs in our community, and take steps to implement them in our operating goals.

Finally, we focus on content building. In Huawei's communities, 'content worth reading' is one of the key elements of attracting and retaining users; that's why we need to constantly encourage, develop, and promote quality content. In our communities' monthly bulletins, we take the best and most popular content written by our users and republish it, and even the leadership will see it. We also collect premium content on hot topics like the Internet and Big Data and republish it for targeted audiences.

Last year we supported a technical CoP that developed extremely well, resolving over 500 business questions and real-world problems in just half a year, with average response times of one hour or less; and all these were detailed questions about hardware design. This community is run not by our KMers but by several high-end hardware experts who saw a need within this domain and took the initiative. It was difficult, of course, because everyone in the company has their own KPIs and finding people with the right enthusiasm was no easy task. This is one of our business domain's most outstanding CoPs ever.

This brings us back to our belief in KM at Huawei:

> The value of knowledge management depends not on knowledge or on IT, but on the use of knowledge by an organization's members.

## Summary

This chapter illustrates many of the themes of this book as it describes the introduction of KM into a huge and complex multinational. The link between KM and value (a strong theme in this book) runs as a thread through this chapter, with Tan Xinde describing how he met the value challenge head-on, like 'climbing the North Face of Everest'. Value, as he explains, comes when KM is applied by the front-line workers. First the idea of value came through stories from outside the company, then through internal pilots such as the R&D project that delivered so much quality. It earned this development team's first ever five-star rating. Mr Tan's KM team was small, but was able to operate through a network of KM champions, or KMers as they are referred to in the chapter. These 30 advocates have been leading the local application of KM in the business departments, and will take a more prominent role as KM takes root.

# KM implementation at the Singapore Youth Olympics

## 30

By **DOREEN TAN**
Head of Knowledge Management, Singapore Youth
Olympic Games Organizing Committee

## Context

When Singapore won the bid to host the first Youth Olympic Games in February 2008, the people were elated. The Youth Olympic Games (referred to by Doreen as 'the Games') was the first innovation by the International Olympic Committee (IOC) in the last 80 years. It would feature all the 26 sports in the Summer Olympic Programme, as well as an integrated culture and education programme, and would be held from 14–26 August 2010. A total of 3,600 athletes and 1,400 team officials from 205 National Olympic Committees would participate.

It would also be the first time that Singapore had hosted an Olympic-level Games, its previous major event having been the Southeast Asian Games in 1973. The people of Singapore looked forward to this great opportunity to showcase their country's hardware, software and 'heartware' to the rest of the world. As a nation, Singapore hoped to maximize this one-off opportunity to learn from and retain the know-how of organizing such a mega event, thus enhancing their ability to host future major Games.

This case study describes the creation and implementation of the Singapore Youth Olympic Knowledge Management Programme.

To plan for and deliver the Games in August 2010, the Singapore Youth Olympic Organizing Committee (SYOGOC) was set up in April 2008. Compared to the usual seven to eight years of preparation for a full-fledged Olympic Games, SYOGOC had a much shorter timeframe of 2.5 years to complete the Games preparation. Time was short. The Games was a brand new product with new components and service standards, and SYOGOC had no equivalent past Games to refer to. An international financial crisis was brewing in the background. And human resources were limited.

SYOGOC had only one opportunity to deliver the Games successfully. They had to do it right the first time. No u-turns were allowed. From the start, SYOGOC's leadership recognized that KM was needed to:

- facilitate the smooth flow and exchange of information to improve operational efficiency across SYOGOC;
- cultivate a learn-as-you-go culture for SYOGOC staff to get on board quickly and improve work processes as Games preparation progressed; and
- retain and transfer Games know-how and lessons learned for future major Games to leverage.

The SYOGOC KM department was set up in June 2008 to spearhead this initiative.

# Facilitating the smooth flow and exchange of information

The key to facilitating a smooth flow and exchange of information in such turbulent times was standardization. All SYOGOC staff needed to speak and write the same 'Games language', understand and use the same templates, follow the same information management processes and refer to the same updated central information source. Information should be made as accessible as possible for cross-referencing and updating. As SYOGOC grew in size, staff with varying degrees of Games experience came on board at different times. One of the challenges was getting all staff to speak and write using the same Games jargon. To help them, two 'dictionary' lists were created containing more than 900 acronyms and 700 technical terms which were categorized into subject matter areas. These lists were shared on the network drive for the staff's reference. Measures were put in place to ensure that the lists were kept updated and staff were using the correct terms.

Due to the tight preparation timeframe, things were moving very fast at SYOGOC. Processes were developed on the fly, and so were corresponding templates. The KM team became the major producer and standardization body of SYOGOC templates, ranging from contact report templates to venue operations manual templates. The release of templates for use by

SYOGOC staff was often accompanied by briefings or mass training sessions for staff so that all were aligned in their usage.

The procurement and set up of any KM technology would take at least six months, and the Games preparation period was only 2.5 years. Hence, SYOGOC decided not to procure an IT system but to leverage on the network drive for information management instead. Simple as it was, the network drive became the default information repository across SYOGOC. It contained both working documents and digitized records.

Document management discipline had to be instilled manually from the start to prevent subsequent information chaos. Business units and meeting forums were assigned folders in the network drive based on three-letter codes. A digital file-naming convention was cascaded downwards so that document owners and versions could be clearly identified. Folder names and the Registry file-numbering system had to conform to the Singapore Sports Council taxonomy so as to enable smooth post-Games knowledge transfer back to the Sports Council.

# Cultivating a learn-as-you-go culture

As the Games preparation progressed, there were new things to learn and new activities to participate in every day. It was important for all SYOGOC staff to be in a continuous 'do-learn-improve-do' mode. KM activities were designed to cultivate a learn-as-you-go habit in conjunction with the Games planning phases (foundation, operations planning, operational readiness and operations).

During the Games foundation phase, the IOC invited SYOGOC staff to observe the Beijing 2008 Olympics. After the observation trip, participants shared their personal experiences and useful insights with their colleagues so that they could improve their own plans and processes. The KM team developed the post-trip reporting and sharing process, resulting in the first SYOGOC-wide sharing session in August–September 2008. Following this session, approval was obtained from senior management to conduct knowledge capture workshops for each business unit at the end of the SYOGOC foundation phase. The first knowledge-capture workshop took place in November 2008. It was designed to answer the following questions:

- What have we accomplished so far?
- Whom did we work with during this period?
- Which were the knowledge resources that we relied upon, created and referred to and where can they be found?
- What have we learned and what can we do better the next time?
- Are there any adjustments that we need to make for the operations planning phase?

Two more workshop series of the same nature were conducted during the operations planning phase for the Singapore Youth Olympics. All three workshops concluded with a SYOGOC-wide sharing session designed to highlight functional cross-dependencies and lessons learned.

Even though the SYOGOC organization structure started off with business units as building blocks, these business units would eventually morph or divide up into functional areas that operated in different venues during Games time. To facilitate this 'venuization' process, knowledge-capture workshops were also conducted for each venue during the Games operations planning phase. From the first series of venue knowledge-capture workshops, a model venue planning toolkit was developed and disseminated in March 2009. The toolkit detailed each micro step required during the venue-planning process, and acted as a guidebook for all venue-planning teams to follow. It also documented the lessons learned from various venue-planning teams. Subsequently, after every major series of venue workshops, the venue-planning toolkit was updated. The released versions were made available to all staff via the network drive.

During the later part of the operations planning phase and the operations readiness phase, SYOGOC venue teams further developed their venue plans into venue-operating manuals. The venue-operating manual was the documented output of the venue-planning sessions and provided an overview of venue-level operations and functional area-specific operations details. It also served as a training guide for the workforce (including volunteers) who needed to operate at the venue. The KM team developed the templates for the venue operations manual as well as the venue functional area operations manuals based on the experience gained and lessons learned during the venue-planning stage, and subsequently trained staff in the usage of them.

Besides collating process information and lessons learned from the operations staff, one-on-one interviews were also conducted with the SYOGOC CEO, deputy CEO, chief operating officer and division directors at the end of each knowledge-capture workshop series. Each interview was conducted using the standard after action review questions (Chapter 14), and captured the senior manager's point of view. The interviews were useful for the senior managers as they helped them to recall and reflect on key project impacts and cross-cutting implications. The KM team captured suggestions on how they would manage issues the next time round.

It was not only important for SYOGOC staff to learn quickly during the Games preparation phases, it was also essential for them to learn on the go while the Games were under way. In order to help staff learn and improve upon their procedures during the Games, a during action review (DAR) process was implemented at all venues. A KM volunteer was deployed to each venue to assist in the facilitation of the DARs, which were conducted by each functional team at the end of each shift. At the end of each day at the venue, the venue manager would use the collated lessons learned as a basis for his or her end-of-day debrief to all functional heads. From there, an end-of-day report would be produced and sent to the Main Operations

Centre. Good practices/lessons learned that were useful across venues would be highlighted and disseminated by the Main Operations Centre to all venues on the next day.

# Retaining and transferring Games know-how

During Games time, SYOGOC had about 22,600 staff and volunteers. After the Games, less than 100 staff would remain to partake in dissolution activities. It was crucial to put in place key processes that would allow the retention and transfer of hard-gained Games know-how to the next Games organizers and Singapore's sports community.

Before Games time, as planning progressed within SYOGOC, working documents were submitted to the IOC at the end of each planning phase for upload onto their Olympic Games KM extranet. These documents were in turn made available to future host cities so that they could refer to them during their own planning phases. In addition, SYOGOC hosted other Games organizing committees via a secondment programme before and during the Games. Secondees were assigned to various Games functional areas to learn about actual Games operations in a hands-on manner.

During the Games, the IOC and SYOGOC jointly conducted the Observers' Programme and Visitors' Programme during which the next Games organizing committees attended seminars and venue tours to learn about SYOGOC's planning considerations and operations. After the Games, debrief and sharing sessions to the Singaporean partner agencies, the IOC and the Nanjing 2014 Youth Olympic Games Organizing Committee were conducted in November 2010 and January 2011. These sessions were complemented by the Singapore 2010 post-Games reports and transfer-of-knowledge materials that were submitted to the IOC for upload onto their Olympic Games KM extranet.

The post-Games reports, together with the entire network drive, physical records, media materials and senior management learning videos, were also transferred to the relevant Singapore government agencies including the Ministry of Community Development, Youth and Sport, Singapore Sports Council, the National Archives of Singapore and the National Library Board to be used as legacy materials and reference materials for future major Games organization. The lessons learned collated from senior management were also made available to the Singapore Civil Service College for the authoring of case studies.

In addition to the explicit documentation, the tacit knowledge and experience gained from the inaugural Youth Olympic Games were transferred in the form of more than 100 assigned staff who returned to the Singapore Sports Council after the Games. As of the time of writing (May 2015), both explicit and tacit knowledge gained from the Singapore Youth Olympic Games have been mobilized for the organization of the South East Asian Games to be held in Singapore in June 2015.

## Summary

It was both easier and harder than expected to do this KM project: easier because there were no grounded mindsets to change in the first place, but harder because we had to implement from scratch the right processes from the start amidst a highly challenging and fast-moving environment. What really made it work was the people: senior management who viewed KM as critical right from the beginning, and the divisional KM coordinators and staff who came to believe that KM was important and embraced it as part of their daily work life. Capturing knowledge for future generations was important, but no one was going to participate if they did not also see immediate work benefits.

# Accelerated learning in a law firm

By **JESSICA MAGNUSSON**
former Head of Knowledge at Osborne Clarke

---

**Context**

Law firms are knowledge-intensive businesses. This case study looks at how a law firm in England implemented a new approach to accelerated learning through a structured training programme. The focus is on how the firm ran and learned from a pilot before implementing its new knowledge and development programme.

## Knowledge and professional development in law firms

Those starting out in law firms as trainee solicitors have traditionally studied law at university followed by three to five years of law school. They would often have had a gap year between law school and joining the firm. Law firms tend to run comprehensive legal training programmes for their trainees that focus on changes in law, client matters and how to navigate the firms' systems and knowledge assets. However, these programmes assume that junior lawyers have retained the knowledge of legal principles that they studied at some point in the past, whereas in reality they have often forgotten. Given this background, the firm has to:

- help junior lawyers bridge the knowledge gap between university/law school and practising law;
- help junior lawyers identify areas that they need to refresh or develop; and

- ensure that junior lawyers provide clients with technically excellent advice at the earliest possible stage in their careers.

These were some of the issues I looked at between 2011 and 2013 when I was Head of Knowledge Management at a prominent English law firm.

# The timeframe

In late 2011 we formed a project team, comprising myself, the real estate professional support lawyer (PSL), the HR director, and the business manager. Our focus was the firm's strategic aim to ensure lawyers' technical excellence. The HR director's role was particularly crucial because, as a strong project sponsor and member of the firm's Executive Board, he secured buy-in from senior management at an early stage. The PSL was also instrumental in shaping the overall structure of the pilot and subsequently the programme.

We invited six universities and law schools to bid for a project to co-develop a programme to address the legal knowledge gap between studying and practising law, and accelerating the learning curve of junior lawyers, and in April 2012, we selected a law school to work with. Who better to ask than those teaching law and preparing students for a career in law?

To test the concept and the collaboration with the law school, we ran a pilot in one of our departments over the summer months in 2012. The feedback and learnings from the pilot shaped the overall programme and helped us refine the approach. We introduced it in each department in 2013.

# Approach

It took about 18 months to introduce and embed the new programme across the firm. The project team took a seven-step approach. We:

- designed a programme to refresh and cement legal knowledge;
- defined the expected benefits of the programme;
- selected a pilot group to test the concept;
- measured results before, during and after the pilot;
- reviewed the results and made adjustments;
- engaged with and kept stakeholders informed;
- took a phased approach to the implementation.

## 1. The programme

The programme was designed to refresh and cement legal knowledge by linking theory with practical application. Each module was to be run once a year, typically 8–10 weeks long. It provided a structured approach to learning and consisted of four elements:

- Self-learning using the law school's Legal Practice Course (LPC) or Graduate Diploma in Law (GDL) online materials and some of the firm's own training materials and know-how documents. The materials were created and maintained by the law school, and made available on the law school's existing e-learning platform.

- Workshops and small group sessions facilitated by partners, PSLs and other experienced lawyers. The sessions were very practical, giving junior lawyers the opportunity to discuss the practical application of law to client matters.

- Assessed presentations. Each lawyer was given a topic which they had to prepare and present to their peers and assessors – the law school tutors, senior lawyers and PSLs. The participants received training in presentation skills, were assessed on their level of knowledge and their delivery and, post presentation, were asked to reflect on areas for improvement.

- Before and after assessments. To provide a baseline measurement on each legal topic, the junior lawyers had to sit a multiple-choice test before a module started. This helped them to understand where they had knowledge gaps and where they should focus their learning. When the module was finished they sat another multiple-choice test but this time needed to achieve a 100 per cent result to pass the test. The use of assessment accelerated the learning, provided an initial benchmark and evidence of knowledge level attained. This was important for providing the firm and its clients quality assurance on the junior lawyers' ability to get the legal fundamentals right every time.

## 2. Benefits

The expected benefits of the programme, which we communicated to all of the stakeholders and departments, were to:

- accelerate learning and improve the level of legal knowledge;
- give quality assurance that the firm's junior lawyers are technically excellent and have mastered the legal fundamentals;
- differentiate our law firm through its excellent learning opportunities and legal grounding for junior lawyers;
- improve the effectiveness of junior lawyers through proactive application of legal knowledge to clients' issues;
- provide efficiencies and cost savings through delegation of work (client advice being worked on at a more junior level);
- obtain tutorial and administrative support from the law school at no additional cost.

## 3. The pilot

We ran a pilot to test the concept. We selected a group of lawyers that had already undergone some changes to their legal technical training. The PSL in this department was keen to use the pilot as an opportunity to bring junior lawyers in different offices up to the same standard of legal knowledge.

The pilot started in June 2012 and ran for nine weeks. It covered nine legal topics, including Alienations, Forfeiture, and the Landlord and Tenant Act 1954. A dozen junior lawyers participated, and their supervisors were also involved as supporters and trainers.

When the pilot was first communicated, the pilot group expressed concern over elements of the assessment. They wanted to understand how the assessment would work and what would happen if they did not pass the final assessment. They also wondered how they would be able to fit the pilot around other client and training commitments. Responding to these questions and reiterating the purpose, aims and benefits of the initiative was critical to keeping the group engaged with the pilot and supportive of its aims.

In September 2012, the project team reported the results back to the firm's Executive Board and got a ringing endorsement to roll out the programme across the firm. Given our measurement strategy and the results this was not surprising for a firm whose overall strategy was focused on technical excellence.

## 4. Measurements before, during and after

Measuring and reviewing the results throughout the pilot was important, both to validate the new approach and also to provide benchmarks for participating individuals.

Before the pilot started the group did a multiple-choice test (MCT) to increase awareness of knowledge gaps and highlight the areas that individual lawyers needed to focus on. The lawyers could see their individual results but these were anonymized to everyone else, including the project team, so as to provide a safe and supportive learning environment. This provided a benchmark of what the level of knowledge was before any training and learning intervention.

During the pilot, qualitative measurement of the presentations was used to assess first the quality of delivery and interaction with audience, and secondly the level of knowledge.

Immediately after the pilot module, the group re-sat their MCT to provide evidence of their increased level of knowledge. Ideally any knowledge gaps would have been plugged, resulting in a 100 per cent score. Although this was not achieved by everyone in the pilot (see Table 31.1) the knowledge increase was evident and the pilot validated the introduction of the new programme.

**TABLE 31.1**    The changes for the various departments: before and after the pilot module

| First modules | Initial MCT (percentage) | Final MCT (percentage) |
| --- | --- | --- |
| Department 1 | 58% | 100% |
| Department 2 | 42.5% | 92.5% |
| Department 3 | 85% | 100% |
| Department 4 | 76.7% | 100% |
| Department 5 | 69.5% | 100% |
| Department 6 | 33% | 100% |
| Department 7 | 58.2% | 88.6% |
| Department 8 | 48.5% | 100% |
| Department 9 | 66% | 100% |
| Average | 55.8% | 97.9% |

## 5. The pilot results

The feedback from the pilot group was invaluable and was used to adjust and refine the programme as well as how it was communicated and supported. Some ideas were incorporated straight away. For example, the assessed presentations were shortened from one hour to half an hour to reduce the time commitment of peers and assessors. Other suggestions were introduced in subsequent modules in the rollout phase. The self-studying and workshops were scheduled further in advance to help lawyers better plan their learning activities and fit them around other commitments. To gauge changes in learning and confidence levels, anecdotal feedback was collated. It was interesting to note that the feedback changed over the course of the pilot. At the point of announcing the pilot, questions and concerns were raised about the need for assessment and the timing of it. However, once the pilot had started and the participants were familiar with the programme the feedback became overwhelmingly positive.

The pilot benchmark and feedback confirmed that the structured approach to learning delivered the expected benefits. For example:

- Accelerated learning: most learning happens on the job but the assessed elements of the programme (MCTs and presentations) provided the impetus to accelerate the development of legal knowledge of junior lawyers.

- Knowledge refresh: feedback from the lawyers universally confirmed that the programme was useful and that it helped them bridge the knowledge gap between study and practice.

- Quality assurance: the programme helped junior lawyers to build a strong foundation and in turn provided the firm and our clients with another level of quality assurance. The law school's involvement and endorsement of the firm's commitment to technical excellence gave the clients external assurance of high quality. The programme embodied and reflected sound educational reasoning and proven academic research. The promotion of learning and application of knowledge through consolidation and revision of materials in a practical context were important tools that had previously been underestimated.

- Efficiency: we already knew that a superior ability to grasp and apply fundamental legal principles results in better-negotiated outcomes for the firm's clients. However, the programme also provided a more efficient and cost effective delivery of our services to clients. This meant the firm could better maintain margins or compete on price without sacrificing quality.

- Attracting talent: feedback from new recruits confirmed that a deciding factor for choosing to train with this law firm was the rigorous and supportive approach to legal knowledge development.

## 6. Stakeholder engagement

Communicating and sharing progress throughout the pilot was done at several levels. It is worth pointing out some activities that worked well with key stakeholder groups.

Decision makers. The firm's managing partner and executive board were clear on the pilot's aims and its potential to deliver on the expected benefits. The project team delivered short and regular progress updates, and the final findings and recommendations were presented in a detailed report and also at a board meeting, to give the decision makers opportunity to ask questions and buy in to the recommendations. This engagement was key to moving from concept to pilot and gaining support for implementation.

Pilot participants. The importance of dealing with and responding to individual feedback, questions and concerns cannot be underestimated. To ensure the pilot group remained engaged, the PSL spoke with the participants and their supervisors regularly and addressed individual concerns and questions. We learned the importance of the timing of the communication as well as allowing people to react to the communication. The first pilot was announced shortly before it was due to kick off. The short notice and lack of engagement with stakeholders resulted in misunderstanding of the purpose of the pilot and a degree of unease amongst junior lawyers.

This was rectified by the setting up of pre-briefing sessions and an orientation meeting which the lawyers and their supervisors attended. For subsequent departments much more time was allocated to communication and preparation.

**Peer assistance and shadow support.** A group of four PSLs was put together to shadow and learn from the pilot. It met with the real estate PSL every three weeks to become familiar with the approach and the programme advocates. It also validated the law school's materials' fitness for purpose for their respective departments, and, of course, for the firm's programme. They shared their views of what they had observed with other PSLs, helping the project team to communicate the benefits as well as the potential of the programme to other departments.

**The law school.** Pilot reflections and observations were also fed back to the law school every two to three weeks. This enabled them to adjust their content and support to the firm. Their involvement in and attendance at the orientation sessions and assessed presentations brought them closer to the firm and even deepened their commitment to collaborating beyond the pilot phase.

## 7. Phased implementation

Once the project team had delivered the initial pilot, a period of communication and preparation followed. The pilot results and lessons learned were shared with all the PSLs and partners with a knowledge management (KM) responsibility. To ensure central KM resource was not overstretched, the new programme was phased in over one or two departments at a time. It took roughly 18 months (January 2013–Summer 2014) to implement and run the first module of the new programme in every department. Feedback and lessons learned in each department were shared and passed on to subsequent departments. That way, the programme continued to improve and got embedded in the overall training curriculum.

# Summary

Running a pilot to test the initial idea and the law school collaboration was a very powerful approach. Not only did the project team get the evidence that was needed to implement the new approach, but it also resulted in greater buy-in from the Executive Board, participants and the participants' supervisors. Why? Firstly, the pilot itself demonstrated the need for, and improvements of, the programme. Secondly, the learnings from each department were acknowledged, and improvements were incorporated in subsequent modules and departments. A pilot suggested that it was a test and might not run perfectly. This expectation and a sense of responsibility to help improve the programme contributed to engagement and acceptance of the changed approach to knowledge development.

# SUMMARY

This book is now complete. If your knowledge management journey has paralleled the structure of this book, then your KM implementation is also complete, and KM is fully embedded in your organizational operations. You should feel proud of yourself – you have successfully done what Machiavelli said (in the quote in our introduction) was most difficult, perilous and uncertain. You have introduced a new order of things. You have introduced a new management discipline to your organization. You have succeeded where many have failed – you have implemented Knowledge Management.

We hope that this book has been helpful to you in your journey, and has guided you away from the pitfalls and presented you with approaches you could copy, case studies you could learn from, and templates you were able to apply.

Now is the time for you to pay some of this knowledge back. Conduct a learning review of your KM implementation programme, and identify the lessons that will be useful both to future KM programmes, and other change programmes in your own organization. Publish these lessons widely so they can help others who will follow in your footsteps, because we can be sure of one thing: no matter how difficult, perilous and uncertain the introduction of knowledge management may be, the topic is important enough that knowledge management implementation will remain a priority for organizations around the globe for decades to come.

# GLOSSARY

**A3 Report**
A structured document following a process for reviewing, analysing and documenting learning about product failures and product design improvements.

**After Action Review**
A short structured meeting, where a team reviews a recent work activity and draws out lessons for the future. This process is generally used for short-term activities such as tasks within a project.

**Ambient Findability**
Ensuring that relevant knowledge resources pop up proactively at the point or in the context where they are needed. This means anticipating where relevant resources will be needed and engineering a 'push' of content to users at that point in the process.

**Autoclassification Tools**
Software tools that automatically assign Tags or Taxonomy topics to information and knowledge resources. They can work by suggesting tags or topics to users, or they can be fully automated, working in the background without human intervention.

**Baton Passing**
A facilitated process for transferring knowledge from one team to another team conducting the same type of work.

**Before Action Review**
A facilitated discussion before a project or activity cycle commences, to identify prior learning and knowledge needs that are relevant to the project.

**Benefits Mapping**
A systematic and visual way of demonstrating the connections between knowledge management interventions and positive business outcomes.

**Best Practice**
A practice or way of doing something that has been identified and validated as the best currently known way of doing it.

**Big Data**
A broad term referring to the processing and mining of very large datasets from multiple sources, to gain meaningful and actionable insights for the business.

**Blog**
An online software application for authoring short articles that shows entries in order of greatest recency. Useful for recording knowledge and insights from projects and activities as they happen.

**Business Intelligence**
Supporting decision making through gathering and analysing information from the environment, to avoid risks and create possibilities for change.

| | |
|---|---|
| Codified Knowledge | Codified knowledge is knowledge that is recorded in text, audio, video or picture form. Also known as Explicit Knowledge. |
| Community of Practice | A network of people who work on a common type of activity or practice area, and who share knowledge regularly on their practice, either in person or virtually, to help each other perform better. |
| Community of Purpose | Similar to a Community of Practice, but focused on a common purpose, process or objective shared by the members. The community focuses on delivering the common purpose (for example the creation of best practice). |
| Competence | A combination of technical knowledge, skills and values that gives somebody the ability to be effective in a role or function. |
| Content Management | The application of processes and systems to managing information content in support of organizational needs, whether it be web content, documents, record, or other forms of Codified Knowledge. |
| Corporate Amnesia | The loss of key capabilities due to knowledge loss when people leave. |
| Culture | Distinctive patterns of behaviours, assumptions and values expressed within a community or organization. Because they are embedded through habits, they are difficult to change simply through appeals to reason, but must be supported through a systematic change programme, putting in place new processes, roles and other enablers. |
| Data | Individual measurements, observations and facts that may be combined and ordered into information. |
| Dialogue | A style of conversation that stresses exploration of different perspectives and achieving mutual understanding, not necessarily agreement. |
| Embedding | A set of processes and interventions intended to ensure that new ways of working become permanent. |
| Enterprise Search Specialist | A role responsible for ensuring that the search technology exploits the Taxonomy effectively, supports the Information Architect's design objectives, and helps users find and access information and knowledge resources useful to them. |
| Enterprise Taxonomist | A role responsible for developing, implementing and maintaining enterprise Taxonomies to support the findability, access and re-use of knowledge resources. |

| | |
|---|---|
| Enterprise Taxonomy Management System | A software application that supports the centralized management of multiple Taxonomies, Metadata elements and other reference vocabularies, and acts as a single source of vocabulary for a number of different information systems. |
| Expert System | A system that embeds the knowledge and decision-making rules of experts into algorithms and workflows in a software application. |
| Explicit Knowledge | The original definition is that Explicit Knowledge is knowledge that can be expressed and described. Nowadays the term has become synonymous with Codified Knowledge. |
| Fail Fair | An organization-wide event to showcase organizational failures that were key learning and improvement opportunities, and to demonstrate leadership's commitment to a cultural willingness to explore failure in search of learning. |
| Governance | Enabling effective administration, oversight and accountability of an organizational function through a combination of structures, policies, metrics, performance management and support. |
| Human Capital | The stock of knowledge, competences, values and social attributes possessed by an organization that enables it to be effective at what it does. Human Capital is one form of Intangible Asset. |
| Information | A collation and presentation of data which tells you something. |
| Information Architect | A role responsible for designing the information and knowledge environment in a system such as a Portal or Knowledge Base so that information resources can be easily navigated and retrieved. |
| Innovation | Introducing significantly improved products, processes and services through the creation of new knowledge, and the implementation and validation of ideas, experimentation and problem solving. |
| Intangible Assets | Assets of an organization that cannot be quantified and put on a balance sheet in the same way as tangible assets such as cash, facilities or equipment. Examples of intangible assets are reputation, goodwill, customer capital, human capital, or capabilities. Knowledge is an important kind of intangible asset. |

| | |
|---|---|
| KNAC | Knowledge Asset Creation process – a five-step process developed by Siemens for creating synthesized knowledge assets around a particular topic or product. |
| Knowledge | Know-how, skill, experience, understanding and rules of thumb that allow you to take effective action. See also Explicit Knowledge and Tacit Knowledge. |
| Knowledge Analyst | A role responsible for retrieving and collating knowledge resources around a specific topic from different knowledge bases, and preparing briefings for internal or external customers. |
| Knowledge Assets | Discrete, identifiable items or collections of knowledge that help to make an organization effective at what it does. Knowledge assets cover the whole range of knowledge types, from explicit to tacit. They can include skills, competencies, methodologies, practices, areas of experience, expertise, and relationship capital. |
| Knowledge Audit | A general term referring to a systematic evaluation of knowledge assets, knowledge gaps, knowledge flows, and knowledge management processes, with the aim of making recommendations for improvement. Often part of the detailed planning process for a KM implementation. |
| Knowledge Bank, Knowledge Base | A place where the Explicit Knowledge of an organization or a community of practice is collected. |
| Knowledge Broker | A person who connects colleagues to knowledge and information resources outside their immediate working context, usually through their own social networks. |
| Knowledge Café | A facilitated large-scale meeting where small group sharing conversations take place at café-style tables. Typically, each table has a host to facilitate the conversation and at the end of each conversation cycle, the other participants at the table split up and join a different table with a different group. Knowledge cafés are good at bringing multiple perspectives to bear on complex problems or challenges, and at improving networking and relationship building. |
| Knowledge Capture, Knowledge Documentation | Processes for documenting Tacit Knowledge into codified form as Explicit Knowledge. |
| Knowledge Engineer | A role with accountability for capturing knowledge from an expert, team, department or division. |
| Knowledge Exchange | A meeting where many people come to discuss and learn from each other. In a knowledge exchange everyone is a contributor and everyone a learner. |

| | |
|---|---|
| **Knowledge Fair** | An organization-wide event to show off its knowledge capabilities and to show the benefits of KM. |
| **Knowledge Handover** | A facilitated process for transferring lessons from a project team that has completed a project to other teams that may need that knowledge. |
| **Knowledge Management** | A systematic and strategic approach to maximizing the value of the collective know-how of an organization. |
| **Knowledge Management Champion** | A person who has been given responsibilities for supporting KM activities in their part of the business, usually as an additional role on top of their normal functional role. |
| **Knowledge Management Framework** | A framework that describes the enablers that need to be in place for knowledge management to become effectively embedded in the way the organization works. |
| **Knowledge Management Plan** | A document that captures the knowledge needs, knowledge gaps, knowledge sources and acquisition strategy, knowledge creation roles, responsibilities and processes for a given project or activity. |
| **Knowledge Manager** | Someone whose primary accountability is making sure that the knowledge of their part of the organization is managed for business benefit. |
| **Knowledge Map** | A visual representation of where knowledge assets are located in an organization and how they relate to key functional areas and activities, and/or a visual representation of knowledge flows and dependencies across an organization. |
| **Knowledge Organization** | A set of processes to organize knowledge assets in an organization so that they can be effectively managed, accessed, and used. |
| **Knowledge Owner** | The person responsible for managing the contents, accuracy, completeness and currency of the Knowledge Base for any particular area of knowledge. |
| **Knowledge Retention** | A set of processes to retain important knowledge in the organization while individual people come and go. Often focused on the retention and transfer of Tacit Knowledge. |
| **Knowledge Synthesis** | Compiling and distilling knowledge from many sources into a single coherent set of guidance for easy reference. |
| **Learning** | Improving the way things are done as a result of acquiring new insight and knowledge. |

| | |
|---|---|
| Learning Historian | A role responsible for creating a learning history through interviews, data gathering and analysis. A narrative that distils learning from a particular activity or event, and gives guidelines on application of the lessons. |
| Lessons Database | A database in which to store, categorize and retrieve lessons learned. |
| Lessons Management System | A system to manage the capture, validation, embedding and application of lessons learned. Differs from a Lessons Database by containing workflows to ensure Lessons are learned (see Learning) rather than merely recorded and stored. |
| Metadata | Data that describes the attributes of data or documents, for example, title, author, date of creation, topic, structure, security classification. Metadata helps in the management of content and supports giving access to content, eg through search. |
| Packaging | Compiling and synthesizing knowledge into a coherent format so that it can be presented to the knowledge customer to maximize the ease of re-use. |
| Partnering | A structured approach to identifying and engaging with partners, negotiating responsibilities and contributions, and recognizing partners' constraints and priorities. |
| Peer Assist | A structured, facilitated meeting or workshop where people are invited from other business units, or other businesses, to provide their experience, insights and knowledge to a team who have requested help in solving a problem or addressing a challenge. |
| Peer Review | A structured, facilitated meeting or workshop where people are invited from other business units, or other businesses, to review the work of another team. |
| People Finder | A knowledge directory matching people's names to knowledge domains to help staff find out 'who knows what' in an organization. |
| Pilot | A limited-scale project to test out the KM Framework in a part of the organization, and to demonstrate the value of KM to business stakeholders. A pilot should also produce insights leading to the refinement of the KM Framework. |
| Policy | A clear statement of what is expected from employees in relation to a specific activity area, spelling out the guiding principles, roles and accountabilities, and supporting instructions. |

| | |
|---|---|
| Portal | An online site that gives access to Knowledge Bases, software applications and collaboration tools. |
| Practice Owner | A subject matter expert who is accountable for maintaining the knowledge of an area of professional practice in the business, both by ensuring that the necessary competencies are developed and maintained, and also that the supporting knowledge base is available and up to date. |
| Professional Support Lawyer | A role within law firms to provide advice, access to precedents and know-how, and provide training and support for client pitches. |
| Proof of Concept | A very small-scale activity to demonstrate the value of KM to management stakeholders. |
| Q&A Forum | An e-mail-based discussion forum structured around questions and answers. These can be a powerful means of exchanging knowledge within a community of practice. Community members can raise questions within the forum, which are answered by their peers around the world. |
| Recordkeeping, Records Management | Systematic processes for keeping formal records of official decisions, activities and transactions, for the purposes of management control, accountability, regulatory compliance, and preservation of organizational memory. |
| Resource Mapping | A structured and visual method of identifying the resources required by a KM implementation, and who will be responsible for contributing those resources. |
| Retrospect | A structured and facilitated meeting at the end of a project or major activity cycle, to capture lessons before the team disbands. |
| Roll-out | The process of extending a new way of working across an organization. |
| Search-Based Application | A software application that uses a search engine to proactively deliver highly targeted content to specific users at a point of need. |
| Social Media | Online software applications that are designed to encourage and facilitate social interactions. |
| Social Network Analysis | A method of mapping the interactions between people in a team, community or organization, to assess the level of connectivity, and to identify any interventions to improve the flow of knowledge and information. |

| | |
|---|---|
| Social Proof | Convincing people of the value of an approach by showing them examples of people like them who are benefiting from the approach. |
| Strategic Knowledge Areas | Knowledge-based capabilities that are critical to an organization's effectiveness and competitiveness. |
| Subject Matter Expert | Someone in a community or a function who has ownership or stewardship of one area of knowledge, and who manages that area on behalf of the community or organization, often at the direction or under the oversight of the Practice Owner. |
| Tacit Knowledge | Knowledge which is held in people's heads and bodies, and which may or may not be possible to write down. |
| Tag Cloud | A cluster of commonly used keywords in a collection of resources, where the size of the font indicates the frequency of use of that keyword. |
| Tagging System | A system that allows users to add their own keywords to an information or knowledge resource. |
| Taxonomy | A structured, controlled vocabulary used to describe what documents or discussions are about. Taxonomies are part of Metadata, and are used to support search and retrieval of relevant content. Taxonomies can also be used to describe expertise topics associated with individuals and communities. |
| Taxonomy Facet | An element of the Taxonomy that focuses on a specific attribute of a knowledge resource, for example the type of document, the activity referenced, the entities involved. |
| Validate | To make sure something – a lesson or other piece of knowledge – is valid and defensible, and can therefore be applied in future as a good practice. |
| Wiki | A set of online pages that can be directly edited by readers through a web browser interface. |
| Wikithon | A facilitated event where a group of Knowledge Owners or Community of Practice members gather to synthesize a collective knowledge base on a wiki platform. |
| Yammer | A commercially available microblogging tool. Microblogging supports the sharing of short messages and updates. |
| Yellow Pages | See People Finder. |

# REFERENCES

Abell, A and Oxbrow, N (2001) *Competing with Knowledge: The information professional in the knowledge management age*, TFPL, London

Adams, S (2004) Practice makes perfect, *Inside Knowledge*, 9 (4), December, pp 25–27

Ajimoko, O (2007) Technical limit thinking produces steep learning curve, *World Oil*, 228 (7), pp 103–06

Ash, J (2007a) Case report, General Motors: Changing Gear, *Inside Knowledge*, 10 (8), pp 18–21

Ash, J (2007b) Case report, Connecting People, *Inside Knowledge*, 10 (9), pp 20–23

Bailey, S and Black, O (2014) *Mind Gym: Achieve more by thinking differently*, HarperOne, New York

Barnes, S and Milton, N (2015) *Designing a Successful KM Strategy: A guide for the knowledge management professional*, Information Today, Medford, NJ

Barrett, F J and Fry, R E (2005) *Appreciative Inquiry: A positive approach to building cooperative capacity*, Taos Institute, Chagrin Falls, OH

Barth, S (2000) KM horror stories, *Knowledge Management Magazine* [online] http://web.archive.org/web/20060612222246/http://destinationkm.com/articles/default.asp?ArticleID=923 [accessed 23 March 2015]

Bicheno, J (2008) *The Lean Toolbox: The essential guide to lean transformation*, Picsie Books, Buckingham, UK

Bishop, K (2002) *New Roles, Skills and Capabilities for the Knowledge-Focused Organisation*, Standards Australia, Sydney

Buckman, R (2004) *Building a Knowledge-Driven Organization*, McGraw Hill, NY

Braganza, A and Möllenkramer, G (2002) Anatomy of a failed knowledge management initiative: lessons from PharmaCorp's experiences, *Knowledge and Process Management*, 9 (1), pp 23–33

Christensen, C M, Cook, S and Hall, T (2006) What Customers Want from Your Products, *Harvard Business School* [online] http://hbswk.hbs.edu/item/what-customers-want-from-your-products [accessed 18 August 2015]

Chua, A and Lam, W (2005) Why KM projects fail: a multi-case analysis, *Journal of Knowledge Management*, 9 (3), pp 6–17

Coleman, C and Barquin, R (2010) The Rule of 151: How to move knowledge management and business intelligence from margin to mainstream, *BeyeNETWORK* [online] http://www.b-eye-network.com/view/12617 [accessed 25 May 2015]

Collins, J (2001) *Good to Great*, Random House Business, London

Conoco (2012) In the news – 2012 Archimedes Award winners, *Conoco Spirit magazine*, Q2 2013 [online] http://www.haleydowning.com/wp-content/uploads/2013/11/Spirit-Magazine_Q2-2013_Archimedes-Awards.pdf [accessed 13 July 2013]

Department of Health (2010) *KM Postcards* [online] http://www.hscic.gov.uk/media/15466/Knowledge-management-postcards/pdf/kmpostcards.pdf [accessed 21 May 2015]

Dixon, N (2009) If the Army Can Put Its Doctrine Up On a Wiki, You've Got No Excuse [online] http://www.nancydixonblog.com/2009/09/if-the-army-can-put-its-doctrine-up-on-a-wiki-youve-got-no-excuse.html [accessed May 2015]

Dora, A, Gibbert, M, Jonczyk and Trillitzsch, U (2002) Networked knowledge: implementing a system for sharing technical tips and expertise, in *Knowledge Management Case Book, Siemens Best Practices*, eds T Davenport and G Probsk, Publicis Corporate Publishing, Germany

Duffy, D (1998) Knowledge champions, *CIO Magazine*, 15 November

FAO (2011) *FAO Knowledge Management Strategy* [online] http://www.fao.org/fileadmin/user_upload/capacity_building/KM_Strategy.pdf [accessed 14 April 2015]

Freudenthaler, K, Borghoff, U, Eisenhauer, R and Stenger, H-J (2003) Entwicklung eines KM Framework und Implementation Guide [online] https://dokumente.unibw.de/pub/bscw.cgi/1076066 [accessed 13 May 2015]

Gartner (2013) Gartner says the vast majority of social collaboration initiatives fail due to lack of purpose: Press release [online] http://www.gartner.com/newsroom/id/2402115 [accessed 17 April 2015]

Ghaedian, S and Chen, B (2012) How to support and facilitate knowledge flow in product development at Volvo group trucks technology, Master of Science Thesis, Chalmers University of Technology, University of Gothenburg, Sweden

Gibbert, M, Probst, G J B, Davenport, T H (2011) Sidestepping implementation traps when implementing knowledge management: lessons learned from Siemens, *Behaviour & Information Technology*, 30 (1)

Gibby, P, Milton, N, Palen, W and Hensley, S (2006) *Implementing a Framework for Knowledge Management*, Society of Petroleum Engineers, SPE-101315-PP

Glick, D (2011) Federal Workers Stage Mobile Gov Wikithon To Aid Agencies, *Breaking Gov* [online] http://breakinggov.com/2011/11/18/federal-workers-stage-mobile-gov-wikithon-to-aid-agencies/ [accessed 12 May 2015]

Gongla, P and Rizzuto, C R (2001) Evolving communities of practice: IBM Global Services experience, *IBM Systems Journal*, 40 (4), pp 842–62

Gorelick, C, April, K and Milton, N (2004) *Performance Through Learning: Knowledge management in practice*, Elsevier, UK

Grant, A (2013) Givers take all: the hidden dimension of corporate culture, McKinsey Quarterly, April [online] http://www.mckinsey.com/insights/organization/givers_take_all_the_hidden_dimension_of_corporate_culture [accessed 31 December 2015]

Hackett, B (2000) Beyond Knowledge Management: New ways to work and learn (Conference Board report) [online] http://www.providersedge.com/docs/km_articles/beyond_km_-_new_ways_to_work_and_learn.pdf [accessed 14 April 2015]

Hedden, H (2010) *The Accidental Taxonomist,* Information Today, Medford, NJ

Ihrig, M and MacMillan, I (2015) Managing your mission-critical knowledge, *Harvard Business Review*, Jan–Feb

Johnson, N Blake (2011) NRC 'knowledge center' helps younger employees benefit from experts' experience, *Federal Times*, August [online] http://archive.federaltimes.com/article/20110829/AGENCY03/108290301/NRC-8216-knowledge-center-helps-younger-employees-benefit-from-experts-experience [accessed 10 April 2015]

Jones, N B, Herschel, R T, Moesel, D D (2003) Using knowledge champions to facilitate knowledge management, *Journal of Knowledge Management*, 7 (1), pp 49–63

Kahan, S (2009) 7 lessons for getting change right, *Fast Company*, 21 May [online] http://www.fastcompany.com/1285129/7-lessons-getting-change-right [accessed 23 March 2015]

Kennedy, M, Harmon, K and Minnock, E (2008) *Ready, Set, Dominate: Implement Toyota's set-based learning for developing products and nobody can catch you*, The Oaklea Press, Richmond, Virginia

Keyes, J (2012) *Enterprise 2.0: Social networking tools to transform your organization*, CRC Press, Boca Raton, Florida

Kleiner, A and Roth, G (1997) How to make experience your company's best teacher, *Harvard Business Review*, 75 (5), pp 172–77

Knoco (2014) Knowledge Management Survey [online] http://www.knoco.com/knowledge-management-survey.htm [accessed 17 August 2015]

Lambe, P (2007) *Organising Knowledge: Taxonomies, knowledge and organisational effectiveness*, Chandos, Oxford

Lambe, P and Tan, E (2003) KM Implementation Challenges: Case studies from Singapore organizations, Singapore: Straits Knowledge [online] http://www.greenchameleon.com/uploads/KM_Implementation_Challenges.pdf [accessed 23 March 2015]

Lambe, P and Tan, E (2006) Guidelines for identifying, motivating and supporting knowledge champions, *Green Chameleon* [online] http://www.greenchameleon.com/uploads/KMChampionGuidelinesAS.doc [accessed 26 November 2015]

Lawley, D (2006) Call Centre KM, *Inside Knowledge*, 9 (6)

Leslie-Skye, B (2014) Time to break out that sharp wit: Columbia Wikithon is upon us, *Columbia Spectator* [online] http://columbiaspectator.com/2014/01/28/time-break-out-sharp-wit-columbia-wikithon-upon-us [accessed 12 May 2015]

Ligdas, N (2009) Using a wiki portal to support operational excellence at Shell, *Knowledge Management Review* (Document ID: 1904057361) [online] http://0-proquest.umi.com.darius.uleth.ca/pqdweb?did=1904057361&sid=2&Fmt=3&clientId=12304&RQT=309&VName=PQD [accessed 19 October 2010]

Lipka, M (2015) My Best Mistake: Mike Lipka's 'Knowledge Now or Later', Office of the Chief Knowledge Officer, *NASA* [online] http://km.nasa.gov/my-best-mistake-mike-lipkas-knowledge-now-or-later/ [accessed 11 May 2015]

Machiavelli, N (1532) *The Prince* [online] http://www.constitution.org/mac/prince.pdf [accessed 20 August 2015]

Maddock, G M and Vitón, R (2010) Knowing vs Learning, *Business Week*, 17 February [online] http://www.businessweek.com/managing/content/jan2010/ca20100119_962696.htm [accessed 25 May 2015]

Magnusson, J (2008) Roles in a Legal Services Context, in *Knowledge Management for Services Operations and Manufacturing*, ed. T Young, pp 98–100, Chandos Publishing, Oxford

Melvin, B (2013) *Knowledge Based Product Development: A practical guide* paperback, self-published

Milton, N J (2005) *Knowledge Management for Teams and Projects*, Chandos Publishing, Oxford

Milton, N J (2010) *The Lessons Learned Handbook: A practical knowledge-based approach to learning from experience*, Chandos Publishing, UK

Milton, N R (2007) *Knowledge Acquisition in Practice: A step-by-step guide (decision engineering)*, Springer-Verlag, London

Morgan, J M and Liker, J K (2006) *The Toyota Product Development System: Integrating people, process and technology*, Productivity Press, New York

Morville, P (2005) *Ambient Findability: What we find changes who we become*, O'Reilly Media, California

NASA (2013) Knowledge Policy on Programs and Projects, NASA Policy Directive 7120.6 [online] http://nodis3.gsfc.nasa.gov/displayDir.cfm?t=NPD&c=7120&s=6 [accessed 10 August 2015]

Nonaka, I and Takeuchi, I I (1995) *The Knowledge Creating Company: How Japanese companies create the dynamics of innovation*, Oxford University Press, New York

Prokesch, S E (1997) Unleashing the power of learning: an interview with British Petroleum's John Browne, *Harvard Business Review*, 75 (5), pp 146–68

Santosus, M (2002) Underwriting knowledge, *CIO Magazine*, 1 Sept

Shearer, M and Tarling, J (2013) Unlocking the data in BBC News, *ISKO UK* [online] http://www.iskouk.org/content/unlocking-data-bbc-news [accessed 21 May 2015]

Singapore Ministry of Defence (2014) *The Army Warrant Officer and Specialist Guidebook*, 2nd ed, *Mindef Singapore* [online] http://www.mindef.gov.sg/dam/publications/eBooks/wospec/ [accessed 21 May 2015]

Snowden, D (2000) The ASHEN model: an enabler of action, *Knowledge Management*, 3 (7), pp 14–17

Snowden, D (2005) Stories from the frontier, *E:CO*, 7 (3–4), pp 155–65

Solomon, D (2010) The tube: IDEO builds a collaboration system that inspires through passion, *Management Exchange* [online]http://www.managementexchange.com/story/tube-ideo-builds-collaboration-system-inspires-through-passion [accessed 23 March 2015]

Suurla, R, Markkula, Mand Mustajärvi, O (2002) Developing and implementing knowledge management in the Parliament of Finland, Parliament of Finland Committee for the Future report [online] http://www.ictparliament.org/sites/default/files/knowledge_management.pdf %09 [accessed 14 April 2015]

Sveiby, K-E and Armstrong, C (2004) Learn to measure to learn! Opening key note address IC Congress Helsinki, 2 Sept [online] http://www.sveiby.com/articles/measuretolearn.pdf [accessed 5 August 2015]

Taylor, L (2014) Pinch with pride, *Association for Project Management news*, November [online] https://www.apm.org.uk/news/pinch-pride [accessed 10 April 2015]

Tennyson, R (2003) *The Partnering Toolbook*, International Business Leaders Forum, London

Valot, W (2010) BP's Knowledge Management, offshore-technology.com, 12 April [online] http://www.offshore-technology.com/features/feature81867/ [accessed 5 January 2016]

Weber, R O (2007) Addressing failure factors in knowledge management, *Electronic Journal of Knowledge Management*, 5 (3), pp 333–46

Weineke, S (2008) Adopting and adapting product best practices across General Motors Engineering six years later, in *Knowledge Management for Services Operations and Manufacturing*, ed. T Young, pp 142–65, Chandos Publishing, Oxford

Wenger, E C, McDermott, R and Snyder, W C (2002) *Cultivating Communities of Practice: A guide to managing knowledge*, Harvard Business School Press, Cambridge, USA

Will, J (2008) The Institutionalization of Knowledge Management in an Engineering Organization, working paper #40, Collaboratory for Research on Global Projects, Stanford University [online] https://gpc.stanford.edu/sites/default/files/wp040_0.pdf [accessed 13 July 2015]

Wurman, R S (2001) *Information Anxiety* 2, Que, Indianapolis

Young, T (2008) *Knowledge Management for Services, Operations and Manufacturing*, Chandos Publishing, Oxford

Young, T and Milton, N (2011) *Knowledge Management for Sales and Marketing*, Chandos Publishing, Oxford

# INDEX